Family Circle

Editorial Director   Arthur Hettich
Editor   Marie T. Walsh
Art Director   Joseph Taveroni
Associate Editor   Gerri Hirshey
Art Associate   Walter C. Schwartz
Food Consultant   Grace Manney
Production Manager   Norman Ellers

Photographs by Richard Jeffery
Illustrations by Maggie Zander

All recipes tested by Family Circle's
Test Kitchen.

CASSEROLE COOKERY

Created by Family Circle Magazine and published 1978 by Arno Press Inc., a subsidiary of The New York Times Company. Copyright © 1976 by The Family Circle, Inc. All rights reserved. Protected under Berne and other international copyright conventions. Title and Trademark FAMILY CIRCLE registered U. S. Patent and Trademark Office, Canada, Great Britain, Australia, New Zealand, Japan and other countries. Marca Registrada. This volume may not be reproduced in whole or in part in any form without written permission from the publisher. Printed in U. S. A. Library of Congress Catalog Card Number 75-42916. ISBN 0-405-06683-X

A New York Times Company Publication NYT

Brunswick Stew is a modern version of a Colonial rabbit dish. Ours combines chicken with chunks of corn and fresh okra. See page 67.

CONTENTS

What is a casserole? Simply defined, it's a baking dish with or without a lid. But to us, it's not the dish, it's what goes into it that counts. It's chicken or beef or fish or vegetables, or all of these deliciously combined. It's a meal for one or a meal for many. It's a dish that's easy on your time and your money. It's a make-ahead, a freeze-ahead, a last-minute creation or one you cook all day long.
On the pages which follow, we show you how to make these many kinds of casseroles, with the artful (and simple) use of sauces, spices and pasta. We offer ways for you to save money and still prepare hearty meals; to save time when there seems to be none to spare; and to entertain

CASSEROLES FROM

A plastic freezer casserole keeper.

A deep bean pot or French marmite.

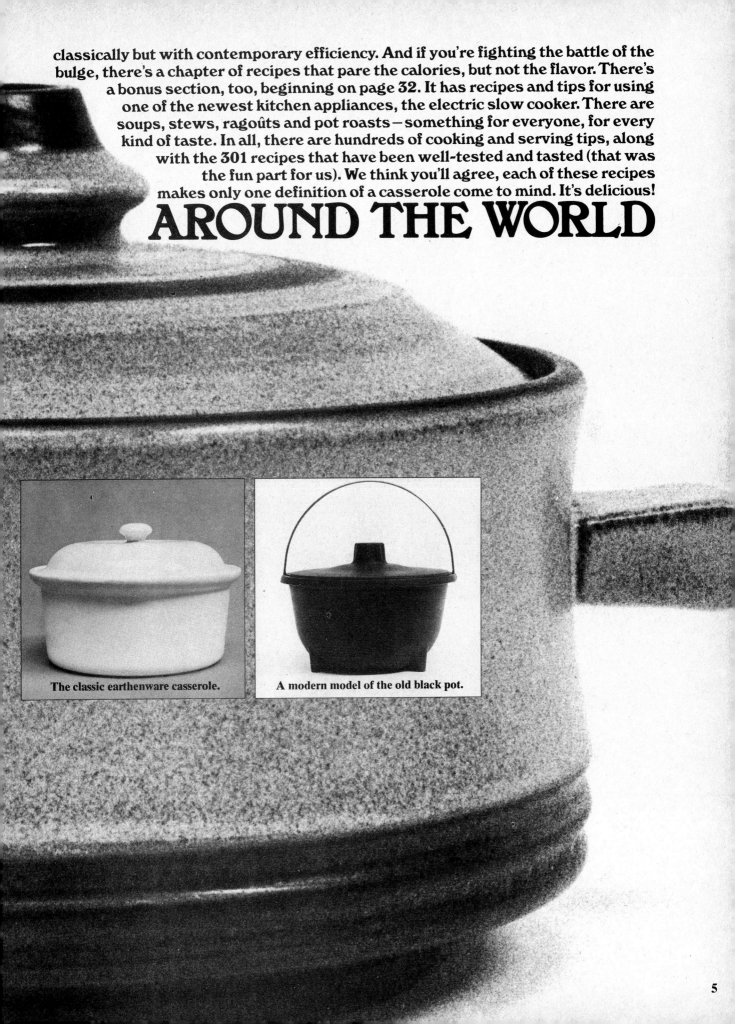

classically but with contemporary efficiency. And if you're fighting the battle of the bulge, there's a chapter of recipes that pare the calories, but not the flavor. There's a bonus section, too, beginning on page 32. It has recipes and tips for using one of the newest kitchen appliances, the electric slow cooker. There are soups, stews, ragoûts and pot roasts — something for everyone, for every kind of taste. In all, there are hundreds of cooking and serving tips, along with the 301 recipes that have been well-tested and tasted (that was the fun part for us). We think you'll agree, each of these recipes makes only one definition of a casserole come to mind. It's delicious!

AROUND THE WORLD

The classic earthenware casserole.

A modern model of the old black pot.

You can make double use of the energy consumed by your oven if you prepare side dishes and desserts that can bake along with a casserole. Here are some recipes for vegetables and desserts that all require oven temperatures between slow and moderate (325° to 375°)—so you can bake them along with many of the casseroles in this book.

AUSTRIAN CABBAGE BAKE

Makes 6 servings. Shred one medium-size cabbage (about 8 cups). Sauté in 3 tablespoons bacon drippings or vegetable oil along with 1 small onion, chopped (¼ cup) in a large skillet until soft. Stir in 2 teaspoons seasoned salt, ½ teaspoon lemon pepper and 1 container (8 ounces) dairy sour cream. Spoon into a 6-cup casserole; cover. Bake in slow to moderate oven (325° to 375°) 30 to 45 minutes, or until bubbly-hot.

DILLED CARROT STICKS

Makes 4 servings. Pare 1 package (1 pound) carrots; cut into thin slices and place in a 4-cup casserole; sprinkle with 2 teaspoons dillweed, 1 teaspoon salt, 1 teaspoon sugar and ¼ teaspoon pepper. Drizzle 3 tablespoons water over and dot with 2 tablespoons butter or margarine. Cover casserole. Bake in a slow to moderate oven (325° to 375°) 45 minutes to 1 hour, or until carrots are tender.

WASHINGTON BAKED APPLES

Makes 6 servings. Wash and core 6 medium-size baking apples. Arrange in an 8-cup shallow casserole. Fill apple centers with ½ cup raisins and a mixture of ½ cup brown sugar, 1 teaspoon lemon rind and ½ teaspoon pumpkin-pie spice. Add ½ cup white wine or apple juice. Cover casserole. Bake in slow to moderate oven (325° to 375°) 40 minutes; remove cover. Baste apples with juices in casserole. Bake 20 minutes longer, or until apples are tender. Cool while eating dinner, then baste with juices in casserole and serve with softened vanilla ice cream.

PARISIENNE PEAS

Makes 6 servings. Place 2 cups frozen peas (from a 1½ pound bag) in a 4-cup casserole. Stir in 1 tablespoon chopped chives, or 1 teaspoon freeze-dried chives, 1 teaspoon leaf basil, crumbled, 1 teaspoon salt and ¼ teaspoon freshly ground pepper. Dot with 2 tablespoons butter or margarine. Run two outer lettuce leaves under cold water to moisten. Place over peas in casserole. Cover casserole. Bake in slow to moderate oven (325° to 375°) 40 minutes to 1 hour, or until peas are tender. Remove lettuce leaves, just before serving. (You can substitute frozen mixed vegetables, cut-up green beans or chopped broccoli for the peas.)

SPICY BAKED BANANAS

Very Good

Makes 6 servings. Peel 6 medium-size firm bananas. Cut in half lengthwise and arrange in a 6-cup shallow casserole. Brush with 2 tablespoons lemon juice. Drizzle with ½ cup honey or dark corn syrup. Sprinkle with a mixture of ½ teaspoon ground nutmeg and ¼ teaspoon ground ginger. Dot with 2 tablespoons butter or margarine. Bake in a slow to moderate oven (325° to 375°) 20 to 40 minutes, or until bananas are well glazed. Cool while eating dinner. Top with softly whipped cream.

BROWN BETTY

Makes 6 servings. Spread ⅓ of a 24-ounce jar of applesauce in the bottom of a 4-cup casserole. Combine 1½ cups graham cracker crumbs, ¼ cup firmly packed brown sugar, 3 tablespoons melted butter or margarine and ½ teaspoon pumpkin-pie spice in a small bowl; sprinkle ⅓ of mixture over applesauce. Repeat to make three layers. Bake in slow to moderate oven (325° to 375°) 30 to 45 minutes, or until crumbs are golden. Serve warm with ice cream, if you wish.

ACORN SQUASH BAKE

Makes 6 servings. Split and seed 3 small acorn squash. Place, cut-side down, in a 13x9x2-inch casserole. Add 1 cup hot water to casserole and cover. Bake in a slow to moderate oven (325° to 375°) 45 minutes to 1 hour, or just until squash is tender. Drain water from casserole. Arrange squash, cut-side up, in casserole. Combine ⅓ cup melted butter or margarine, ¼ cup orange juice, 3 tablespoons dry sherry (optional), 1 teaspoon orange rind, 1 teaspoon salt and ½ teaspoon pepper in a small saucepan. Divide among the squash shells. Bake 15 minutes longer, or until bubbly-hot.

the energy savers

to save money, bake a side dish along with the main event.

ORANGE BAKED BEETS

Makes 6 servings. Scrub 2 bunches beets; pare and shred on a vegetable shredder. Toss with 2 tablespoons brown sugar, 1 teaspoon salt and ¼ teaspoon ground cloves. Spoon into a 4-cup casserole and pour ¼ cup orange juice over. Dot with 2 tablespoons butter or margarine; cover casserole. Bake in slow to moderate oven (325° to 375°) 1 hour to 1 hour, 30 minutes, or until beets are tender.

CRUMB COATED GREEN BEANS

Makes 6 servings. Cook 2 packages (9 ounces each) cut-up green beans, following label directions; drain. Toss with 1 can condensed cream of onion soup, ½ teaspoon garlic powder and ½ teaspoon lemon pepper. Spoon into a 4-cup casserole. Toss 1½ cups soft white bread crumbs (3 slices) with 2 tablespoons melted butter or margarine until well coated. Sprinkle over green beans. Bake in slow to moderate oven (325° to 375°) 20 to 40 minutes, or until crumbs are golden.

SPINACH BAKE

Makes 4 servings. Cook 1 package (10 ounces) frozen chopped spinach, following label directions; drain well. Combine with 3 tablespoons sliced green onion, 3 tablespoons all-purpose flour, 1 teaspoon seasoned salt and ¼ teaspoon seasoned pepper in a medium-size bowl. Stir in 2 eggs, lightly beaten, and 1 cup milk until well-blended. Pour into a well-buttered 4-cup casserole. Bake in slow to moderate oven (325° to 375°) 30 to 45 minutes, or until a knife inserted in center comes out clean.

CREAMY RICE PUDDING

Makes 6 servings. Beat 2 eggs lightly in a medium-size bowl. Stir in 2 cups hot milk, ½ cup sugar, 1 teaspoon vanilla and 1 teaspoon lemon rind. Combine with 1 cup cooked rice in a 4-cup casserole; sprinkle top with grated nutmeg. Place casserole in a baking pan and place pan on oven rack. Fill pan to a depth of 1 inch with boiling water. Bake in slow to moderate oven (325° to 375°) 1 hour to 1 hour, 30 minutes, or until a knife inserted near center comes out clean. Serve warm.

APRICOT BREAD PUDDING

Makes 6 servings. Combine 6 slices white bread, cubed, and ½ cup chopped dried apricots or golden raisins in a 6-cup casserole. Scald 3 cups milk in a medium-size saucepan; remove from heat and stir in ½ cup sugar, ¼ cup sherry (optional), 2 eggs, lightly beaten, and ½ teaspoon ground nutmeg. Pour over bread cubes. Place casserole in a baking pan and place pan on oven rack. Fill pan to a depth of 1 inch with boiling water. Bake in slow to moderate oven (325° to 375°) 1 hour to 1 hour, 30 minutes, or until a knife inserted near the center comes out clean. Serve warm with a topping of apricot jam, if you wish.

SCALLOPED TOMATOES

Makes 6 servings. Coat the bottom of a well-buttered 6-cup shallow casserole with 1 cup soft white bread crumbs (2 slices). Combine 1 can (1 pound, 13 ounces) tomatoes, ½ cup celery, 1 tablespoon minced dried onion, 1 tablespoon minced dried green pepper (optional), 1 teaspoon salt, 1 teaspoon sugar, 1 teaspoon leaf basil, crumbled and ¼ teaspoon pepper in a bowl; spoon over crumbs in casserole. Dot with 2 tablespoons butter or margarine and top with 1 cup soft white bread crumbs (2 slices). Bake in slow to moderate oven (325° to 375°) 30 to 50 minutes, or until top is golden.

NECTARINE AND APPLE BETTY

Makes 8 servings. Wash 3 large firm nectarines and 3 large firm apples. Quarter core, pare and slice fruit. Arrange in a 6-cup shallow casserole. Combine 1½ cups quick-cooking oatmeal, ¾ cup firmly packed brown sugar, 3 tablespoons butter or margarine and ½ teaspoon ground mace in a medium-size bowl until well-blended. Cover fruits with mixture. Bake in a slow to moderate oven (325° to 375°) 1 hour to 1 hour, 30 minutes, or until fruit is tender. Serve with pour cream if you wish.

PEAR SCALLOP

Makes 8 servings. Drain 1 can (1 pound, 13 ounces) pear halves, reserving syrup for another recipe. Place pear halves in an 8-cup casserole; top with ½ cup raisins. Sprinkle with 1 tablespoon lemon juice and 1 teaspoon ground cinnamon. Combine 1 cup sifted all-purpose flour and ½ cup firmly packed brown sugar in a medium-size bowl; cut in ¼ cup (½ stick) butter or margarine with a pastry blender until mixture is crumbly; spread mixture over pears. Bake in slow to moderate oven (325° to 375°) 40 to 50 minutes, or until golden. Serve warm.

YELLOW SQUASH BAKE

Makes 6 servings. Slice 4 medium-size yellow squash. Sauté in 3 tablespoons vegetable oil in a skillet until soft; place in a 6-cup casserole; sauté 1 green pepper, halved, seeded and chopped and 1 small onion, chopped (¼ cup) in same skillet until soft. Add to yellow squash with 1 teaspoon leaf oregano, crumbled, 1 teaspoon salt and ½ teaspoon pepper. Sprinkle top with a mixture of ½ cup packaged dry bread crumbs and ½ cup grated Parmesan cheese. Bake in slow to moderate oven (325° to 375°) 30 to 45 minutes, or until topping is golden. You can substitute Zucchini for yellow squash and leaf basil for oregano.

GREAT BUDGET DISHES

There'll be no "martyrs on a budget" with this chapter. Our recipes (none cost more than **59¢** a serving) show you how to scrimp deliciously. Try Tamale Bake, Caribbean Chicken and Kentucky Tuna Casserole, and you'll see what we mean.

Trying to hold onto a food budget doesn't mean you have to cut down on good eating. Eggplant Parmigiana (recipe on page 10) proves the point. It's just one of our many family-size dinners made with little or no meat—and for very little money!

PENNSYLVANIA DUTCH CASSEROLE

Thrifty Pennsylvania Dutch housewives often served this creamy noodle and sliced egg casserole.

Bake at 350° for 20 minutes.
Make 6 servings at 25¢ each.

- 1 package (8 ounces) fine noodles
- 1 can condensed cream of onion soup
- ½ cup milk
- ¼ cup mayonnaise or salad dressing
- 2 teaspoons Worcestershire sauce
- 8 hard-cooked eggs, shelled and sliced
- ⅓ cup grated Parmesan cheese

1. Cook noodles, following label directions; drain. Place in a greased 8-cup shallow casserole.
2. Combine onion soup, milk, mayonnaise or salad dressing and Worcestershire sauce in a small saucepan; heat slowly, stirring constantly, until smooth and hot; stir half into noodles.
3. Place egg slices over noodle mixture; spoon remaining sauce over eggs. Sprinkle Parmesan cheese on top.
4. Bake in moderate oven (350°) 20 minutes, or until bubbly.

EGGPLANT PARMIGIANA

Fresh oregano from your own herb garden could go into this classic dish. Pictured on page 9.

Bake at 350° for 45 minutes.
Makes 8 servings at 52¢ each.

Sauce
- ½ pound ground chuck
- 1 large onion, chopped (1 cup)
- 1 clove garlic, minced
- 1 can (1 pound, 1 ounce) Italian tomatoes, chopped
- 2 tablespoons chopped fresh oregano
  OR: 2 teaspoons leaf oregano, crumbled
- 1½ teaspoons salt

Eggplant
- 1 large eggplant (about 2 pounds)
- 1 egg
- 1 tablespoon water
- 1 teaspoon salt
- ¼ teaspoon freshly ground pepper
- 1 cup packaged dry bread crumbs
- ⅓ cup olive oil or vegetable oil
- 1 cup grated Parmesan cheese
- 1 package (6 ounces) sliced Provolone cheese, quartered

1. Make Sauce: Shape beef into a large patty; brown in a large skillet 5 minutes on each side; break into chunks and push to one side. Sauté onions and garlic in drippings until soft; stir in tomatoes, oregano and salt. Simmer, uncovered, for 30 minutes.
2. Prepare eggplant: Cut eggplant into ¼-inch thick slices; pare slices. Beat egg, water, salt and pepper in a pie plate; sprinkle bread crumbs in a second pie plate. Dip eggplant slices, first into the egg mixture and then into the crumbs to coat lightly.
3. Brown eggplant slices, a few at a time in part of the oil in a large skillet; remove and reserve.
4. Spread ⅓ of the sauce on the bottom of a 10-cup shallow casserole. Layer half the eggplant slices over and top with half the Parmesan and Provolone cheese; spoon ⅓ of the sauce over and top with remaining eggplant slices and Parmesan cheese and sauce.
5. Bake in moderate oven (350°) 40 minutes; top with remaining Provolone cheese and bake 5 minutes longer, or until cheese is melted. Cool 10 minutes before serving. Pass a small bowl of freshly grated Parmesan cheese for those who like an extra topping.
HOSTESS TIP: EGGPLANT PARMIGIANA can be made ahead. Cook, but do not top with remaining Provolone cheese. Cover, then refrigerate. One hour before serving, place casserole in oven; turn oven control to moderate (350°) and bake 55 minutes, or until bubbly-hot, then top with remaining cheese and bake 5 minutes longer. Cool 10 minutes; serve.

NOODLES ROMANO

Romans enjoy a variety of pasta dishes. It's both economical and delicious.

Bake at 350° for 50 minutes.
Makes 6 servings at 52¢ each.

- 1 medium-size onion, chopped (½ cup)
- 1 clove garlic, minced
- 2 tablespoons vegetable oil
- 1 pound ground chuck
- 1 can (8 ounces) tomato sauce
- 1 can (6 ounces) tomato paste
- ¼ cup dry red wine
- 1 bay leaf
- 2 teaspoons salt
- 1 teaspoon leaf oregano, crumbled
- 2 eggs
- 1 package (10 ounces) frozen chopped spinach, thawed and drained
- 1 cup cottage cheese
- ¼ cup grated Romano cheese
- 1 teaspoon leaf basil, crumbled
- 1 package (8 ounces) wide noodles, cooked and drained
- 2 slices Swiss cheese

1. Sauté onion and garlic lightly in oil in a large skillet. Brown beef in same skillet; crumble. Stir in tomato sauce, tomato paste, wine, bay leaf, 1 teaspoon of the salt and oregano; simmer 15 minutes.
2. Beat eggs in a medium size bowl; add spinach, cottage cheese, Romano cheese, remaining 1 teaspoon salt and basil; mix until well-blended.
3. Spread half the tomato mixture into a 10-cup shallow casserole. Layer half the noodles on top; spread with all of the spinach-cheese mixture. Repeat noodle layer; top with rest of tomato mixture; cover casserole.
4. Bake in moderate oven (350°) 45 minutes; remove from oven. Cut cheese into strips; arrange on top of casserole. Bake 5 minutes longer, or until cheese melts.

QUICK TIPS

To save the most on vegetables, buy them at the peak of the growing season. Look for produce to be on special:
- Winter—Artichokes, avocados, broccoli, Brussel sprouts, cauliflower, mushrooms, parsnips, potatoes
- Spring—Asparagus, cabbage, carrots, green onions, spinach
- Summer—Green and wax beans, beets, corn, okra, onions, peas, sweet green and red peppers, summer squash, tomatoes, zucchini
- Fall-Broccoli, cauliflower, eggplant, mushrooms, onions, parsnips, potatoes, sweet potatoes, acorn and Hubbard squash.
- Be frugal. Don't throw out bits of chopped onion. Store in the refrigerator in a tightly sealed jar. That way the onion stays fresh and the refrigerator remains free of onion odor.

TUCSON HASH

Kidney beans and chili powder give this hash its distinctive character.

Bake at 350° for 30 minutes.
Makes 4 servings at 57¢ each.

- 1 large onion, chopped (1 cup)
- 2 tablespoons olive oil or vegetable oil
- 1 to 2 tablespoons chili powder
- 2 cups diced cooked beef
- 1 can (1 pound) red kidney beans, drained
- 1 cup chopped celery
- 1 can (1 pound) tomatoes
- 1 teaspoon salt
- ¼ teaspoon pepper
- 1 bag (4 ounces) corn chips

1. Sauté onion until soft in oil in a large skillet; stir in chili powder and cook 2 minutes; add beef and cook 3 minutes.
2. Stir in kidney beans, celery, tomatoes, salt and pepper; spoon into an 8-cup casserole.
3. Bake in moderate oven (350°) 20 minutes; top with corn chips; bake 10 minutes longer, or until bubbly-hot.

KENTUCKY TUNA CASSEROLE

First one home can put this dish together, it's that easy.

Bake at 400° for 35 minutes.
Makes 4 servings at 48¢ each.

   1   package (about 6 ounces) au
         gratin potatoes
2¼   cups hot water
   1   envelope (2 to a package)
         onion soup mix
   1   package (9 ounces) frozen
         French-cut green beans,
         partially thawed
   1   can (about 7 ounces) tuna, drained
         and flaked
   ¾   cup milk
   2   tablespoons butter or margarine

1. Combine potatoes, hot water and onion soup mix in an 8-cup casserole until well-blended. Stir in green beans, tuna and milk; dot with butter or margarine.
2. Bake in hot oven (400°) 35 minutes, or until potatoes are tender and golden; sprinkle with chopped parsley, if you wish and serve with a tossed green salad topped with diced apple.

PRESTO LASAGNA

The fastest recipe we know for home-made lasagne.

Bake at 350° for 30 minutes.
Makes 6 servings at 58¢ each.

   1   package (8 ounces) medium-size
         noodles
   1   tablespoon vegetable oil or olive oil
   1   package (8 ounces) heat-and-serve
         sausage patties
   1   can (1 pound, 1 ounce) Italian
         tomatoes
   1   can (8 ounces) tomato sauce
   1   tablespoon minced dried onion
   1   teaspoon mixed Italian herbs,
         crumbled
   1   container (8 ounces) pot cheese
   ¼   cup grated Parmesan cheese
   1   package (6 ounces) sliced
         mozzarella cheese, cut into ½-
         inch strips

1. Cook noodles, following label directions; drain; return to same kettle; toss with oil to keep from sticking.
2. While noodles cook, dice sausage patties; brown with no fat, stirring often, in medium-size skillet; stir in tomatoes, tomato sauce, onion and Italian herbs; bring to boiling; lower heat; simmer, stirring often, about 5 minutes.
3. Layer half the noodles, pot cheese, Parmesan cheese, tomato mixture and mozzarella cheese in 6-cup shallow casserole; repeat, crisscrossing mozzarella strips on top.
4. Bake in moderate oven (350°) 30 minutes, or until bubbling at edges and cheese is lightly browned.

KIELBASA AND KRAUT

Polish sausage and sauerkraut are foods to a man's taste.

Bake at 325° for 1 hour, 30 minutes.
Makes 6 servings at 44¢ each.

   2   packages (1 pound each)
         sauerkraut
         OR: 1 can (1 pound, 11 ounces)
         sauerkraut
   1   large onion, sliced
   2   tablespoons butter, margarine or
         bacon drippings
   1   large apple, pared, quartered,
         cored and sliced
   2   tablespoons brown sugar
   ½   teaspoon caraway seeds
   ½   teaspoon leaf marjoram, crumbled
   ½   cup dry white wine or water
   1   kielbasa sausage (about 1 pound)

1. Drain sauerkraut and rinse under cold running water.
2. Sauté onion lightly in butter, margarine or bacon drippings in an 8-cup flame-proof casserole or a large skillet. Stir in drained sauerkraut, apple, brown sugar, caraway seeds, marjoram and wine or water; bring to boiling.
3. While sauerkraut mixture heats, make deep cuts, 1 inch apart, in sausage. Lay on top of sauerkraut mixture; cover. (If using a skillet, spoon sauerkraut mixture into an 8-cup casserole; top with kielbasa; cover.)
4. Bake in slow oven (325°) 1 hour, 30 minutes, stirring several times and adding more wine or water if necessary, or until sauerkraut is soft and delicately browned. Serve with freshly boiled potatoes and prepared mustard.

OXFORDSHIRE APPLE AND HAM BAKE

A jumbo pancake bakes over ham and apple slices in this old English favorite.

Bake at 350° for 1 hour.
Makes 6 servings at 53¢ each.

   3   cups diced cooked ham
   4   medium-size tart apples, pared,
         cored and sliced
   ¼   cup firmly packed brown sugar
   ¼   teaspoon ground mace
   ¼   teaspoon pepper
   ¼   cup apple juice or water
   1   cup pancake mix
   1   cup milk
   2   tablespoons melted butter or
         margarine

1. Make a layer of half of the ham and apples in an 8-cup casserole.
2. Combine brown sugar, mace and pepper in a cup; sprinkle half over layer. Repeat with remaining ham, apples and sugar mixture. Pour apple juice or water over; cover casserole.
3. Bake in moderate oven (350°) 40 minutes, or just until apples are tender.
4. For pancakes, blend the mix, milk

and melted butter or margarine in a medium-size bowl to make a thin batter; pour over hot ham-apple mixture.
5. Bake, uncovered, 20 minutes longer, or until topping is puffed and golden.
Suggested Variations: Follow recipe for OXFORDSHIRE APPLE AND HAM BAKE, substituting 3 cups diced cooked pork for the ham and 1 teaspoon curry powder for the mace; add 1 teaspoon salt.

BEEF TAVERNA

Casseroles get a nutrition boost when wheat germ is used as an ingredient.

Bake at 375° for 30 minutes.
Makes 4 servings at 51¢ each.

   1   cup elbow macaroni
   ½   pound ground beef
   1   medium-size onion, chopped
         (½ cup)
   ½   teaspoon salt
   ¼   teaspoon pepper
   ¼   teaspoon leaf thyme, crumbled
   1   egg
   2   egg whites
   ½   cup milk
   2   tablespoons chopped parsley
   1   cup regular wheat germ
   ½   cup shredded mozzarella cheese
         Mozzarella Cheese Sauce (recipe
         follows)

1. Cook macaroni, following label directions; drain and keep warm.
2. Brown ground beef in a large skillet; break into chunks and push to one side. Sauté onion in drippings until soft; season with salt, pepper and thyme; remove from heat and cool slightly.
3. Stir cooked macaroni, whole egg, egg whites, milk and parsley into skillet until mixture is well-blended.
4. Grease a 6-cup casserole and sprinkle with half the wheat germ; spoon beef mixture into casserole; top with remaining wheat germ, then shredded cheese. Spoon MOZZARELLA CHEESE SAUCE over top of casserole.
5. Bake in moderate oven (375°) 30 minutes, or until top is golden. Serve with shredded iceberg lettuce, diced apple and bottled oil-and-vinegar dressing, if you wish.

MOZZARELLA CHEESE SAUCE:
Makes about 1½ cups.
Melt 2 tablespoons butter or margarine in a small saucepan; stir in 2 tablespoons all-purpose flour and cook, stirring constantly, until bubbly. Stir in 1 cup milk. Cook, stirring constantly, until sauce thickens and bubbles 3 minutes; beat 2 egg yolks in a small bowl; beat ½ cup of the hot sauce into eggs, then beat back into saucepan. Cook over low heat 2 minutes. Blend in ½ cup shredded mozzarella cheese, ½ teaspoon salt and a dash of grated nutmeg. This sauce also makes an excellent topping for lasagna, manicotti, canneloni and other pasta dishes.

the art of cooking in one pot

The big black kettle has been updated! For centuries women greeted their families with the aroma of dinner simmering in the big black kettle on the back of a wood-burning stove. The foods and flavorings varied with the nationality of the cook, but there were certain points they all had in common—they made the most from inexpensive cuts of meat, beans and vegetables, and they used little fuel energy. You now have an electrical version of the old black kettle, called a slow cooker, and it can deliver delicious dinners every night, even if the cook's away all day. Polish Hot Pot, Glazed Rock Cornish Hens and Vermont Corned Beef Platter are just three of the delicious recipes from our bonus section on Slow Cookers that begins on page 32.

TAMALE BAKE

Cornmeal goes Southwestern-style with a chili-tomato sauce and chunks of ripe olives and a Cheddar cheese topping.

Bake at 400° for 45 minutes.
Makes 6 servings at 48¢ each.

3½ cups water
1 cup yellow cornmeal
1½ teaspoons salt
1 pound ground beef
1 large onion, chopped (1-cup)
1 large green pepper, halved, seeded and chopped
1 tablespoon chili powder
1 envelope (1½ ounces) spaghetti sauce mix
1 can (1 pound) tomatoes
1 cup halved ripe olives
1 cup shredded Cheddar cheese (4 ounces)

1. Bring water to boiling in a large heavy saucepan; stir in cornmeal and salt, very slowly; lower heat. Continue stirring constantly until cornmeal thickens and starts to leave the side of the pan; pour into 13x9x2-inch casserole; chill until cornmeal is firm.
2. While cornmeal chills, brown beef in a large skillet; break into chunks; remove with slotted spoon; reserve. Sauté onion and green pepper in pan drippings until soft; stir in chili powder and cook 2 minutes longer.
3. Stir in spaghetti sauce mix, tomatoes and ripe olives; return meat to skillet; lower heat; simmer 15 minutes.
4. Invert cold cornmeal onto a cutting board; cut lengthwise into thirds, then into triangles. Wash and dry casserole.
5. Spoon part of the sauce into the bottom of the casserole; overlap cornmeal triangles in casserole; top with remaining meat-tomato sauce.
6. Bake in hot oven (400°) 40 minutes; sprinkle cheese over; bake 5 minutes longer or until cheese melts.

QUICK TIPS

In casserole cooking, always leave at least a ½-inch above the food when filling your dish. This gives room for the casserole to bubble without spill-overs. Bake extra in a little casserole.
To know the exact volume of your casserole, pour water from a measuring cup into the pan until water level reaches the top. Mark number of cups on the back with nail polish or paint.

CANADIAN MACARONI AND CHEESE

This version includes a tomato-onion sauce with lots of cheese and herbs.

Bake at 350° for 30 minutes.
Makes 6 servings at 36¢ each.

1 package (8 ounces) elbow macaroni
1 small onion, chopped (¼ cup)
2 tablespoons butter or margarine
1 can (1 pound, 4 ounces) tomatoes
2 cups shredded Cheddar cheese (8 ounces)
½ teaspoon salt
½ teaspoon leaf basil, crumbled
¼ teaspoon pepper

1. Cook macaroni in boiling salted water in a large kettle, following label directions; drain; spoon into an 8-cup casserole; set aside.
2. Sauté onion until soft in butter or margarine in a large skillet; stir in tomatoes, half of the cheese, salt, basil and pepper. Heat, stirring constantly, just until cheese melts. Stir into macaroni; sprinkle with remaining cheese.
3. Bake in moderate oven (350°) 30 minutes, or until bubbly-hot. Garnish with tomato slices, if you wish.

OXTAILS ROMANO

This recipe was inspired by a Roman trattoria specialty. Serve with linguini and a full red wine.

Bake at 350° for 2 hours.
Makes 6 servings at 55¢ each.

3 pounds oxtails, cut up
3 tablespoons olive oil or vegetable oil
1 large onion, chopped (1 cup)
2 cloves garlic, minced
2 large carrots, pared and diced
⅓ cup chopped parsley
1 can (1 pound, 1 ounce) Italian tomatoes
1 cup dry red wine or beef broth
2 teaspoons salt
½ teaspoon freshly ground pepper
2 cups chopped celery

1. Brown oxtails, a few pieces at a time, in oil in a 10-cup flame-proof casserole or a large skillet; remove and keep warm. Sauté onion, garlic, carrots and parsley in drippings until soft.
2. Stir in tomatoes, wine or broth, salt and pepper until sauce bubbles. Return oxtails to casserole; cover. (If using a skillet, place browned oxtails in a 10-cup casserole; pour sauce over; cover.)
3. Bake in moderate oven (350°) 1 hour, 30 minutes; stir in celery; cover. Bake 30 minutes longer, or until oxtails are very tender. Let stand 5 minutes to allow fat to rise; skim off fat. Serve with buttered linguini and a tossed green salad.
COOK'S TIP: OXTAILS ROMANO are even more flavorful if made the day ahead, cooled and refrigerated. To serve, re-

move fat from top of sauce; place, covered, in oven. Set oven thermometer to moderate (350°) and bake 1 hour, or until casserole is bubbly-hot.

ARIZONA RICE BAKE

Chili powder flavored sauce bakes with quick-cooking rice for a meal in minutes.

Bake at 350° 20 minutes.
Make 6 servings at 32¢ each.

½ cup frozen chopped onion
½ cup chopped celery
2 tablespoons vegetable oil
1 to 3 teaspoons chili powder
2½ cups tomato juice
¼ teaspoon pepper
2½ cups packaged pre-cooked rice
1 package (1 pound) frankfurters

1. Sauté onion and celery lightly in oil in a large skillet; stir in chili powder and cook 2 minutes. Add tomato juice and pepper; bring to boiling; stir in rice; spoon into a 6-cup casserole.
2. Cut each frankfurter into thirds and score; arrange on top of rice; cover.
3. Bake in moderate oven (350°) 20 minutes, or until bubbly-hot.

SAN PEDRO SUPPER CASSEROLE

Keep the ingredients for this dish on hand and you can be sure of a hearty supper in less than an hour.

Bake at 400° for 45 minutes.
Makes 4 servings at 38¢ each.

½ cup frozen chopped onions
1 tablespoon vegetable oil
1 can condensed cream of celery soup
1 can (about 7 ounces) tuna, drained and flaked
1 cup frozen peas (from a 1½-pound bag)
⅓ cup milk
2 pimiento, cut into strips
1 teaspoon salt
½ teaspoon dillweed
4 cups frozen Southern-style hash brown potatoes (from a 24-ounce bag)

1. Sauté onion in oil in a large skillet until soft. Stir in soup, tuna, peas, milk, pimiento strips, salt and dill; bring to boiling; remove from heat.
2. Spread half of the hash brown potatoes in a greased 6-cup shallow casserole; spread with half the sauce; repeat layers; cover.
3. Bake in hot oven (400°) 30 minutes. Remove cover and bake 15 minutes longer, or until potatoes are golden and casserole is bubbly-hot.
Suggested Variations: One can (7 ounces) salmon, drained, boned, and flaked, may be substituted for the tuna in this dish. Also, one can of cream of mushroom soup may be substituted for the celery soup.

ALABAMA HAM AND VEGETABLES

Cooked cucumber can add an interesting touch to casseroles, especially those made with a smoked meat.

Bake at 350° for 30 minutes.
Makes 4 servings at 52¢ each.

- 1 package (10 ounces) frozen lima beans
- 2 medium-size carrots, pared and thinly sliced
- 1 medium-size cucumber, pared, quartered lengthwise and cubed
- 2 cups diced cooked ham or pork or sliced frankfurters
- ½ cup frozen chopped onion
- 2 tablespoons butter or margarine
- 1 can condensed cream of celery soup
- ⅔ cup milk
- 1 teaspoon leaf sage, crumbled teaspoon pepper
- 1 package (about 4 ounces) corn chips, crushed

1. Cook lima beans and carrots together, following label directions for limas, in a medium-size saucepan; add cucumber for last 2 minutes of cooking; drain.
2. Sauté ham and onion in butter or margarine in a large skillet 5 minutes, or until onion is softened. Stir in soup, milk, sage and pepper; heat, stirring constantly, just until blended.
3. Pour into a buttered 6-cup casserole; stir in cooked vegetables; sprinkle crushed corn chips over.
4. Bake in moderate oven (350°) 30 minutes, or until bubbly-hot. Serve with refrigerated crescent rolls.

BASQUE GARBANZO CASSEROLE

A simplified version of Olla Podrida, the popular Spanish soup-stew.

Bake at 325° for 1 hour.
Makes 8 servings at 52¢ each.

- ½ pound piece pepperoni, sliced
- 1 chicken breast (about 12 ounces)
- 1 large leek, chopped
  OR: 1 large onion, chopped (1 cup)
- 2 cloves garlic minced
- 4 medium-size carrots, sliced
- 2 cups shredded cabbage (¼ head)
- 2 cans (1 pound, 4 ounces each) chick peas (garbanzos), drained
  OR: 2 cans (1 pound each) red kidney beans, drained
- 1 can (1 pound) tomatoes
- 2 teaspoons salt
- 1 teaspoon leaf thyme, crumbled
- ½ teaspoon pepper

1. Sauté pepperoni in a 12-cup flame-proof casserole or large skillet for 5 minutes; remove with slotted spoon. Cut chicken breast into 2-inch pieces with poultry or kitchen scissors.
2. Brown chicken pieces in pan drippings; remove with slotted spoon. Sauté leek or onion and garlic in pan drippings; stir in carrots and cook 3 minutes; stir in cabbage and cook 2 minutes. Add chick peas or kidney beans, tomatoes, salt, thyme and pepper; stir to blend well.
3. Return browned chicken and pepperoni to casserole; cover. (If using a skillet, combine meats and beans in a 12-cup casserole; cover.)
4. Bake in slow oven (325°) 1 hour, or until casserole bubbles.

QUICK TIPS

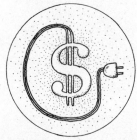

Less cooking time = less energy used = money saved:
- Make mashed potatoes faster? Pare potatoes and cut into small pieces; cook in boiling salted water 15 minutes; drain; add milk and butter to pan with potatoes; heat until butter melts; then remove pan from heat and mash potatoes.
- Brown a batch of meat balls quickly by placing them, in a single layer, in a jelly-roll pan. Bake at 350° for 15 minutes; then add to casserole and cook following recipe instructions.

SWISS STEAK

When chuck steak is on special, try baking it in this savory sauce.

Bake at 350° for 1 hour, 30 minutes.
Makes 6 servings at 47¢ each.

- 1 bone-in chuck steak, about 2 pounds
- 2 tablespoons all-purpose flour
- 1 teaspoon salt
- ¼ teaspoon ground cloves
- 2 tablespoons vegetable oil
- 1 medium-size onion, chopped (½ cup)
- ½ cup chopped celery
- 1½ cups tomato juice
- 1 jar (about 8 ounces) junior carrots (baby-pack)
- 1 bay leaf

1. Trim fat from steak; rub both sides with mixture of flour, salt and cloves. Brown quickly in oil in a 10-cup shallow flame-proof casserole or a large skillet; remove and keep warm.
2. Sauté onion and celery in pan drippings until soft; stir in tomato juice, carrots and bay leaf; bring to boiling; return steak to casserole; spoon some of the sauce over; cover. (If using a skillet, place steak in a 10-cup casserole; pour sauce over; cover.)
3. Bake in moderate oven (350°) 1 hour, 30 minutes, or until steak is tender when pierced with a two-tined fork.
COOK'S TIP: You can bake potatoes, small acorn squash or butternut squash along with casserole to serve with meat. Oven-baked apples or pears would make an energy-saving dessert. For additional bake-alongs, see page 6.

CARIBBEAN CHICKEN

A chicken and pork combination for those who like food on the fiery side.

Bake at 350° for 1 hour.
Makes 8 servings at 58¢ each.

- 1 Spanish onion, sliced
- 2 tablespoons olive oil or vegetable oil
- 1 broiler-fryer, cut up (about 3 pounds)
- 1 pound smoked pork butt, cut into 1-inch cubes
  OR: 2 cups cubed cooked ham or frankfurters
- 2 cups water
- 1 can (8 ounces) tomato sauce
- ¼ cup shredded coconut
- 1½ teaspoons salt
- 1½ teaspoons red pepper flakes
- 4 whole cloves
- 1 bay leaf
- ¼ teaspoon leaf thyme
- 2 pounds sweet potatoes
- 2 bananas, peeled and sliced, ¾-inch thick
- ¼ cup sliced green onion

1. Sauté onion until golden in a 12-cup flame-proof casserole or in a heavy kettle in oil, about 5 minutes. Remove with a slotted spoon; reserve.
2. Brown chicken, half at a time, in same casserole. Return chicken and onion to pan. Add smoked pork, water, tomato sauce, coconut and salt and stir to combine. Tie pepper, cloves, bay leaf and thyme in cheesecloth; add to liquid. Bring to boiling; lower heat; cover. (If using a skillet, place chicken, onions and pork in a 12-cup casserole. Heat water, tomato sauce, coconut and salt in skillet and pour over ingredients in casserole. Add cheesecloth bag; cover.)
3. Bake in moderate oven (350°) 30 minutes before adding potatoes.
4. Meanwhile, pare sweet potatoes and cut into about ½-inch slices. Add to casserole, pushing them down into liquid. Bake 25 minutes longer, or until meats and potatoes are tender.
5. Stir bananas and green onion into stew. Cover and bake 5 minutes longer. Garnish with additional coconut and green onion, if you wish.

FOR QUICKER MEALS

Too busy for time-consuming dinner recipes? Start with packaged ingredients that do some of the work for you, such as dry soup and gravy mixes, rice mixes and frozen vegetables. Some foods are actually cheaper in this packaged form, so you'll save money, as well as time and effort. This chapter includes family-size recipes that are fast (less than one hour)—but flavorful. And some are simple enough for the children to prepare when they arrive home from school.

Munich Kraut and Knackwurst
combines plump sausage
with sauerkraut, a bright red
apple and wine or beer, for a
quick-into-the-oven dish
that goes so well with pumpernickel bread and a sharp,
tangy mustard. The recipe
appears on page 18.

MUNICH KRAUT AND KNACKWURST

Try this quick version of Choucroute a l'Alsacienne. Shown on page 16.

Bake at 375° for 30 minutes.
Makes 4 servings.

- 1 large onion, sliced
- ¼ cup (½ stick) butter or margarine
- 1 large red apple, quartered, cored and diced
- 1 can (1 pound, 13 ounces) sauerkraut, washed and drained
- 3 tablespoons brown sugar
- 1 teaspoon caraway seeds
- 1 pound knackwursts, scored
- ½ cup beer or dry white wine

1. Sauté onion in 3 tablespoons butter or margarine in a large skillet just until soft; sauté apple 2 minutes. Stir in sauerkraut, brown sugar and caraway seeds; toss lightly with a fork to mix well; spoon into an 8-cup shallow casserole.
2. Sauté knackwursts in remaining 1 tablespoon butter or margarine in same pan 5 minutes, or until browned; arrange on sauerkraut; drizzle beer or wine over; cover casserole.
3. Bake in moderate oven (375°) 30 minutes, or until bubbly-hot. Serve with a zippy mustard, dill pickles and pumpernickel bread, if you wish.

MANDARIN BEEF

Sauté meat quickly, the Oriental way, then combine with a soy seasoned sauce and bake.

Bake at 375° for 50 minutes.
Makes 6 servings.

- 1 round or boneless chuck steak (about 2 pounds)
  Instant unseasoned meat tenderizer
- ¼ cup peanut oil or vegetable oil
- 1 cup frozen chopped onion
- 2 cups sliced celery
- 1 can (3 or 4 ounces) sliced mushrooms
- 1 can condensed cream of chicken soup
- ½ cup water
- ¼ cup soy sauce
- 2 cups shredded Chinese cabbage
- ¼ cup toasted slivered almonds

1. Moisten meat and sprinkle with tenderizer, following label directions; cut in 2-inch-long strips about ½-inch thick.
2. Brown strips, a few at a time, in part of the oil in a large skillet, adding more oil as needed; spoon into an 8-cup casserole. Sauté onion just until soft in pan drippings; add with celery to meat.
3. Stir mushrooms and liquid, soup, water and soy sauce into skillet; bring to boiling; pour over meat mixture; cover.
4. Bake in moderate oven (375°) 40 minutes, or until meat is tender. Place shredded cabbage on top; cover.

5. Bake 10 minutes longer, or just until cabbage wilts. Before serving, sprinkle with almonds. Serve over rice.

MEXICAN JACK CASSEROLE

The perfect casserole for a last-minute picnic.

Bake at 375° for 30 minutes.
Makes 6 servings.

- 1 cup frozen chopped onion
- 1 cup chopped celery
- 2 tablespoons vegetable oil
- 1 can (12 ounces) pork luncheon meat, cubed
- 1 to 3 teaspoons chili powder
- 1 teaspoon leaf oregano, crumbled
- 1 can (8 ounces) tomato sauce
- 2 cans (1 pound each) red kidney beans, drained
- 1 cup shredded Monterey Jack or Cheddar cheese (4 ounces)

1. Sauté onion and celery in oil in a large skillet just until soft; push to one side. Add meat and brown lightly. Stir in chili powder and oregano; cook 2 minutes. Stir in tomato sauce and beans; bring to boiling.
2. Spoon into an 8-cup casserole; stir in cheese lightly.
3. Bake in moderate oven (375°) 30 minutes, or until bubbly-hot. Garnish with sliced ripe olives, if you wish.

SHEPHERD'S PIE

An old favorite that's perfect for meat and potato lovers. Cooked pork, lamb or turkey can be substituted for the beef in this recipe.

Bake at 350° about 30 minutes.
Makes 6 servings.

- 3 cups cooked cubed beef
- 1 small onion, grated
- 1 can (about 11 ounces) beef gravy
  OR: 1½ cups leftover gravy
- 1 cup cooked carrots, green beans or corn
  OR: 1 can (8 ounces) carrots, green beans or corn, drained
- 1 tablespoon prepared mustard
- 1 teaspoon Worcestershire sauce
  Instant mashed potatoes to make 4 cups

1. Combine beef, onion, gravy, cooked vegetables, mustard and Worcestershire sauce in large saucepan; bring to boiling.
2. Prepare instant mashed potatoes following label directions (or use 4 cups seasoned hot mashed potatoes). Spread half in buttered 8-cup shallow casserole; spoon hot meat mixture over; top with remaining potatoes.
3. Bake in moderate oven (350°) 30 minutes, or until heated through and potatoes are lightly browned. Serve with a tossed greens salad, if you wish.

CREOLE FISH FILLETS

Green peppers and tomato sauce give fish a whole new flavor.

Bake at 400° for 30 minutes.
Makes 4 servings.

- ½ cup frozen chopped onion
- 1 large green pepper, halved, seeded and chopped
- ½ cup chopped celery
- ¼ cup (½ stick) butter or margarine
- 1 can (8 ounces) tomato sauce
- 1 teaspoon salt
- 1 teaspoon curry powder
  Few drops bottled red-pepper seasoning
- 1 package (1 pound) frozen Greenland turbot or cod fillets
- 1 can (1 pound) white potatoes, drained
- 1 cucumber, pared and sliced

1. Sauté onion, green pepper and celery in butter or margarine in a large skillet until soft; stir in tomato sauce, salt, curry powder and red-pepper seasoning.
2. Cut fish in serving-size pieces; place in a single layer in a 6-cup casserole; spoon sauce over; arrange potatoes and cucumber slices on sides.
3. Bake in hot oven (400°) 30 minutes, or until fish flakes easily. Sprinkle chopped parsley on top, if you wish.

SAUSAGE AND EGGPLANT BAKE

Breakfast sausages make an interesting addition to casserole cooking.

Bake at 375° for 40 minutes.
Makes 6 servings.

- 1 package (1 pound) sausage links
- 1 medium-size eggplant, pared and cut into 1-inch cubes
- 1 large onion, chopped (1 cup)
- 1 clove garlic, minced
- ¼ cup chopped parsley
- 1 teaspoon curry powder
- 1 teaspoon leaf oregano, crumbled
- 3 large tomatoes, peeled and cut into thick slices

1. Brown sausage links slowly in a large skillet; remove and reserve.
2. Pour off all but 2 tablespoons of the fat; sauté eggplant cubes, one third at a time, in drippings; remove and reserve, using additional fat as needed to sauté eggplant. Then add several tablespoons vegetable oil, if needed.
3. Sauté onion and garlic in pan drippings until soft; stir in parsley, curry powder and oregano; cook 2 minutes. Return sausages to skillet and blend well; remove from heat.
4. Layer half the eggplant, sausage mixture and sliced tomatoes in an 8-cup shallow casserole; repeat.
5. Bake in moderate oven (375°) 40 minutes, or until bubbly-hot; top with chopped parsley, if you wish.

DEVILED TUNA

Deviled in the title means a dish will be spicy—often with a liberal dash of mustard and red pepper.

Bake at 350° for 20 minutes.
Makes 4 servings.

  2 tablespoons butter or margarine
  2 tablespoons all-purpose flour
  ½ teaspoon salt
  1½ cups milk
  1 tablespoon prepared mustard
  ¼ teaspoon bottled red-pepper seasoning
  1 can (about 7 ounces) tuna, drained and flaked
  ¾ cup soda cracker crumbs (4 large crackers)
  4 hard-cooked eggs, shelled

1. Melt butter or margarine in medium-size saucepan; stir in flour and salt; cook, stirring constantly until bubbly; stir in milk. Cook, stirring constantly, until sauce thickens and bubbles 3 minutes; lower heat.
2. Stir in mustard, bottled red-pepper seasoning, tuna and ½ cup of the cracker crumbs; remove from heat.
3. Chop 3 eggs coarsely; stir into tuna mixture; pour into a buttered 4-cup shallow casserole or a 9-inch pie plate. Sprinkle remaining ¼ cup cracker crumbs over top.
4. Bake in moderate oven (350°) 20 minutes, or until crumbs are golden. Slice remaining egg lengthwise; arrange on casserole and garnish with parsley.

EGGS AU GRATIN

Eggs make a grand dinner dish when given a cheese sauce.

Bake at 375° for 15 minutes.
Makes 6 servings.

  2 packages (10 ounces each) frozen broccoli spears
    OR: 2 packages (9 ounces each) frozen whole green beans
  12 hard-cooked eggs, shelled and sliced
  1 can condensed Cheddar cheese soup
  ⅔ cup milk
  1 teaspoon Worcestershire sauce
  6 slices white bread, toasted, buttered and cut into triangles

1. Cook frozen broccoli or green beans, following label directions; drain. Place in a 6-cup shallow casserole. Layer egg slices on top of vegetables.
2. Combine soup and milk in a medium-size saucepan; heat slowly to boiling; stir in Worcestershire sauce. Pour over eggs and vegetables.
3. Bake in moderate oven (375°) 15 minutes, or until bubbly; arrange toast triangles around edge of casserole just before serving.

NAPA VALLEY BEANS

The Italian influence is still tasted in the cooking of this great wine producing region of California.

Bake at 375° for 30 minutes.
Makes 8 servings.

  ½ pound piece salami, diced
  1 large onion, chopped (1 cup)
  2 cloves garlic, minced
  2 large tomatoes, peeled and diced
    OR: 1 can (1 pound) tomatoes, chopped
  1 teaspoon leaf basil, crumbled
  1 teaspoon salt
  ½ teaspoon pepper
  ¼ cup dry red wine
  2 cans (1 pound, 4 ounces each) white kidney beans (cannellini) or red kidney beans, drained
  1 package (6 ounces) sliced Provolone cheese

1. Sauté salami in a large skillet; remove with slotted spoon; sauté onion and garlic in pan drippings.
2. Stir tomato, basil, salt, pepper and wine into skillet and cook 2 minutes. Stir in drained beans; bring to bubbling. Spoon into a 10-cup casserole.
3. Bake in a moderate oven (375°) 25 minutes; lay slices of Provolone cheese over top of casserole. Bake 5 minutes longer, or until cheese melts and beans are bubbly-hot.

TONGUE AND POTATO CASSEROLE

You can use sliced bologna, ham or even quartered frankfurters, in place of the tongue in this recipe.

Bake at 350° for 15 minutes.
Makes 6 servings.

  6 medium-size potatoes, cooked, peeled and sliced
  ¼ cup sliced green onions
  1 can condensed cream of onion soup
  ½ cup milk
  ¼ cup mayonnaise or salad dressing
  4 teaspoons prepared mustard
  1 teaspoon Worcestershire sauce
  1 cup frozen peas (from a 1½-pound bag)
  12 slices cooked tongue
  1 tablespoon white corn syrup

1. Place potato slices in a large bowl; add green onions.
2. Combine soup and milk in a small saucepan; stir until smooth. Cook until bubbly-hot. Stir in mayonnaise or salad dressing, 3 teaspoons of the mustard, Worcestershire sauce and frozen peas.
3. Pour hot sauce over potatoes and onions; toss lightly until potatoes are coated. Spoon into an 8-cup casserole.
4. Overlap tongue slices in a ring on top of potatoes; mix corn syrup and remaining mustard in a cup; brush over tongue.

5. Bake in moderate oven (350°) 15 minutes, or until potatoes are hot and tongue is lightly glazed. Garnish with strips of pimiento, if you wish.

VEAL CONTINENTAL

Chicken breasts can be substituted for the veal in this recipe.

Bake at 350° for 35 minutes.
Makes 4 servings.

  1 package (about 5 ounces) noodles Romanoff
  4 frozen veal patties (about 1 pound)
  3 tablespoons all-purpose flour
  1 teaspoon salt
  ¼ teaspoon pepper
  ¼ cup (½ stick) butter or margarine
  ½ cup packaged croutons

1. Cook noodles Romanoff, following label directions. Spoon into a shallow 6-cup casserole; set aside.
2. While noodles cook, sprinkle veal with flour seasoned with salt and pepper on wax paper.
3. Sauté veal quickly in butter or margarine in large skillet 5 to 8 minutes on each side, or until golden. Tuck into noodle mixture.
4. Bake in moderate oven (350°) 30 minutes, or until bubbly in middle. Pile croutons on top; bake 5 minutes longer, or until golden. Garnish with parsley.

BAKED BOLOGNA JUBILEE

Bologna is available unsliced and you save money by buying the bulk pieces.

Bake at 350° for 30 minutes.
Makes 6 servings.

  1½ pound piece bologna
    Whole cloves
  1 can (1 pound) fruit cocktail
  1 can (1 pound) sweet potatoes
  ½ cup firmly packed light brown sugar
  1 teaspoon ground cinnamon
  ¼ cup orange juice
  2 tablespoons butter or margarine

1. Peel covering, if any, from bologna; cut bologna in half lengthwise. Score rounded side of each half in diamond pattern; stud meat with whole cloves. Place halves, cut-sides down, in a 13x9x2-inch casserole. Arrange fruits and sweet potatoes around meat.
2. Blend brown sugar, cinnamon and orange juice in a small bowl; drizzle over meat. Dot fruits and potatoes with butter or margarine.
3. Bake in moderate oven (350°) 20 minutes. Spoon juices in dish over meat. Bake 10 minutes longer, or until glazed.
Suggested Variation: A 1-inch thick slice of canned ham or a ham steak can be substituted for the bologna.

LONG BEACH TURKEY BAKE

Teens vote this casserole one of their favorites.

Bake at 450° for 10 minutes.
Makes 4 servings.

- 2 cups finely crushed potato chips (from a 4-ounce package)
- ½ cup shredded Cheddar cheese
- 1 package (8 ounces) frozen mixed vegetables in onion sauce
- 2 cups cubed cooked turkey
- 1 cup thinly sliced celery
- ½ cup chopped walnuts or dry-roasted peanuts
- ½ cup mayonnaise or salad dressing
- 2 teaspoons grated onion
- 1 teaspoon salt
- 2 tablespoons lemon juice

1. Mix potato chips and cheese in a small bowl; pat half of mixture into bottom of a 6-cup shallow casserole.
2. Cook frozen mixed vegetables, following label directions, in a large saucepan; stir in turkey, celery, nuts, mayonnaise or salad dressing, onion, salt and lemon juice.
3. Spoon into prepared casserole; sprinkle reserved potato-chip mixture on top.
4. Bake in very hot oven (450°) 10 minutes, or until hot and golden. Serve with hot buttered noodles.

YORKSHIRE PUDDING AND BEEF

This is a favorite of Carolyn Bishop, Family Circle's Home Furnishings and Equipment, Editor.

Bake at 400° for 35 minutes.
Makes 4 servings.

- 3 tablespoons butter or margarine
- 1 pound ground chuck
- 3 tablespoons bottled steak sauce
- 1 small onion, chopped (¼ cup)
- 1 tablespoon chopped parsley
- 1 teaspoon salt
- ⅛ teaspoon ground nutmeg
- 2 eggs
- 1 cup milk
- 1 cup sifted all-purpose flour
- ¼ teaspoon salt

1. Melt butter or margarine in a 6-cup shallow casserole in preheating oven.
2. Combine ground chuck, steak sauce, onion, parsley, salt and nutmeg in a medium-size bowl until well-blended.
3. Beat eggs until foamy in a second bowl with a wire whisk; stir in milk; beat in flour and salt until very smooth.
4. Pour half the batter into heated casserole; drop meat mixture by teaspoons over batter; top with remaining batter to cover meat mixture.
5. Bake in hot oven (400°) 35 minutes, or until batter is crisp and brown around the edges. Serve with a bowl of sliced pickled beets or a marinated bean salad, if you wish.

CALIFORNIA SUPPER PIE

Try this corned beef hash and pineapple pie for supper on the patio.

Bake at 350° for 40 minutes.
Makes 4 servings.

- 1 can (1 pound) corned beef hash
- 1 can (8¼ ounces) crushed pineapple, drained
- ¼ cup chopped parsley
- 1 tablespoon prepared mustard
- 1 frozen 9-inch pie shell
- 2 eggs
- ¼ cup milk

1. Combine corned beef hash, pineapple, parsley and mustard in a medium-size bowl; spoon into frozen pie shell. Beat eggs and milk together in the same bowl; pour over hash mixture.
2. Bake in moderate oven (350°) 40 minutes, or until center is firm. Cool 10 minutes before cutting.

WISCONSIN MACARONI BAKE

The kids can make this one—and then enjoy eating it half an hour later.

Bake at 350° for 30 minutes.
Makes 4 servings.

- 2 cans (15 ounces each) macaroni and cheese
- 1 package (12 ounces) smokie sausage links, sliced
- ½ cup thinly sliced celery
- 1 tablespoon prepared mustard
- 1 cup packaged corn-bread stuffing mix (from an 8-ounce package)

1. Combine macaroni and cheese, sliced sausages, celery and prepared mustard in a 6-cup casserole; stir lightly to mix. Sprinkle stuffing mix over top.
2. Bake in moderate oven (350°) 30 minutes, or until bubbly and topping is lightly toasted.

QUICK TIPS

- Save time and energy by using your toaster oven to cook small casseroles. The toaster oven requires less than half the amount of power needed to heat a large oven. Just be sure to freeze food in casserole that fits into your toaster oven.
- Use your toaster-oven to put the broiled top in individual casseroles. Just turn the lever to browning.

SAVANNAH CHICKEN AND HAM

Unexpected guests for dinner will cause no alarm. Pick up the groceries on the way home and have dinner on the table in less than an hour.

Bake at 375° for 30 minutes.
Makes 6 servings.

- 3 chicken breasts, split (12 ounces each)
- 2 tablespoons butter or margarine
- 1 package (8 ounces) fine noodles, cooked and drained
- 1 package (4 ounces) sliced ham, halved
  OR: 6 slices cooked ham
- ½ cup frozen chopped onion
- 1 can (about 11 ounces) chicken gravy
- 2 tablespoons dry white wine or lemon juice
- 1 teaspoon leaf rosemary, crumbled

1. Brown chicken breasts in butter or margarine in a large skillet.
2. Spread hot noodles in an 8-cup shallow casserole; arrange chicken breasts on top; brown ham slices quickly in same pan and tuck around chicken.
3. Sauté onion until soft in pan drippings; stir in chicken gravy, wine or lemon juice and rosemary; cook, stirring constantly, until bubbly; pour over chicken and ham; cover.
4. Bake in moderate oven (375°) 30 minutes, or until chicken is tender; top with chopped parsley, if desired.

HAM STEAK JAMAICA

Ham and vegetables bake together in a spicy glaze.

Bake at 400° for 45 minutes.
Makes 4 servings.

- 1 slice ready-to-eat ham, cut about 1-inch thick
- 1 can (13¼ ounces) pineapple chunks
- ¼ cup firmly packed brown sugar
- 1 tablespoon prepared mustard
- ½ teaspoon ground ginger
- ¼ teaspoon ground allspice
- 1 can (1 pound) sweet potatoes
- 1 package (10 ounces) frozen broccoli spears, cooked and drained

1. Score ham steak and place in center of an 8-cup shallow casserole.
2. Drain syrup from pineapple into a 2-cup measure. (There will be about ½ cup.) Stir in brown sugar, mustard, ginger and allspice; pour over ham.
3. Bake in hot oven (400°) 30 minutes; arrange pineapple chunks, sweet potatoes and broccoli in piles around ham; baste with syrup in dish; bake 15 minutes longer, or until top is glazed. Serve with a tall glass of limeade made with part quinine water, if you wish.

QUICK CASSOULET

The French, too, are taking on quicker methods of cooking. Here is a short-cut version of a classic.

Bake at 400° for 45 minutes.
Makes 6 servings.

- 4 slices bacon, diced
- 2 cups cubed cooked lamb or ham or sliced knackwurst
- 1 cup frozen chopped onion
- ¼ pound salami, cut into ¼-inch cubes
- 2 cans (1 pound, 4 ounces each) white kidney beans (cannellini)
- 1 can (1 pound) stewed tomatoes
- 1 teaspoon salt
- ¼ teaspoon pepper
- 1 bay leaf

1. Cook bacon until crisp in a large skillet; remove and place in a 10-cup bean pot or deep casserole.
2. Brown meat in bacon drippings. Remove with slotted spoon and place in bean pot with bacon; pour off all but 2 tablespoons pan drippings.
3. Sauté onion until soft in same skillet; stir in salami and sauté about 2 minutes. Add beans and liquid, tomatoes, salt, pepper and bay leaf; bring to boiling. Stir into meat mixture.
4. Bake in hot oven (400°) 45 minutes.

MEXICAN POTATO CASSEROLE

Try this at the next barbecue. It goes along well with franks and hamburgers.

Bake at 375° for 20 minutes.
Makes 6 servings.

- 1 package (16 ounces) frozen crinkle-cut potatoes
- ½ cup frozen chopped onion
- 1 tablespoon vegetable oil
- 1 can (1 pound) stewed tomatoes
- 1 green chili pepper, seeded and chopped (from a 4-ounce can) optional
- 1 teaspoon leaf oregano, crumbled
- 1 teaspoon salt
- ¼ teaspoon garlic powder
- 1½ cups shredded Monterey Jack or Muenster cheese (6 ounces)

1. Spread frozen potatoes on a cooky sheet. Heat in moderate oven (375°) 15 minutes, while making sauce.
2. Sauté onion in oil in a large skillet; stir in tomatoes, green chili pepper, oregano, salt and garlic powder; bring to boiling; lower heat; simmer 10 minutes.
3. Spread half the heated potatoes in a 6-cup shallow casserole; top with half the sauce and cheese; repeat layering.
4. Bake in moderate oven (375°) 20 minutes, or until bubbly-hot.
Suggested Variations: You can add 2 cups cooked cubed beef, lamb or pork to sauce. Shredded American cheese can be used in place of the Monterey Jack cheese as well.

FILLETS OF HADDOCK VERONIQUE

Fish fans often order the delicacy when eating out. It's really so easy to make.

Bake at 350° for 30 minutes.
Makes 6 servings.

- 2 packages (1 pound each) frozen haddock fillets
- 2 cups water
- 1 small onion, sliced
- 1 bay leaf
  Handful celery leaves
- 4 peppercorns
- 1 teaspoon salt
- 2 tablespoons butter or margarine
- 1 cup soft white bread crumbs (2 slices)
- 2 tablespoons all-purpose flour
- 1 small can skimmed evaporated milk
- 1 cup seedless green grapes, halved

1. Place blocks of frozen fillets in single layer in a large skillet. Add water, onion, bay leaf, celery leaves, peppercorns and salt. Bring to boiling; lower heat; cover. Simmer 10 minutes.
2. Lift fish from pan with slotted wide spatula; place in 13x9x2-inch casserole; cut fish into 8 serving-size pieces. Strain stock into a 2-cup measure; add water, if needed, to make 1¼ cups; reserve.
3. Melt butter or margarine in same skillet; measure out 1 tablespoon and toss with bread crumbs in a small bowl.
4. Stir flour into remaining butter or margarine in skillet; cook, stirring constantly, just until mixture bubbles. Stir in the 1¼ cups fish stock and evaporated milk slowly; continue cooking and stirring until sauce thickens and bubbles 3 minutes. Fold in grapes; pour over fish; sprinkle with crumbs.
5. Bake in moderate oven (350°) 30 minutes, or until bubbly-hot.

SALMON FLORENTINE

Florentine in a recipe's name means spinach in the dish.

Bake at 400° for 15 minutes.
Makes 6 servings.

- 2 packages (10 ounces each) fresh spinach
- 1 can (1 pound) pink salmon
- 3 tablespoons butter or margarine
- 3 tablespoons all-purpose flour
- ½ teaspoon salt
- ½ teaspoon dillweed
- 1½ cups milk
- 1 egg, separated
- 2 tablespoons lemon juice

1. Trim stems and any coarse leaves from spinach. Wash leaves well; place in a large saucepan; cover. (There's no need to add any water.)
2. Cook 1 minute over low heat, or just until spinach wilts; drain well; chop.
3. Drain salmon and reserve liquid; remove skin and bones; flake.
4. Melt butter or margarine in a small saucepan; stir in flour, salt and dillweed. Cook, stirring constantly, until bubbly. Stir in milk and reserved salmon liquid; continue cooking and stirring until sauce thickens and bubbles 3 minutes. Stir half of hot mixture into beaten egg yolk in a small bowl; return to saucepan; cook, stirring constantly, 1 minute, or until sauce thickens again. Fold 1 cup of the hot sauce into salmon with lemon juice.
5. Line 6 scallop shells, au gratin dishes or individual casseroles with chopped spinach. Spoon salmon mixture onto center of spinach. Beat egg white until stiff in a small bowl; fold into remaining hot sauce; spoon over salmon.
6. Bake in hot oven (400°) 15 minutes, or until tops are golden. Garnish with a slice of lemon and a sprig of parsley.
Suggested Variation: Two cans (6½ ounces each) crabmeat can be substituted for the salmon. Serve with refrigerated crescent rolls.

VEGETABLE STUFFED HALIBUT STEAKS

Fish is an excellent choice for the dieter; it's low in calories, yet rich in nutrients.

Bake at 350° for 30 minutes.
Makes 4 servings.

- 1 cup finely chopped carrots
- 1 cup finely chopped celery
- ½ cup thinly sliced green onions
- 2 tablespoons butter or margarine
- 1 teaspoon salt
- ⅛ teaspoon bottled red-pepper seasoning
- 2 tablespoons lemon juice
- 1 tablespoon chopped parsley
- 2 packages (12 ounces each) frozen halibut steaks
- 2 large tomatoes, peeled and quartered
- 2 large green peppers, halved, seeded and sliced

1. Sauté carrots, celery and green onions in 1 tablespoon of the butter or margarine in a heavy skillet for 5 minutes. Stir in salt, red-pepper seasoning, 1 tablespoon of the lemon juice and parsley; remove from heat.
2. Melt remaining 1 tablespoon butter or margarine; brush small amount over bottom of a 6-cup shallow casserole; place halibut steak from one package in bottom of dish. (If there is more than one piece in package, fit pieces tightly together.) Top with vegetable mixture, then with halibut from second package.
3. Place tomatoes and green pepper in casserole around steaks. Blend remaining lemon juice with remaining melted butter or margarine; brush over surface of halibut; season with salt, if you wish; cover.
4. Bake in moderate oven (350°) 30 minutes, or until halibut flakes easily. Sprinkle with chopped parsley.

THIRTY MINUTE PAELLA

No need to cook all day to enjoy this quick version of a Spanish paella.

Bake at 350° for 30 minutes.
Makes 8 servings.

- 1 broiler-fryer, cut up (about 3 pounds)
- 2 tablespoons all-purpose flour
- 1 teaspoon salt
- ⅛ teaspoon pepper
- ¼ cup vegetable oil
- 2 packages (6 ounces each) Spanish-rice mix
- 1 package (6 to 8 ounces) sliced, Italian-assortment cold cuts
- 2 envelopes or teaspoons instant chicken broth
- 4 cups hot water
- 1 package (5 ounces) frozen cooked deveined shrimp

1. Shake chicken in plastic bag with flour, salt and pepper to coat evenly.
2. Brown quickly in vegetable oil in a large skillet; place in a 10-cup casserole.
3. Sprinkle Spanish rice right from package over chicken; top with meats.
4. Bring instant chicken broth and water to boiling in same skillet; add shrimp; cook 1 minute; pour over mixture in casserole; cover.
5. Bake in moderate oven (350°) 30 minutes, or until bubbly-hot.

CHOPSTICK PORK

Leftovers gain new character when combined with soy sauce and crisply cooked vegetables.

Bake at 350° for 30 minutes.
Makes 6 servings.

- 3 cups cubed cooked pork
- ¼ cup soy sauce
- 6 medium-size carrots, pared and sliced
- 2 medium-size green peppers, halved, seeded, and cut into strips
- 1 can (1 pound) sliced cling peaches
- 3 tablespoons vegetable oil or peanut oil
- 1 cup frozen chopped onion
- 1 can (about 14 ounces) chicken broth
- ¼ cup cider vinegar
- 3 tablespoons cornstarch
- ⅓ cup water
- 3 medium-size bananas
- 1 can (3 ounces) Chinese fried noodles

1. Combine pork and soy sauce in a medium-size bowl; toss lightly to mix; let stand to season.
2. Cook carrots in boiling salted water in a medium-size saucepan 10 minutes; add green peppers; cook 5 minutes longer, or just until crisply tender; drain.
3. Drain syrup from peaches into a 1-cup

measure; reserve peaches.
4. Drain meat, saving soy sauce. Brown meat in oil in a large skillet; remove and reserve. Stir onion into drippings in pan; sauté just until soft. Stir in ½ cup of the peach syrup, chicken broth, vinegar and saved soy sauce; bring to bubbling.
5. Smooth cornstarch and water to a paste in a cup; stir into bubbling mixture; cook, stirring constantly, until mixture thickens and bubbles 1 minute. Remove from heat and set aside.
6. Peel bananas and slice. Arrange with cooked carrots, green peppers and peach slices in separate mounds in an 8-cup shallow casserole; pile browned meat in center; pour hot onion sauce over top.
7. Sprinkle noodles over; top with a ring of water chestnut slices, if you wish.
8. Bake in moderate oven (350°) 30 minutes, or until bubbly-hot.
Suggested Variations: Cubed cooked ham, chicken or turkey or sliced frankfurters can be substituted for the pork in this recipe.

QUICK TIPS

Casserole Substitution Chart
No need to have a variety of special dishes for casserole cooking. Use some of the pans you already have on hand. If the recipe calls for:
4-cup dish: 9-inch pie plate
8x1¼-inch cake pan
7x3x2-inch loaf pan
6-cup dish: 9x1½-inch cake pan
10-inch pie plate
8x3½x2½-inch loaf pan
8-cup dish: 8x8x2-inch-square pan
11x7x1½-inch baking pan
9x5x3-inch loaf pan
10-cup dish: 9x9x2-inch square pan
15x10x1-inch jelly roll pan
12-cup dish: 13x9x2-inch baking pan
16-cup dish: 13x9x3-inch roasting pan
Ingredient Substitution Chart
Some safe substitutions, if you're out of the ingredients listed in our recipes:

1 teaspoon dry leaf herb	=	1 tablespoon chopped fresh herb
1 cup dairy sour cream	=	1 tablespoon lemon juice to 1 cup evaporated milk
1 tablespoon finely chopped fresh chives	=	1 teaspoon freeze-dried chives
1 tablespoon cornstarch	=	2 tablespoons all-purpose flour

CRAB PARISIENNE

A little costly to prepare, but if you keep these ingredients on hand, you're always ready for unexpected dinner guests.

Broil for 5 minutes.
Makes 6 servings.

- 2 packages (10 ounces each) frozen asparagus spears
- 1 package (1 ounce) onion-sauce mix Milk
- 1 egg, separated
- 2 cans (6½ ounces each) crab meat, drained and flaked
  - OR: 2 packages (6 ounces each) frozen king crab, thawed and drained
- 1 tablespoon dry white wine
- ¼ cup mayonnaise or salad dressing

1. Cook asparagus, following label directions; drain. Divide among 6 scallop shells, au gratin dishes or flame-proof individual casseroles.
2. While asparagus cooks, prepare onion-sauce mix with milk, following label directions; beat into egg yolk gradually in a medium-size bowl; fold in crab meat and wine and blend well.
3. Beat egg white until it forms soft peaks in a small bowl; fold in mayonnaise or salad dressing.
4. Spoon hot crab mixture over asparagus spears in each dish, dividing evenly, then top with mayonnaise mixture.
5. Broil, about 4 inches from heat, 5 minutes, or until sauce puffs and turns golden. Serve at once.

SAN JOSÉ SALMON CURRY

A quick answer to what's for lunch.

Bake at 350° for 20 minutes.
Makes 4 servings.

- 1 package (1 ounce) sour cream sauce mix
- 1 can (1 pound) salmon, drained, boned and flaked
- 1 can (1 pound, 4 ounces) pineapple chunks in juice, drained
- 1 medium-size cucumber, pared and diced
- ¼ cup sliced green onions
- ½ cup mayonnaise or salad dressing
- 1 teaspoon curry powder
  Chinese fried noodles (from a 3-ounce can)

1. Prepare sour cream sauce mix, following label directions; stir in mayonnaise or salad dressing and curry powder; set aside.
2. Combine salmon, pineapple chunks, cucumber and green onions in a 6-cup shallow casserole; pour sauce over; sprinkle with Chinese fried noodles.
3. Bake in moderate oven 350°) 20 minutes, or until heated through. Serve with tossed greens and hot buttered rolls, if you wish.

PORTICO WHEAT GERM CASSEROLE

Ground beef is combined with corn and sprinkled with a wheat germ topping.

Bake at 375° for 20 minutes.
Makes 6 servings.

¾ cup regular wheat germ
½ cup soft white bread crumbs (1 slice)
2 tablespoons melted butter or margarine
1 tablespoon chopped parsley
1 pound ground beef
1 medium-size onion, chopped (½ cup)
1 can (about 1 pound) cream-style corn
¼ cup milk
2 teaspoons prepared mustard
1 teaspoon salt
1 teaspoon mixed Italian herbs, crumbled

1. Combine wheat germ and bread crumbs in a small bowl. Grease a 6-cup casserole and sprinkle with half the crumb mixture. Toss remaining mixture with melted butter or margarine and parsley; reserve.
2. Brown ground beef in a large skillet; break into chunks and push to one side. Sauté onion in drippings until soft; stir in corn, milk, mustard, salt and Italian herbs. Spoon into prepared casserole. Sprinkle reserved crumb mixture on top.
3. Bake in moderate oven (375°) 20 minutes, or until bubbly-hot. Serve with a tossed green salad and fresh fruit for dessert, for a simple and nutritious meal.

SANTA FE BAKE

Cornmeal drop biscuits top a quick-to-fix dish of franks and beans.

Bake at 425° for 40 minutes.
Makes 6 servings.

1 pound frankfurters
2 cans (1 pound each) pork and beans
1 can (8 ounces) tomato sauce
¼ cup firmly packed brown sugar
½ cup frozen chopped onion
2 teaspoons dry mustard
1 cup cornmeal
½ cup sifted all-purpose flour
2 teaspoons baking powder
½ teaspoon salt
⅛ teaspoon garlic powder
1 egg, beaten
2 tablespoons vegetable shortening
⅔ cup milk

1. Cut frankfurters into slices; combine with pork and beans, sugar, onion and mustard in a 6-cup shallow casserole.
2. Bake in hot oven (425°) 15 minutes.
3. Sift cornmeal, flour, baking powder, salt and garlic powder together into a medium-size bowl. Add egg, shortening and milk. Beat with rotary beater until smooth, 1 minute; do not overbeat.

4. Drop by spoonfuls over hot bean mixture. Bake 25 minutes more, or until biscuits are golden-brown.

CALIFORNIA FRANKS AND POTATOES

Hearty enough for the hungriest appetite, yet simple to prepare.

Bake at 350° for 45 minutes.
Makes 6 servings.

1 package (6 ounces) hash brown potatoes
1½ cups boiling water
1 pound frankfurters, cut in 1-inch pieces
1 container (1 pound) cream-style cottage cheese
1 container (8 ounces) dairy sour cream
1 teaspoon minced dried onion
1 envelope (about 1 ounce) blue cheese salad dressing mix
½ cup shredded Cheddar or process American cheese
Paprika

1. Combine hash brown potatoes and water in an 8-cup casserole; cover; let stand 10 minutes.
2. Combine frankfurters, cottage cheese, sour cream, onion and blue cheese dressing mix in a medium-size bowl; spoon over potatoes and mix gently to blend.
3. Bake in moderate oven (350°) 40 minutes, or until potatoes are tender; sprinkle with cheese and paprika. Bake 5 minutes longer, or until cheese melts. Serve with marinated green beans and sliced cucumbers, if you wish.

BAKED NEST EGGS

Eggs bake 'en casserole' with frozen mixed vegetables and smoked sausages. It's a fast dish to make, and filling, too.

Bake at 400° for 20 minutes.
Makes 6 servings.

2 packages (8 ounces each) frozen mixed vegetables with onion sauce
Milk
Butter or margarine
4 smokie sausage links, sliced
6 eggs
Paprika
3 English muffins, halved and toasted

1. Cook frozen vegetables with milk and butter or margarine, following label directions. Stir in sausages. Spoon into a greased, 6-cup shallow casserole.
2. Break eggs, 1 at a time, into a cup, then pour each into vegetable mixture, spacing evenly. Sprinkle with paprika.
3. Bake in hot oven (400°) 20 minutes, or until eggs are set and vegetables are bubbly-hot.

4. Place each muffin half on a heated serving plate; lift eggs and vegetables with a pancake turner or slotted spoon and place on muffins.

QUICK TIPS

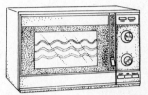

Casserole cooking is quick when you use a microwave oven. Here are some tips:
• Reduce the cooking liquid in a favorite recipe by about ½ cup.
• Cover casserole with wax paper.
• Stir and turn casserole several times while cooking.
• Remove all foil from frozen casseroles before putting in to microwave oven.
• Reheat individual casserole servings on a paper plate and top with a second plate to save after dinner clean-up.

SOUTH DAKOTA DINNER

This recipe was developed by Mrs. Delphine Benkert for conventional ranges. Her daughter, Carolyn Bishop, has adapted it to microwave cooking.

Microwave for 20 minutes.
Makes 4 servings.

1 pound ground chuck
1 cup frozen chopped onion
1 can (12 or 16 ounces) whole-kernel corn
4 medium-size potatoes, pared and thinly sliced
3 tablespoons all-purpose flour
3 tablespoons butter or margarine
3 tablespoons milk
1 teaspoon salt
½ teaspoon paprika
¼ teaspoon pepper

1. Brown ground chuck and onion in a 6 to 8-cup microwave-safe casserole. (The microwave browning dish is perfect.) Stir frequently; drain off fat.
2. Drain liquid from corn and sprinkle corn over meat; layer potato slices over; dust with flour; dot with butter or margarine and drizzle milk over; season with salt, paprika and pepper. Cover casserole loosely with wax paper.
3. Microwave 20 minutes, rotating the dish several times, or until potatoes are tender when pierced with a fork.
COOK'S TIP: To bake this casserole in a conventional range: Brown meat and onion in a skillet; place in a 6-cup casserole; add corn and liquid, then potatoes and increase the milk to ¼ cup; cover casserole. Bake in moderate oven (350°) 1½ hours, taking the cover off for the last 10 minutes to brown potatoes.

Dried beans were known to the Indians of Mexico when the Spanish explorers first arrived. Tijuana Bean Pot combines dried pea or navy beans with chunks of green pepper, tomatoes and cumin. Recipe is on page 26. Serve with a crisp salad.

24

MEATLESS AND HEARTY

After years of being the biggest meat-eaters in the world, Americans are now learning to appreciate all of the protein-rich foods, including seafood, beans, eggs, cheese and grains. These can be combined to make memorable dishes that are lower in cost, yet high in good nutrition. We have included quick-cooking recipes and long, slow-cooking favorites for meals to fit your daily time pattern. They are so flavorful you'll never miss the meat.

TIJUANA BEAN POT

Not every bean dish from Mexico needs to be made with chili powder. This flavorful casserole has oregano and cumin along with chunks of tomato and green peppers. (Shown on page 24.)

Bake at 325° for 3 hours.
Makes 8 servings.

1 package (1 pound) dried pea beans
5 cups water
1 Spanish onion, chopped (1½ cups)
3 tablespoons olive oil or vegetable oil
2 large green peppers, halved, seeded and cut into 1-inch pieces
1 can (1 pound) tomatoes
½ cup dark molasses
2 teaspoons salt
2 teaspoons leaf oregano, crumbled
½ teaspoon cumin seeds, crushed
½ teaspoon pepper

1. Pick over beans and rinse under running water. Combine beans and water in a large kettle. Bring to boiling; cover kettle; boil 2 minutes; remove from heat; let stand 1 hour. Return kettle to heat; bring to boiling; add onion; lower heat and simmer 1 hour, or until beans are firm-tender.
2. Heat oil in a large skillet; sauté green peppers until soft; stir in tomatoes, molasses, salt, oregano, cumin and pepper; heat until bubbling.
3. Drain beans, reserving liquid. Combine beans and green pepper mixture in a 12-cup casserole; add enough reserved liquid to just cover the beans; cover.
4. Bake in slow oven (325°) 2½ hours, adding more reserved liquid, if needed, to prevent beans from drying. Remove cover; bake 30 minutes longer, or until beans are very tender.

TUNA NOODLE CASSEROLE

The All-American favorite casserole with a special topping of crunchy cashews.

Bake at 350° for 35 minutes.
Makes 8 servings.

1 package (8 ounces) wide noodles
2 cups frozen peas (from a 1½-pound bag)
1 can condensed cream of mushroom soup
1 can (3 or 4 ounces) sliced mushrooms
1 cup milk
Few drops Worcestershire sauce
1 package (8 ounces) process American cheese, diced
1 can (13 ounces) tuna, drained and flaked
1 package (about 3 ounces) salted cashew nuts, chopped coarsely

1. Cook noodles in boiling unsalted water in a large saucepan, following label directions; drain; return to kettle; stir in

frozen peas; reserve.
2. Heat soup, mushrooms and liquid, milk, Worcestershire sauce and cheese, stirring frequently in a medium-size saucepan until cheese melts; stir into noodles and peas; mix well. Gently fold in tuna. Pour into a 12-cup casserole; cover casserole.
3. Bake in moderate oven (350°) 30 minutes; uncover; sprinkle cashew nuts over top; bake 5 minutes longer, or until bubbly-hot.
Suggested Variation: SALMON NOODLE CASSEROLE—Follow recipe for TUNA NOODLE CASSEROLE, except use frozen cut green beans for the peas, process Swiss cheese for the American and 1 can (1 pound) salmon, drained and flaked for the tuna. Top with 1 can (1½ ounces) French fried potato sticks.

MACARONI LOUIS

Scallops and macaroni are sauced with a Louis dressing, then baked til bubbly.

Bake at 350° for 30 minutes.
Makes 6 servings.

1 pound fresh or frozen sea scallops
1 teaspoon shrimp spice
1 slice lemon
2 cups water
1 package (8 ounces) elbow macaroni
3 tablespoons butter or margarine
1 cup soft white bread crumbs (2 slices)
2 tablespoons all-purpose flour
1 teaspoon dry mustard
½ teaspoon salt
2½ cups milk
¼ cup chili sauce
1 cup shredded Cheddar cheese (4 ounces)

1. Wash fresh scallops under running cold water or partly thaw frozen ones; cut into small pieces.
2. Combine shrimp spice, lemon and water in a medium-size saucepan; bring to boiling; add scallops; cover. Remove from heat; let stand 5 minutes; drain.
3. Cook macaroni in a large kettle of boiling salted water, for 10 minutes; drain; return to kettle.
4. While macaroni cooks, melt butter or margarine in a medium-size saucepan; then toss 1 tablespoon with the bread crumbs in a small bowl; reserve. Stir flour, mustard and salt into remaining butter; cook, stirring constantly until bubbly; stir in milk; cook, stirring constantly, just until sauce thickens slightly and bubbles 3 minutes; remove from heat, then stir in chili sauce.
5. Pour sauce over macaroni, then stir in scallops. Spoon into buttered 8-cup casserole; sprinkle with cheese, then with buttered crumbs.
6. Bake in moderate oven (350°) 30 minutes, or until bubbly-hot. For an elegant appetizer, serve avocado halves drizzled with a tangy lemon dressing.

NORTH ATLANTIC PAPRIKA PERCH

Ocean perch fillets bake on top of a creamy noodle and tomato casserole.

Bake at 350° for 30 minutes.
Makes 4 servings.

1 package (8 ounces) medium-size egg noodles
1 container (8 ounces) dairy sour cream
1 tablespoon paprika
2 medium-size tomatoes, cut into 6 slices each
1 package (1 pound) frozen perch fillets
2 tablespoons bottled lemon juice
1 tablespoon melted butter or margarine
1 teaspoon salt
¼ teaspoon pepper

1. Cook noodles, following label directions; drain; return to kettle. Stir in sour cream and paprika. Place in a 6-cup shallow casserole; arrange tomato slices over noodles.
2. Thaw frozen perch; cut away skin, if desired; separate into fillets. Arrange over tomatoes; brush with a mixture of lemon juice and butter or margarine and sprinkle with salt and pepper.
3. Bake in moderate oven (350°) 30 minutes, or until fish is golden. Serve with lettuce and Green Goddess dressing.

SAN FERNANDO VALLEY BAKE

Vegetable casseroles become main dishes when they are layered with plenty of shredded cheese.

Bake at 325° for 45 minutes.
Makes 4 servings.

2 medium-size zucchini
2 medium-size yellow squash
1 medium-size onion, chopped (½ cup)
2 tablespoons vegetable oil
2 tablespoons chopped parsley
½ teaspoon salt
½ teaspoon leaf oregano, crumbled
¼ teaspoon freshly ground pepper
3 eggs, slightly beaten
1 cup unsalted soda cracker crumbs (about 6 large crackers)
2 cups shredded Monterey Jack or Cheddar cheese (8 ounces)

1. Wash zucchini and yellow squash; cut off ends; grate squash coarsely (you should have about 4 cups).
2. Sauté onion until golden in oil in a large skillet; remove from heat; stir in grated squash, parsley, salt, oregano and eggs; blend well.
3. Spoon one third of the squash mixture into an 8-cup casserole; top with one third of the crumbs and cheese; repeat to make 3 layers.
4. Bake in slow oven (325°) 45 minutes, or until mixture is set and top golden.

MICHIGAN LIMA BEAN CASSEROLE

Grated Parmesan cheese gives the final touch to this hearty bean dish.

Bake at 350° for 2 hours, 30 minutes.
Makes 8 servings.

- 1 package (1 pound) dried lima beans
- 6 cups water
- 2 large onions, chopped (2 cups)
- 1 clove garlic, minced
- 2 medium-size carrots, pared and chopped
- 3 tablespoons vegetable oil
- 2 envelopes or teaspoons instant vegetable broth
- 2 teaspoons salt
- 1 teaspoon leaf rosemary, crumbled
- ¼ teaspoon pepper
- 1 cup grated Parmesan cheese

1. Pick over beans and rinse. Place in a large kettle and add water. Bring to boiling; boil 2 minutes; remove from heat and cover kettle. Let stand 1 hour.
2. Return kettle to heat; bring to boiling; lower heat; simmer 1 hour, or until beans are firm-tender. Sauté onion, garlic and carrot in oil in a large skillet until soft.
3. Drain beans and measure liquid. Add enough water to make 4 cups. Stir bean liquid into skillet with instant vegetable broth, salt, rosemary and pepper; bring to boiling; remove from heat.
4. Spoon beans into a 12-cup casserole. Pour liquid in skillet over casserole; cover casserole.
5. Bake in moderate oven (350°) 2 hours; remove cover. Bake 30 minutes longer, or until beans are tender and soft. Sprinkle with cheese before serving.

SOYBEAN STUFFED ZUCCHINI

A purée of soybeans, a handful of chopped parsley and green onions blend with brown rice for a hearty main dish.

Bake at 375° for 15 minutes.
Makes 4 servings.

- 1 cup dried soybeans
- 3 cups cold water
- ½ cup uncooked brown rice
- 4 medium-size zucchini
- ½ cup sliced green onions
- ½ cup chopped parsley
- 1 teaspoon salt
- ¼ teaspoon pepper
- 2 tablespoons butter or margarine
- ¾ cup plain wheat germ

1. Pick over soybeans and rinse under running water. Cover soybeans with cold water in a glass bowl; cover bowl and let stand at room temperature overnight.
2. Pour soybeans and soaking liquid into a large saucepan. Bring to boiling; cover saucepan; lower heat and simmer 3 hours. (Soybeans will still not be tender.) Drain beans and reserve liquid.
3. While soybeans are cooking, prepare brown rice, following label directions.
4. Halve zucchini, lengthwise, parboil in boiling salted water in a large skillet 5 minutes; drain, cut-side down, on paper towels.
5. Measure ¾ cup soybean liquid into electric blender container; add cooked soybeans; cover container; process at high speed until mixture is very smooth.
6. Combine soybean purée, cooked brown rice, green onions, parsley, salt and pepper in a medium-size bowl.
7. Arrange zucchini, cut-side up, in an 8-cup shallow casserole; fill zucchini shells with soybean mixture. Melt butter or margarine in a small saucepan; stir in wheat germ until well-blended. Sprinkle over zucchini shells.
8. Bake in moderate oven (375°) 15 minutes, or until topping is golden and zucchini shells are heated through.

MARVELOUS MACARONI AND CHEESE

This traditional favorite of young and old is filled with good nutrition, too, from enriched macaroni and cheese.

Bake at 350° for 40 minutes.
Makes 6 servings.

- 1 package (1 pound) elbow macaroni
- ½ cup (1 stick) butter or margarine
- 1½ cups soft white bread crumbs (3 slices)
- ⅓ cup all-purpose flour
- 2 teaspoons dry mustard
- 2 teaspoons salt
- 4 cups milk
- 2 tablespoons Worcestershire sauce
- 4 cups shredded process sharp American or Cheddar cheese (1 pound)

1. Cook macaroni in a kettle of boiling salted water until firm-tender, about 10 minutes; drain and return to kettle.
2. Melt butter or margarine in a large saucepan; remove 2 tablespoons from pan and toss with bread crumbs in a small bowl; reserve.
3. Stir flour, dry mustard and salt into butter in saucepan; cook, stirring constantly, until mixture bubbles; stir in milk and Worcestershire sauce; cook, stirring constantly, until sauce thickens slightly and bubbles 3 minutes; stir in 3 cups of the shredded cheese.
4. Stir sauce into macaroni in kettle until well-blended; spoon mixture into a 13x9x2-inch casserole; sprinkle remaining 1 cup cheese over; top with reserved buttered crumbs.
5. Bake in moderate oven (350°) 40 minutes, or until crumbs are golden and casserole is bubbly.
COOK'S TIP: MARVELOUS MACARONI AND CHEESE can be prepared ahead of time, covered and refrigerated. One hour before serving, place casserole, covered, in oven and turn oven control to moderate (350°). Bake 40 minutes; remove cover and bake 20 minutes longer.

BROCCOLI AND TUNA DIVAN

Fresh broccoli is topped with a tuna sauce then baked, until bubbly.

Bake at 400° for 20 minutes.
Makes 4 servings.

- 1 bunch broccoli (about 2 pounds)
- 1 can condensed cream of onion soup
- ¼ cup milk
- 2 tablespoons lemon juice or dry white wine
- 1 can (about 7 ounces) tuna, drained and flaked
- ¼ cup grated Parmesan cheese

1. Trim and discard outer leaves and tough ends of broccoli stalks; split largest pieces lengthwise. Add to a small amount boiling salted water in a medium-size saucepan; cover. Cook 10 minutes, or until tender; drain on paper towels.
2. Combine soup and milk in small saucepan; heat until smooth and bubbly. Stir in lemon juice or wine and tuna.
3. Arrange broccoli in a 6-cup shallow casserole; top with tuna sauce; sprinkle with cheese.
4. Bake in hot oven (400°) 20 minutes, or until lightly golden. Garnish with lemon slices, if you wish.

CAPTAIN'S CASSEROLE

No need to own your own boat to enjoy this flavorful casserole.

Bake at 375° for 30 minutes.
Makes 6 servings.

- 1 small green pepper, halved, seeded and chopped
- 1 small onion, chopped (¼ cup)
- ¼ cup (½ stick) butter or margarine
- 3 tablespoons all-purpose flour
- 1½ teaspoons salt
- ½ teaspoon dillweed
- ¼ teaspoon pepper
- 1 tall can evaporated milk
- 1 can (3 or 4 ounces) sliced mushrooms
- 2 cans (about 7 ounces each) tuna, drained and flaked
- 1 package (10 ounces) frozen peas, thawed
- 1 tablespoon Worcestershire sauce
- 1 package (1 pound) frozen French fried potato rounds

1. Sauté green pepper and onion in butter or margarine in a large saucepan until soft. Blend in flour, salt, dillweed and pepper. Cook, stirring constantly, until bubbly; gradually add milk and liquid drained from the mushrooms.
2. Cook, stirring constantly, until sauce thickens and bubbles 3 minutes. Then add tuna, peas, mushrooms and Worcestershire sauce; spoon mixture into a 6-cup casserole. Top with potato rounds.
3. Bake in moderate oven (375°) 30 minutes, or until bubbly-hot.

PARTY JAMBALAYA

Here's a version of the famous Deep South specialty combining shrimp, tomatoes and rice.

Bake at 350° for 1 hour.
Makes 8 servings.

- 1 large onion, chopped (1 cup)
- 1 large green pepper, halved, seeded and chopped
- 1 cup chopped celery
- 1 clove garlic, minced
- 3 tablespoons vegetable oil
- 2 cups uncooked rice
- 2 teaspoons salt
- ⅛ teaspoon cayenne
- 1 tablespoon Worcestershire sauce
- 1 can (1 pound) tomatoes
- 1 bag (1½ pounds) frozen shelled deveined raw shrimp
- 3½ cups boiling water
- 1 bay leaf

1. Sauté onion, green pepper, celery and garlic until soft in vegetable oil in a large skillet; remove from heat.
2. Combine sautéed vegetables, rice, salt, cayenne, Worcestershire sauce and tomatoes, breaking up tomatoes with a fork, in a 12-cup casserole.
3. Separate frozen shrimp and add to casserole. Pour boiling water in and stir with a fork to mix well. Place bay leaf on top; cover.
4. Bake in moderate oven (350°) 1 hour, or until rice is tender and almost all liquid is absorbed. Remove bay leaf; fluff up rice-shrimp mixture with a fork.

LETTUCE SOUFFLÉ

This very French dish is from Gallatin's Restaurant in Monterey, California.

Bake at 350° for 50 minutes.
Makes 4 servings.

- 4 cups shredded iceberg lettuce
- 1 teaspoon onion salt
- 4 tablespoons (½ stick) butter or margarine
- ¼ cup all-purpose flour
- 1 cup light cream or milk
- 1 teaspoon Worcestershire sauce
- ½ teaspoon salt
- 1 cup shredded Swiss cheese (4 ounces)
- 4 eggs, separated
- ¼ cup grated Parmesan cheese

1. Cook shredded lettuce and onion salt in 1 tablespoon of the butter or margarine in a medium-size saucepan until very soft and liquid is almost evaporated; cool slightly. Place in an electric blender container; cover; process on high 30 seconds, or until smooth.
2. Melt remaining 3 tablespoons butter or margarine in a medium-size saucepan; stir in flour; cook, stirring constantly, just until mixture bubbles.

3. Stir in cream or milk, Worcestershire sauce and salt; continue cooking and stirring until sauce thickens and bubbles 3 minutes; stir in Swiss cheese until cheese is melted.
4. Beat egg whites until they form soft peaks in a large bowl; reserve. Beat egg yolks until creamy-thick in a medium-size bowl; gradually beat in cheese mixture until well-blended; stir in lettuce purée.
5. Fold lettuce mixture over egg whites with a wire whip until no streaks of white remain.
6. Butter a 6-cup soufflé dish or straight-sided casserole; sprinkle with part of the Parmesan cheese; spoon in soufflé mixture. Sprinkle top with remaining Parmesan cheese.
7. Bake in moderate oven (350°) 50 minutes, or until soufflé is puffy-light.

QUICK TIPS

The ready-to-cook yield from 1 pound fresh vegetables:

Vegetable	Amount	Servings
Asparagus	16 spears	2 servings
Beets	3 medium	3 servings
Broccoli	6 stalks	3 servings
Brussels Sprouts	1 pint	4 servings
Cabbage	4 cups	4 servings
Carrots	2 cups	4 servings
Cauliflower	small	3 servings
Corn	3 ears	3 servings
Eggplant	small	3 servings
Green Beans	2 cups	4 servings
Green Pepper	3 large	3 servings
Lima Beans	⅔ cup	1 serving
Mushrooms	12 large	4 servings
Onions	2 cups	4 servings
Peas	1 cup	2 servings
Potatoes	2½ cups	3 servings
Spinach	4 cups	4 servings
Yellow Squash	2½ cups	3 servings
Sweet Potatoes	2½ cups	4 servings
Tomatoes	2½ cups	3 servings
Turnips	2½ cups	3 servings
Winter Squash	2½ cups	4 servings
Zucchini	2½ cups	3 servings

ONION AND MACARONI BAKE

Want to try a new casserole topper? Canned French fried onion rings add crispness and extra flavor.

Bake at 375° for 30 minutes.
Makes 6 servings.

- 1 package (8 ounces) elbow macaroni
- 1 can condensed cream of mushroom soup
- 1¼ cups milk
- 2 tablespoons prepared mustard
- 1 teaspoon Worcestershire sauce
- ¼ teaspoon pepper
- 1½ cups shredded Cheddar cheese (6 ounces)
- 2 cans (3 ounces each) French fried onion rings

1. Cook macaroni in a large kettle of boiling salted water, following label directions, drain and return to kettle.
2. Add soup, milk, mustard, Worcestershire sauce and pepper; stir until well-blended; fold in cheese.
3. Layer half the mixture into an 8-cup casserole; top with 1 can of the onions; repeat for another layer.
4. Bake in moderate oven (375°) 30 minutes, or until bubbly-hot.

DEEP SEA BAKE

Fish fillets bake with potatoes and green beans in onion-butter sauce.

Bake at 325° for 1 hour.
Makes 6 servings.

- 2 packages (12 ounces each) frozen haddock, cod or flounder fillets
- ¼ cup (½ stick) butter or margarine
- 1 large onion, chopped (1 cup)
- 1 package (9 ounces) frozen green beans with sliced mushrooms
- 3 large potatoes, cooked, peeled and sliced
- 2 teaspoons salt
- 1 teaspoon paprika
- 1 teaspoon leaf basil, crumbled

1. Cut each package of frozen fish fillets into 3 equal-size servings (do not thaw).
2. Melt butter or margarine in a small saucepan; add onion; heat until bubbly.
3. Spoon half the onion-butter into a 13x9x2-inch casserole. Layer frozen fish pieces, green beans with mushroom slices and potato slices in casserole; season with salt, paprika and basil; drizzle with remaining onion-butter; cover casserole.
4. Bake in slow oven (325°) 45 minutes; uncover; bake 15 minutes longer, or until potatoes are golden.

LOUISIANA CORN PUDDING

When frozen shrimp is on special, here is a recipe to make a little go a long way.

Bake at 325° for 50 minutes.
Makes 4 servings.

1 package (about 12 ounces) frozen shelled deveined raw shrimp
  OR: 1 package (12 ounces) frozen cod fillets
3 eggs
1 cup milk
1 can (about 1 pound) cream-style corn
1 cup soft white bread crumbs (2 slices)
1 medium-size onion, chopped (½ cup)
1 teaspoon salt
⅛ teaspoon pepper
1 tablespoon melted butter or margarine
1 teaspoon Worcestershire sauce
1 tablespoon chopped parsley

1. Cook shrimp or cod, following label directions for poaching; drain well; quarter shrimp or flake cod.
2. Beat eggs slightly in a large bowl; stir in milk, corn, bread crumbs, onion, salt, pepper, butter or margarine, Worcestershire sauce, parsley and prepared fish.
3. Turn into a buttered 4-cup casserole; place in baking pan on oven rack; pour boiling water into pan to 1-inch depth.
4. Bake in slow oven (325°) 50 minutes, or until a knife inserted near center comes out clean; remove from water at once; garnish with chopped parsley.

RIGATI CASSEROLE

Rigati is a finely ridged pasta that gives this casserole its distinctive character. Your supermarket may sell the same shape pasta under a different name.

Bake at 350° for 30 minutes.
Makes 8 servings.

1 package (1 pound) rigati, ziti or elbow macaroni
1 large eggplant (about 2 pounds)
½ cup olive oil or vegetable oil
1 large onion, chopped (1 cup)
1 jar (24 ounces) marinara sauce
1 container (1 pound) cream-style cottage cheese
½ cup chopped Italian parsley
1 teaspoon mixed Italian herbs, crumbled
1 package (6 ounces) sliced Provolone cheese

1. Cook pasta in a large kettle of boiling salted water, for 10 minutes; drain; return to kettle.
2. Trim ends from eggplant; cut into ½-inch slices; pare. Sauté slices, a few at a time, in part of the oil, until soft in a large skillet; drain on paper towels.

3. Sauté onion until soft in same skillet; stir in marinara sauce and simmer until piping-hot. Pour sauce over pasta in kettle and blend well.
4. Combine cottage cheese, parsley and Italian herbs in a small bowl.
5. Place half the pasta mixture in a 12-cup shallow casserole. Add half the eggplant, overlapping slices if necessary. Add cheese mixture, spreading evenly. Add remaining pasta mixture and top with remaining eggplant.
6. Bake in moderate oven (350°) 20 minutes. Cut Provolone cheese into strips and arrange over eggplant.
7. Bake 10 minutes longer, or until cheese melts and casserole is bubbly.

PASTA SOUFFLÉ

This is a dish the diners must wait for. A soufflé must never wait for a guest.

Bake at 350° for 1 hour.
Makes 8 servings.

1 package (8 ounces) maruzzelle (small shells) or elbow macaroni
6 tablespoons (¾ stick) butter or margarine
¼ cup all-purpose flour
1½ teaspoons salt
½ teaspoon paprika
2 cups milk
2 cups shredded Cheddar or Monterey Jack cheese (8 ounces)
1 tablespoon sharp prepared mustard
6 eggs, separated
  Sesame seeds

1. Cook pasta in a large kettle of boiling salted water following label directions; drain; return to kettle.
2. While pasta cooks, melt butter or margarine in a medium-size saucepan. Blend in flour, salt and paprika; cook, stirring constantly, just until bubbly. Stir in milk; continue cooking and stirring until sauce thickens and bubbles 3 minutes. Stir in cheese and mustard until cheese melts. Remove from heat; cool.
3. Beat egg whites just until they double in volume and form soft peaks in a large bowl; reserve.
4. Beat egg yolks until creamy-thick in a second large bowl; gradually add cooled sauce, stirring until well-blended. Stir in cooked, drained pasta. Lightly stir in about 1 cup of the beaten egg whites; gently fold in remainder until no streaks of white remain.
5. Pour into an ungreased 8-cup soufflé dish or straight-sided casserole; gently cut a deep circle in mixture about an inch in from edge with spatula. (This gives the puff its tiered top.) Sprinkle top evenly with sesame seeds.
6. Bake in moderate oven (350°) 1 hour, or until puffy-firm and golden. Serve with an "antipasto" plate of marinated vegetables, fish, and crisp greens.

CONFETTI SCALLOP

A hearty meal-in-a-dish. The perfect choice for an after the football game supper.

Bake at 350° for 1 hour.
Makes 8 servings.

1 package (8 ounces) macaroni twists
4 cups shredded cabbage (about 1 pound)
1 can (1 pound) tomatoes
1 can (13 ounces) tuna, drained and flaked
1 cup frozen chopped onion
1 can (8 ounces) tomato sauce
1 can (3 or 4 ounces) chopped mushrooms
1 cup shredded sharp Cheddar cheese (4 ounces)
¼ cup seedless raisins
1 teaspoon salt
1 teaspoon leaf oregano, crumbled
4 slices mozzarella cheese (from an 8-ounce package), cut into triangles

1. Cook macaroni for 10 minutes; drain; return to kettle.
2. Stir in cabbage, tomatoes, tuna, onion, tomato sauce, mushrooms and liquid, Cheddar cheese, raisins, salt and oregano into kettle. Spoon mixture into a greased 12-cup casserole; cover.
3. Bake in moderate oven (350°) 50 minutes; uncover casserole; arrange mozzarella cheese on top. Bake 10 minutes longer, or until cheese melts. Let stand 10 minutes; serve.

IDAHO TUNA PUFF

A quick-to-fix casserole that's made from items on hand.

Bake at 350° for 1 hour.
Makes 4 servings.

1 can (about 7 ounces) tuna
4 eggs, beaten
⅓ cup grated Parmesan cheese
  Instant mashed potatoes to make 2 cups
2 tablespoons fine dry bread crumbs
1 envelope (1 ounce) white sauce mix
  Water
1 tablespoon lemon juice
1 teaspoon freeze-dried chives

1. Drain and flake tuna; combine with eggs and cheese in a large bowl.
2. Prepare 2 cups instant mashed potatoes, following label directions; stir tuna mixture in until well-blended.
3. Butter a 4-cup casserole, then sprinkle with crumbs. Fill casserole evenly with potato mixture.
4. Bake in moderate oven (350°) 1 hour, or until puffy and golden-brown.
5. Prepare white sauce mix with water in a small saucepan, following label directions. Stir in lemon juice and chopped chives. Serve separately.

ITALIAN BAKED BEANS

You can substitute Great Northern or dried lima beans for the kidney beans in this recipe.

Bake at 325° for 3 hours.
Makes 8 servings.

- 1 package (1 pound) dried red kidney beans
- 6 cups water
- 1 large onion, chopped (1 cup)
- 3 tablespoons olive oil or vegetable oil
- 1 small eggplant, sliced, pared and cubed
- 1 can (1 pound) tomatoes
- 2 teaspoons salt
- 1 teaspoon leaf marjoram, crumbled
- 1 cup dry red wine or water

1. Pick over beans and rinse. Place in a large kettle and add water. Bring to boiling; boil 2 minutes; remove from heat and cover. Allow to stand 1 hour.
2. Bring beans in kettle to boiling; reduce heat and simmer 1 hour.
3. While beans cook, sauté onion in oil in a large skillet; push to one side; sauté eggplant until soft in same pan. Stir in tomatoes, salt and marjoram; simmer 5 minutes; remove from heat.
4. Drain beans, reserving liquid. Combine beans and eggplant mixture in a 10-cup casserole. Stir in wine or water and 1 cup of reserved bean liquid. Cover.
5. Bake in slow oven (325°) 2 hours, 30 minutes remove cover. Bake 30 minutes longer, or until beans are tender. (Should beans begin to dry during baking, add just enough of the reserved bean liquid to moisten the surface.)

QUICK TIPS

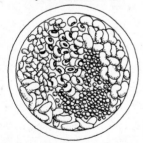

The dried beans shown on page 24 are, from top to bottom:
- Large limas—These are the beans that look the most like the fresh variety. Use in French dishes with lamb.
- Pinto beans—These are medium-size kidney-shaped beans. Use them in Mexican and Southwestern dishes.
- Black beans—These are small, black beans, white on the inside. Use in soups and Caribbean dishes.
- Garbanzos—These are also called chick peas. They are medium-size, round and wrinkled. Use in Spanish and Italian dishes.
- Blackeyed peas—These are small, grayish-white beans with a black circle on one end. Use in Southern dishes.

MARJORAM BAKED HALIBUT

A marjoram-flavored sauce transforms and enhances the fish flavor; even fish-haters will like this dish.

Bake at 400° 20 minutes for fresh fish,
or   at 400° 30 minutes for frozen.
Makes 4 servings.

- 2 leeks, washed and sliced
  OR: 2 large onions, chopped (2 cups)
- 2 cloves garlic, minced
- ¼ cup (½ stick) butter or margarine
- 1 can (2 pounds, 3 ounces) Italian tomatoes
- 1 tablespoon chopped fresh marjoram
  OR: 2 teaspoons leaf marjoram, crumbled
- 1 teaspoon salt
- ¼ teaspoon pepper
- 4 halibut steaks (4 ounces each)
  OR: 1 package (1 pound) frozen fillets of haddock or cod

1. Sauté leeks or onions and garlic in butter or margarine until soft in a large skillet. Drain liquid from tomatoes into skillet; cook, stirring often, until liquid has almost evaporated.
2. Stir in tomatoes, marjoram, salt and pepper, breaking up tomatoes with the back of a wooden spoon.
3. Place fish in a 6-cup casserole; spoon sauce over; cover.
4. Bake in hot oven (400°) 20 minutes, for fresh fish or 30 minutes for frozen fish, or until fish flakes easily. Serve with boiled potatoes, if you wish.
Suggested Variations: A 1-pound package of frozen Greenland turbot or pollock fillets can be substituted for the halibut steaks in this recipe.

CRAB AND MUSHROOM ROYAL

This is truly a dish fit for a king.

Bake at 325° for 1 hour.
Makes 8 servings.

- 1 pound mushrooms
- ¼ cup (½ stick) butter or margarine
- 1 medium-size onion, chopped (½ cup)
- 1 small green pepper, halved, seeded and chopped
- ½ cup finely chopped celery
- ½ cup mayonnaise or salad dressing
- 1 teaspoon salt
- ¼ teaspoon pepper
- 1 pound fresh crabmeat
  OR: 1 can (12 ounces) crabmeat
- 9 slices white bread
- 2 eggs
- 1½ cups milk
- 1 cup condensed cream of mushroom soup

1. Wipe and slice mushrooms; sauté in butter or margarine in a large skillet until soft; push to one side; sauté onion, green pepper and celery until soft in same pan.

Remove from heat; stir in mayonnaise or salad dressing, salt, pepper and crab.
2. Cut bread into 1-inch squares and arrange one-third of them in the bottom of a 10-cup casserole. Top with half of the crab mixture, then one-third more of the bread and remaining crab; reserve remaining bread squares.
3. Beat egg lightly in a small bowl; stir in milk; pour over casserole; cover; refrigerate at least one hour, or overnight for best results.
4. Remove from refrigerator; remove cover; top with reserved bread; spoon soup over top.
5. Bake in slow oven (325°) 1 hour, or until casserole is bubbly-hot. Serve with a crisp romaine and sliced avocado salad for a delightful party menu.

CHEESE ENCHILADAS

Enchiladas are an excellent company dish that's festive, yet not expensive.

Bake at 325° for 25 minutes.
Makes 6 servings.

- 1 large onion, chopped (1 cup)
- 1 medium-size green pepper, halved, seeded and chopped
- 1 clove garlic, minced
- 2 tablespoons vegetable oil
- 2 tablespoons all-purpose flour
- 1 tablespoon chili powder
- ½ teaspoon salt
- 1 cup water
- 1 envelope or teaspoon instant vegetable broth
- 1 large tomato, peeled and chopped
  OR: 1 can (8 ounces) tomatoes
- 1 can (1 pound) red kidney beans, mashed
- 1 package (9 ounces) frozen tortillas
- 4 cups shredded Cheddar cheese (1 pound)
- 1 cup sliced green onion

1. Sauté chopped onion, pepper and garlic in oil in a large skillet until soft. Stir in flour, chili powder and salt; cook, stirring constantly, just until bubbly.
2. Stir in water and instant vegetable broth; continue cooking and stirring until sauce thickens and bubbles 3 minutes. Add chopped tomatoes and kidney beans; bring to boiling; lower heat; simmer 15 minutes.
3. Cook tortillas, following label directions. Place tortillas on a flat surface; sprinkle each with ¼ cup cheese and a 1 tablespoon green onion; roll up. Place filled tortillas in a single layer in a 12-cup shallow casserole; pour sauce over and sprinkle liberally with the remaining Cheddar cheese.
4. Bake in slow oven (325°) 25 minutes or until sauce bubbles.
COOK'S TIP: It isn't twice as much work to make two-times a recipe. So double this recipe and other stew, chili and pasta casseroles and freeze the balance for another day.

FRENCH MARKET FONDUE

The trick to making this casserole puff handsomely is to make ahead and chill before baking. Overnight is best.

Bake at 350° for 45 minutes.
Makes 6 servings.

- 1 large Bermuda onion, sliced and separated into rings
- ¼ cup (½ stick) butter or margarine
- 12 slices French bread (about ½ loaf)
- 3 eggs
- 3 cups milk
- 1 tablespoon prepared mustard
- 1 teaspoon Worcestershire sauce
- ½ teaspoon salt
- 2 cups shredded Swiss cheese (8 ounces)
- ¼ cup grated Parmesan cheese
  Paprika

1. Sauté onion rings just until soft in 2 tablespoons of the butter or margarine in a large skillet.
2. While onion cooks, spread bread slices with remaining 2 tablespoons butter or margarine.
3. Beat eggs with milk, mustard, Worcestershire sauce and salt in a medium-size bowl until blended.
4. Place 4 slices of bread in a single layer in buttered 8-cup shallow casserole; top with layers of one third of the onion rings and Swiss cheese; repeat to make 2 more layers; top with Parmesan cheese.
5. Pour egg mixture over; sprinkle with paprika. Cover; chill at least 4 hours, or even overnight; uncover.
6. Bake in moderate oven (350°) 45 minutes, or until puffed and golden. Serve at once with a tossed green salad and a dry white wine.

PANCAKE STRATA

Pancakes are stacked with a tuna and cheese filling, then topped with a custard and baked to make this deliciously different main dish

Bake at 325° for 30 minutes.
Makes 6 servings.

- 4 eggs
- 1¼ cups water
- 3 tablespoons vegetable oil
- 1½ cups buttermilk pancake mix
- 1 package (8 ounces) process sharp American cheese, shredded
- 1 can (about 7 ounces) tuna, drained and flaked
- 1 cup milk

1. Beat 2 of the eggs with water and oil until foamy in a medium-size bowl; beat in pancake mix just until smooth.
2. Heat griddle or large skillet slowly; test temperature by sprinkling on a few drops of water. When drops bounce about, temperature is right; grease griddle lightly.
3. Pour batter, ½ cup for each pancake, onto griddle or pan to make an 8-inch round; bake 1 to 2 minutes, or until bubbles appear on top and underside is golden; turn; brown other side. Repeat with remaining batter, lightly greasing griddle before each baking, to make 5 large pancakes.
4. Layer pancakes with cheese and tuna between in a buttered 9-inch round casserole; top with cheese.
5. Beat remaining 2 eggs with milk in a medium-size bowl; pour over top pancake slowly (not down side of dish); cover casserole.
6. Bake in slow oven (325°) 30 minutes, or until a knife inserted in center comes out clean. Cut in wedges.

NORWEGIAN FISH BAKE

A trio of Scandinavian favorites; fish, dill and sour cream are topped with buttered crumbs.

Bake at 350° for 40 minutes.
Makes 6 servings.

- 2 pounds fresh cod, haddock or flounder fillets
  OR: 2 packages (1 pound each) frozen cod, haddock or flounder fillets
- ¼ cup all-purpose flour
- 2 teaspoons salt
- ¼ teaspoon pepper
- 1 cup milk
- 2 cups soft white bread crumbs (4 slices)
- ¼ cup (½ stick) butter or margarine, melted
- 1 tablespoon chopped fresh dill
  OR: 1 teaspoon dillweed
- 1 container (8 ounces) dairy sour cream

1. Cut fresh or frozen fish into serving-size pieces; coat with mixture of flour, salt and pepper. Arrange in a single layer in a 13x9x2-inch casserole; pour milk over coated fillets.
2. Bake in moderate oven (350°) 30 minutes, or until fish flakes easily.
3. While fish bakes, mix crumbs and melted butter or margarine in a small bowl. Stir dill into sour cream container.
4. Remove fish from oven; spoon sour-cream mixture over, then top with buttered crumbs.
5. Bake 10 minutes longer, or just until the sour cream mixture is set.

QUICK TIPS

For fish to taste its best in your casseroles, care must be taken in its storage:
- Store fresh fish between 35° and 40° in refrigerator and use within 2 days.
- Hold frozen fish at 0° in freezer and use within 6 months.
- Never re-freeze thawed fish; cook it, even if you wait a day to eat it.
- Canned fish can be stored in a cool, dry place up to 1 year.

HOW TO COOK PASTA

1. Use a large kettle because the pasta needs plenty of room to bubble if it's to cook without sticking together.
2. Do not cook more than 1 pound of pasta at a time in the same kettle. It will merely clump and stick together.
3. Fill a large kettle with water, leaving about 4 inches at the top (for 1 pound of pasta, you should use at least 12 cups of water). Add a drop of olive oil or vegetable oil (this helps keep pasta from sticking), place kettle over high heat and bring to boiling. Salt the cooking water or not, according to directions given on the package label.
4. When cooking long macaroni or spaghetti, slowly lower a handful at a time into the rapidly boiling water until it softens enough to fit into the kettle. Stir once or twice to separate strands, if necessary.
5. Boil rapidly, uncovered, until a strand of pasta cut in half shows no raw starch in the center—it shows up as a white dot—or until the pasta has no raw starch taste, but *does* feel a bit firm between the teeth (al dente is the Italian term for this firm-tenderness).
6. Drain pasta in a large colander the instant it's al dente. But do not rinse in cool water unless you are cooking lasagna or manicotti noodles.
7. If pasta must wait a few minutes before being served, toss with a little oil, butter or margarine, and set the colander over a kettle containing about 1 inch of simmering water and cover.

NEW ENGLAND SCALLOPED OYSTERS

Oysters were once eaten only in months with the letter "r." Now you can enjoy them year-round.

Bake at 350° for 30 minutes.
Makes 4 servings.

- ¼ cup (½ stick) butter or margarine
- 2 cups coarse soda cracker crumbs (about 12 large)
- ½ cup chopped parsley
- 1 teaspoon salt
- ¼ teaspoon pepper
- 1 pint (about 24) oysters
  OR: 2 cans (8 ounces each) oysters
- ½ cup light cream
- 1 teaspoon Worcestershire sauce

1. Melt butter or margarine in a medium-size saucepan; remove from heat; stir in cracker crumbs, parsley, salt and pepper; set aside.
2. Drain juice from oysters into a 2-cup measure; reserve. Sprinkle ⅓ of crumb mixture into a 9-inch pie plate or a 4-cup shallow casserole; layer half the oysters on top, then half of remaining crumbs and rest of oysters.
3. Combine saved oyster juice, cream and Worcestershire sauce and pour over oysters; sprinkle with remaining crumbs.
4. Bake in moderate oven (350°) 30 minutes, or until top is golden.

31

Would you believe that this festive party dish of **Bountiful Barbecued Turkey**, (recipe is on page 35), is from a slow cooker? It's just one of the 101 recipes in this bonus section devoted to the modern art of cooking one-pot meals. They'll simmer in your slow cooker whether you're at home or away.

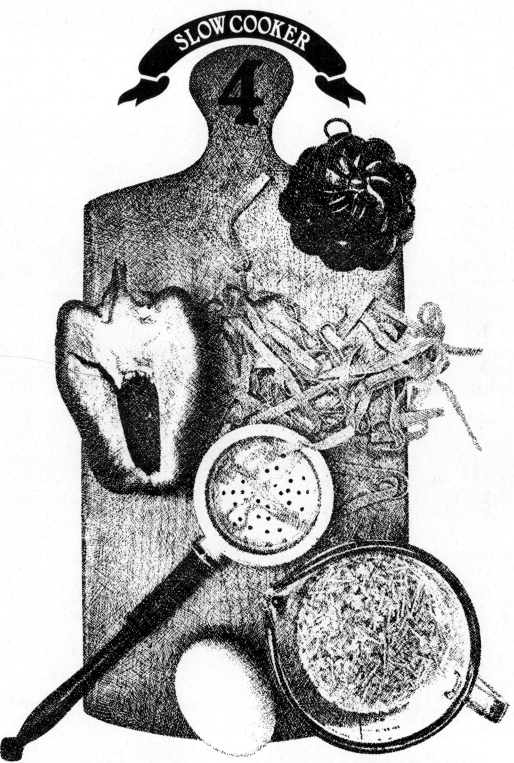

4

CAREFREE COOKING

Slow cookers speed things up. In less than 30 minutes you can combine the ingredients for a slow cooker meal, turn a switch and walk away. This wizard of an electric appliance cooks all day long or overnight, without any supervision. Try our slow cooker recipes for some of your favorites — pot roasts, stews and soups.

POLISH HOT POT

Red cabbage and pie-sliced apples turn this dish into a colorful, as well as flavorful family dish. Shown on page 12.

Cook on 190° to 200° for 6 hours, or on 290° to 300° for 3 hours. Makes 4 servings.

1 kielbasa or Polish sausage (about 1 pound)
1 Bermuda onion, sliced
4 cups shredded red cabbage
1 can (1 pound, 4 ounces) pie-sliced apples
1 teaspoon salt
¼ teaspoon pepper
¼ teaspoon caraway seeds (optional)
1 bay leaf
½ cup beer
1 can condensed chicken broth

1. Score kielbasa all around and place in an electric slow cooker.
2. Layer onion, cabbage, and apples in cooker, sprinkling each with part of the salt and pepper; sprinkle with caraway, if used; add bay leaf. Pour beer and chicken broth over; cover cooker.
3. Cook on low (190° to 200°) for 6 hours, or on high (290° to 300°) 3 hours, or until cabbage is very tender. Spoon vegetables into a heated casserole; top with whole cooked sausage.

GLAZED ROCK CORNISH HENS

Elegant enough to serve to the most discriminating guest, yet a breeze to prepare. You'll need your 5-quart slow cooker for this one. Photo on page 13.

Cook on 190° to 200° for 7 hours. Makes 4 servings.

1 large red cooking apple, quartered and cored
1 tablespoon soy sauce
4 frozen Rock Cornish game hens, thawed
¼ cup dry white or rosé wine
3 tablespoons orange marmalade
Rind and juice of ½ lemon
½ teaspoon salt
⅛ teaspoon pepper

1. Dip apple quarters into soy sauce in a 1-cup measure; tuck one piece into the cavity of each hen.
2. Stir wine, marmalade, lemon rind and juice, salt and pepper into remaining soy sauce; brush over hens.
3. Place hens, breast side down, in a 5-quart electric slow cooker; pour remaining glaze over; cover.
4. Cook on low (190° to 200°) for 3 hours. Baste at this point, if possible. Cook 4 hours longer, or until tender.
5. Arrange hens on a heated serving platter and serve with canned pear halves filled with prepared chicken-flavored stuffing mix, if you wish.

MUSHROOM STEAK

Try finding a more popular food combination—and so quick to fix.

Cook on 190° to 200° for 8 hours or on 290° to 300° for 4 hours. Makes 8 servings.

1 chuck roast, cut 1½-inches thick (about 3 pounds)
1 envelope (2 to a package) mushroom soup mix
1 tablespoon minced dried onion
1 cup dry red wine or water

1. Trim excess fat from roast; combine dry soup mix and onion on a sheet of aluminum foil or wax paper. Roll roast in mixture to coat well.
2. Place coated roast in an electric slow cooker; pour wine or water over; cover.
3. Cook on low (190° to 200°) 8 hours, turning after 4 hours, if possible, or on high (290° to 300°) 4 hours, turning after 2 hours, if possible, or until meat is tender. Serve with mashed potatoes and buttered green beans, if you wish.

HONG KONG PORK STEW

If you like sweet-and-sour pork, you'll rave about this colorful stew.

Cook on 190° to 200° for 8 hours, or on 290° to 300° for 4 hours. Makes 8 servings.

2 pounds boneless pork shoulder, cubed
1 teaspoon salt
¼ teaspoon ground ginger
⅛ teaspoon pepper
1 can (13¼ ounces) pineapple chunks
¼ cup firmly packed brown sugar
1 envelope or teaspoon instant chicken broth
¼ cup light molasses
¼ cup vinegar
2 tablespoons cornstarch
1 can (1 pound) sweet potatoes
2 firm tomatoes, cut in eighths
1 green pepper, halved, seeded and cut in 1-inch squares

1. Trim excess fat from pork; place in an electric slow cooker; season with salt, ginger and pepper.
2. Drain syrup from pineapple, adding water to syrup to make 1½ cups; reserve pineapple chunks. Add syrup mixture to pork; stir in sugar, instant broth, molasses and vinegar; cover.
3. Cook on low (190° to 200°) 8 hours, or on high (290° to 300°) 4 hours.
4. Turn heat control to high (290° to 300°). Combine cornstarch and ¼ cup cold water in a cup; stir into pork mixture until well-blended.
5. Add sweet potatoes, tomatoes, pineapple chunks and green pepper; cover; simmer 20 minutes longer.

VERMONT CORNED BEEF

Our favorite way with corned beef, but it must be the "mild cure" corned beef, otherwise the dish is too salty. Pictured on page 13.

Cook on 190° to 200° for 10 hours, or on 290° to 300° for 5 hours. Makes 8 servings.

1 "mild cure" corned beef brisket (about 4 pounds)
¼ cup firmly packed brown sugar
1 California orange, sliced
1 tablespoon mixed pickling spices
1 bay leaf
2 large carrots, pared and sliced
2 large onions, peeled and quartered
3 small white turnips, pared and quartered
1 cup dry white wine
½ cup water

1. Wash corned beef in cold running water. Place in an electric slow cooker; top with sugar, orange slices, mixed pickling spices and bay leaf.
2. Arrange carrots, onions and turnips around meat in slow cooker; pour wine and water over; cover.
3. Cook on low (190° to 200°) 10 hours, or on high (290° to 300°) 5 hours, or until meat is tender when pierced with a two-tined fork.
4. Slice meat and place on a heated serving platter and arrange boiled potatoes, chopped turnip greens and lima beans around it.

OLD-COUNTRY CHICKEN IN THE POT

This is the kind of soup mother brought you when you were sick in bed.

Cook on 190° to 200° for 8 hours, or on 290° to 300° for 4 hours. Makes 6 servings.

1 broiler-fryer, cut up (about 3 pounds)
1 pound small new potatoes, washed
4 large carrots, pared and diced
2 white turnips, pared and diced
2 stalks celery with leaves, chopped
1 leek, trimmed and sliced
OR: 1 large onion, chopped (1 cup)
1 tablespoon salt
6 cups water
Handful parsley
6 peppercorns
1 bay leaf

1. Layer chicken, potatoes, carrots, turnips, celery and leek or onion in an electric slow cooker, sprinkling salt between layers; add water.
2. Tie parsley, peppercorns and bay leaf in a piece of cheesecloth. Push under liquid; cover.
3. Cook on low (190° to 200°) 8 hours, or on high (290° to 300°) 4 hours, or until chicken is tender. Ladle into soup bowl.

BOUNTIFUL BARBECUED TURKEY

An excellent party dish that needs the 5-quart slow cooker. For something colorful and delicious, serve with herb buttered cauliflower and broccoli. Pictured on page 32.

Cook on 190° to 200° for 9 hours, then on 290° to 300° for 3 hours. Makes 12 servings.

- 1 frozen turkey, thawed and cut up, (about 8 pounds)
- ¾ cup all-purpose flour
- 1 tablespoon salt
- ½ teaspoon pepper
- ½ cup vegetable shortening
- 1 Bermuda onion, sliced
- 1 clove garlic, minced
- 1 or 2 green chili peppers, seeded and chopped (from a 4-ounce can)
- 6 slices lemon
- 1 can condensed chicken broth
- 1 can (8 ounces) tomato sauce
- ½ cup dry white wine
- 1 tablespoon brown sugar
  Hot linguini

1. Shake turkey pieces, a few at a time, in a mixture of flour, salt and pepper in a plastic bag to coat evenly.
2. Brown turkey pieces in shortening in a large skillet or a 5-quart electric slow cooker with a browning unit; remove and reserve. Pour off all but 2 tablespoons of the pan drippings. Sauté onion and garlic in drippings until soft. Stir in peppers and lemon slices and cook 2 minutes.
3. Place turkey pieces in slow cooker and coat with onion mixture. Combine chicken broth, tomato sauce, wine and brown sugar in a 4-cup measure; pour over turkey; cover.
4. Cook on low (190° to 200°) 9 hours. Turn heat control to high (290° to 300°); cook 3 hours, or until turkey pieces are tender when pierced with a fork.
COOK'S TIP: To thicken gravy, remove turkey to a heated platter lined with linguini and keep warm. Combine ½ cup all-purpose flour with 1 cup cold water in a 2-cup measure until smooth; stir into liquid; cover; cook 15 minutes.

SLOW COOKER TIPS

Here are a few general guidelines for adapting your favorite one-pot recipes to a slow cooker:
- Uncooked meat and vegetable combinations will require 8 to 10 hours on low (190° to 200°) or 4 to 5 hours on high (290° to 300°).
- One hour of simmering on the range or baking at 350° in the oven is equal to 8 to 10 hours on low (190° to 200°), or 4 to 5 hours on high (290° to 300°).
- Reduce the liquid in your recipe to about 1 cup since the slow cooker method of simmering foods saves all the food's natural juices.
- Use canned soups and broths, wine or water as the liquid in your slow cooker.
- Don't add dairy products, such as milk, sour cream, or cream until the final 30 minutes of cooking.
- Cook noodles and macaroni products, following label directions, then add to slow cooker near the end of the cooking.
- Frozen vegetables and frozen fish should be thawed slightly, (especially if your slow cooker is made of crockery) and added only during the last hour of cooking, since they require so little cooking.
- Don't lift the cover of your slow cooker, just to peek and see how the food is cooking. Every time the cover comes off, you lose heat that is equal to 30 minutes of cooking time.
- Trim as much excess fat as possible from the meat going into your slow cooker. Fat can increase the temperature of the liquid in the slow cooker and cut down on the cooking time so much, you might have an overcooked dish.
- Browning meats and poultry is not essential, but it does help to develop a richer flavor in the food and remove some of the fat, especially in pork, lamb and sausages. Turn the heat control to 350° and brown meat on all sides; remove and sauté vegetables in pan drippings, then remove vegetables and pour out all fat remaining in cooker before returning food, then lower heat control to slow-cooking temperature.

SCOTCH LAMB BROTH

The last of a leg of lamb can be substituted for the lamb combination.

Cook on 190° to 200° for 10 hours, or on 290° to 300° for 5 hours. Makes 8 servings.

- 2 pounds lamb shoulder combination
- 2 leeks, trimmed and sliced
- 2 cups chopped celery
- 2 large carrots, pared and chopped
- 1 medium-size onion, chopped
- 8 cups water
- 2 teaspoons salt
- ½ teaspoon pepper
- ½ cup pearl barley
- 1 cup light cream

1. Trim excess fat from lamb. Place in an electric slow cooker with leeks, celery, carrots, onion, water, salt and pepper. Stir in pearl barley; cover.
2. Cook on low (190° to 200°) 10 hours, or on high (290° to 300°) 5 hours, or until meat is tender and barley is cooked. Stir in cream just before serving.

ELECTRIC FRYPAN VEAL AND DILL

Have no slow cooker, but want to make recipes in this section? Use your electric frypan and follow the cooking directions in this recipe.

Cook on "simmer" for 8 hours. Makes 6 servings.

- 1½ pounds boneless veal shoulder, cubed
- 6 medium-size boiling potatoes, pared and quartered
- 12 small white onions, peeled
- 6 small zucchini, cut into 1-inch pieces
- 1½ cups water
- 2 envelopes or teaspoons instant chicken broth
- 2 teaspoons salt
- 1 teaspoon dillweed
- ½ pound mushrooms, quartered

OR: 1 can (3 or 4 ounces) sliced mushrooms
- ¼ cup all-purpose flour
- ½ cup cold water

1. Find "simmer" on your electric frypan by pouring 2 cups cold water into frypan and turn heat control to about 200°. (If there is no marking for 200°, try some place between the lowest setting on the control and the first temperature marking.) Allow water to heat until tiny pin-point bubbles begin to form on the bottom of the frypan. This is the simmer point. If water begins to boil, then lower temperature control, just a little. You want the pin-point bubbles, but not the rolling boil. Pour out water, and mark the simmer spot on heat control with red paint or nail polish.
2. Place veal, potatoes, onions, zucchini, water, instant chicken broth, salt and dillweed in electric frypan; stir to blend well. (Don't worry that the water level is so low; the steam will baste the food.) Cover with frypan dome, being sure that the vents are closed.
3. Turn heat control to "simmer" and cook 8 hours, or until veal and vegetables are tender.
4. Turn heat control to 250° and add mushrooms; cook 5 minutes. Combine flour and cold water in a cup; stir into liquid in frypan; cover; cook 15 minutes.
COOK'S TIP: Recipes that have been tested on a higher setting (250°) of the electric frypan cook much more quickly than on the setting (290° to 300°) of the slow cooker. So it is wisest to follow only the "simmer" setting on the electric frypan for the low setting of the slow cooker recipes in this section.
Suggested Variations: Cubed boneless lamb shoulder or pork shoulder can be substituted for the cubed veal in the recipe.

CLASSIC CHICKEN BROTH

You see it called for in gourmet recipes. Now let your slow cooker do the work while you're away—or even asleep.

Cook on 190° to 200° for 10 hours, or on 290° to 300° for 5 hours. Makes 12 cups.

- 1 stewing chicken (about 5 pounds)
- 2 medium-size carrots, pared
- 1 large white parsnip, pared
- 1 large onion, chopped (1 cup)
- 2 stalks celery with leaves, chopped
    Handful parsley
- 10 cups water
- 2 tablespoons salt
- 12 peppercorns

1. Combine chicken with giblets, but not livers, in a 5-quart electric slow cooker. Add carrots, parsnip, onion, celery, and parsley; pour water over; sprinkle with salt and peppercorns; cover.
2. Cook on low (190° to 200°) 10 hours, or on high (290° to 300°) 5 hours, or until chicken is tender; remove chicken and vegetables from broth.
3. Strain broth through cheesecloth into a large bowl. (There should be about 12 cups.) Cool chicken until cool enough to handle; remove and discard skin and bones. Save chicken meat for use in casseroles or cold salads.
4. Refrigerate broth, up to 4 days, leaving the fat layer on surface until ready to use; then lift off and discard. To freeze broth, pour into recipe-size plastic freezer containers to within ½-inch of top; seal; label and date. Freeze. Plan to use within 3 months.

CLASSIC BEEF BROTH

Slow cookers are taking the place of the old soup pot which simmered for hours on the back of a wood-burning stove.

Bake at 450° for 40 minutes.
Cook on 190° to 200° for 10 hours, or on 290° to 300° for 5 hours. Makes 12 cups.

- 3 pounds meaty beef bones
- 1 veal bone, cracked (optional)
- 3 large carrots, pared and chopped
- 2 large onions, halved
- 1 leek, trimmed
- 2 celery stalks with leaves, chopped
- 10 cups water
    Handful parsley
- 2 cloves garlic, peeled
- 1 tablespoon salt
- 1 bay leaf
- 3 whole cloves

1. Put the meat bones, carrots, onions, leek and celery into a roasting pan.
2. Roast in hot oven (450°) 40 minutes, or until bones are well browned.
3. Place browned bones and vegetables in a 5-quart electric slow cooker; add water, parsley, garlic, salt, bay leaf and cloves; cover cooker.
4. Cook on low (190° to 200°) 10 hours, or on high (290° to 300°) 5 hours, or until broth is rich and flavorful; strain broth through cheesecloth into a large bowl.
5. Refrigerate broth, up to 4 days, leaving the fat layer on surface until ready to use; then lift off fat and discard. To freeze broth, pour into recipe-size plastic freezer containers to within ½-inch of top; seal; label and date. Freeze. Plan to use within 3 months.

POT-ROASTED CHICKEN

Beef broth and thyme are the flavor secrets to this French-style chicken dish.

Cook on 190° to 200° for 10 hours, or on 290° to 300° for 5 hours. Makes 6 servings.

- 1 stewing chicken (about 5 pounds)
- 3 tablespoons butter or margarine
- 2 teaspoons leaf thyme, crumbled
- 1 can condensed beef broth
- 3 tablespoons all-purpose flour
- 1 small can evaporated milk

1. Brown chicken on all sides in butter or margarine and thyme until golden in a large skillet or an electric slow cooker with a browning unit.
2. Combine browned chicken and beef broth in slow cooker; cover.
3. Cook on low (190° to 200°) 10 hours, or on high (290° to 300°) 5 hours, or until chicken is tender when pierced with a two-tined fork. Remove chicken to a heated platter and keep warm.
4. Turn heat control to high (290° to 300°). Combine flour and evaporated milk in a cup; stir into liquid in slow cooker until well-blended. Cover; cook 15 minutes. Taste and season with salt and pepper, if you wish. Serve sauce separately in heated gravy boat.

SANTA CLARA PORK POT

Dried apricots and prunes cook along with the pork in this hearty dish.

Cook on 190° to 200° for 10 hours, or on 290° to 300° for 5 hours. Makes 6 servings

- 1 rib-end pork loin (about 3 pounds)
- 2 teaspoons salt
- ½ teaspoon ground ginger
- ¼ teaspoon pepper
- ¼ teaspoon dry mustard
- 1 large orange
- 1 lemon
    Water
- 2 tablespoon dark corn syrup
- 1 pound small white onions, peeled
- 1 cup dried apricots
- 1 cup dried pitted prunes
- 2 tablespoons cornstarch

1. Trim excess fat from pork; brown on all sides in a large skillet or an electric slow cooker with a browning unit; sprinkle with salt, ginger, pepper and mustard to coat well.
2. Meanwhile, remove the thin, bright-colored rind from the orange and lemon with a sharp knife; reserve. Squeeze juice from orange and lemon into a 1-cup measure; add water to fruit juices to make 1 cup liquid.
3. Place pork in slow cooker with rinds and juices and corn syrup; add onions and cover cooker.
4. Cook on low (190° to 200°) 10 hours, or on high (290° to 300°) 5 hours; add apricots and prunes.
5. Turn heat control to high (290° to 300°). Simmer 15 minutes. Combine cornstarch and ¼ cup cold water in a cup; stir into liquid in slow cooker until well-blended. Cover; cook 15 minutes longer. Serve with boiled potatoes and cold beer, if you wish.

HOPPING JOHN

Some say this dish was named for a famous waiter in a fashionable Charleston, South Carolina hotel.

Cook on 190° to 200° for 8 hours, or on 290° to 300° for 4 hours. Makes 8 servings.

- 2 slices bacon, diced
- 1 pound ground meatloaf mixture
- 1 medium-size onion, chopped (½ cup)
- 1 cup chopped celery
- 2 packages (10 ounces each) frozen blackeyed peas, partly thawed
- 1 teaspoon salt
- 1 teaspoon leaf basil, crumbled
- ½ teaspoon leaf thyme, crumbled
- 1 bay leaf
    Few drops bottled red-pepper seasoning
- 1 envelope or teaspoon instant beef broth
- ½ cup water
- ½ cup uncooked rice
- 2 cups tomato juice

1. Sauté bacon until crisp in a large skillet or an electric slow cooker with a browning unit; remove with a slotted spoon and drain on paper towels.
2. Shape meatloaf mixture into a patty in same pan; brown 5 minutes on each side, then break up into chunks; push to one side. Add onion to pan and sauté just until soft. Stir in cooked bacon, celery, blackeyed peas, salt, basil, thyme, bay leaf, red-pepper seasoning, instant beef broth, and water. Bring to boiling.
3. Combine ground beef mixture, uncooked rice and tomato juice in an electric slow cooker; cover.
4. Cook on low (190° to 200°) 8 hours, or on high (290° to 300°) 4 hours, stirring, if possible, halfway through cooking, or until rice is tender. Serve with crisp cucumber and onion slices, if you wish.

PICADILLO

This Cuban supper dish is usually served with rice and fried bananas.

Cook on 190° to 200° for 6 hours.
Makes 8 servings

- 1 large onion, chopped (1 cup)
- 1 large green pepper, halved, seeded and chopped
- 1 clove garlic, minced
- ¼ cup olive oil
- 4 large ripe tomatoes, peeled and chopped
- ½ teaspoon sugar
- 3 cups finely diced cooked beef
- 1 can condensed beef broth
- 1 teaspoon salt
- 1 bay leaf
- ¼ teaspoon ground cloves

1. Sauté onion, green pepper and garlic in oil in a large skillet or an electric slow cooker with a browning unit until soft; stir in tomatoes and sugar; simmer 5 minutes. Stir in diced beef.
2. Combine in slow cooker with beef broth, salt, bay leaf and cloves; cover.
3. Cook on low (190° to 200°) 6 hours, or until ready to serve.

DANISH OXTAIL SOUP

Laugh at rainy days when you have this bubbling soup waiting at home in your slow cooker.

Bake at 450° for 45 minutes.
Cook on 190° to 200° for 8 hours,
or   on 290° to 300° for 4 hours.
Makes 6 servings.

- 3 pounds oxtails, cut up
- 1 large onion, chopped (1 cup)
- 2 large carrots, pared and sliced
- 1 large parsnip, pared and sliced
- 1 white turnip, pared and sliced
- 2 tablespoons brandy
- 6 cups water
- 1 tablespoon salt
- ½ teaspoon pepper
- ½ teaspoon leaf savory, crumbled
- 1 bay leaf
  Eggs Mimosa (recipe follows)
  Chopped parsley

1. Spread oxtails in a single layer in shallow roasting pan. Roast in very hot oven (450°) 45 minutes, or until nicely browned. Drain off fat, reserving 2 tablespoons in pan.
2. Sauté onion, carrots, parsnip and turnip in reserved fat in a large skillet or an electric slow cooker with a browning unit, 10 minutes, or until soft. Add browned oxtails. Drizzle brandy over; ignite carefully with a lighted match.
3. Place oxtail mixture in slow cooker; add water, salt, pepper, savory and bay leaf; cover slow cooker.
4. Cook on low (190° to 200°) 8 hours, or on high (290° to 300°) 4 hours, or until oxtails are tender.

5. Ladle into soup bowls; place half an EGG MIMOSA in each, sprinkle with parsley. Serve with crusty French bread.
EGGS MIMOSA—Cut 3 hard-cooked eggs in half lengthwise. Carefully remove yolks, keeping whites whole. Press yolks through a sieve; spoon back into whites. A double batch can also be served on BRAZILIAN FEIJOADA (page 50).

LIVER RAGOÛT

Here's an unusually good way to prepare beef liver. Economical, too.

Cook on 190° to 200° for 8 hours,
or   on 290° to 300° for 4 hours.
Makes 6 servings.

- 1½ pounds unsliced beef liver
- 2 tablespoons vegetable oil
- 1½ cups water
- 1 envelope (about 1½ ounces) beef-stew seasoning mix
- 1 bag (1 pound) frozen whole carrots
- 1 can (1 pound) small boiled onions, drained
  Chopped parsley

1. Brown the whole piece of liver slowly in oil in a large skillet or an electric slow cooker with a browning unit; remove and reserve. Stir in water and seasoning mix; bring to boiling.
2. Place liver with carrots and onions in slow cooker; pour hot liquid over; cover.
3. Cook on low (190° to 200°) 8 hours, or on high (290° to 300°) 4 hours, or until liver is tender when pierced with a two-tined fork.
4. Remove liver to a serving platter; arrange vegetables in mounds around edge; sprinkle with chopped parsley. Serve gravy separately.

HUNGARIAN GOULASH SOUP

This dish, sometimes called "Gulyas", tastes best with Hungarian paprika.

Cook on 190° to 200° for 8 hours,
or   on 290° to 300° for 4 hours.
Makes 8 servings.

- 2 tablespoons vegetable shortening
- 1½ pounds lean beef, cubed
- 1 tablespoon paprika
- ¼ cup tomato purée
- 6 cups Classic Beef Broth (recipe on page 36)
  OR: 6 envelopes or teaspoons instant beef broth and 6 cups water
- 2 large potatoes, pared and diced
- 2 large onions, chopped (2 cups)
- 1 cup chopped celery
- 1 large carrot, pared and chopped
- 1 teaspoon caraway seeds, crushed
- 1 teaspoon salt
- ¼ teaspoon pepper

1. Melt shortening in a large skillet or a 5-quart electric slow cooker with a

browning unit. Add beef cubes and stir over high heat for 5 minutes.
2. Add paprika and mix well. Stir in tomato purée. Pour into a 5-quart slow cooker; stir in CLASSIC BEEF BROTH or instant beef broth and water, potatoes, onions, celery, carrot, caraway seeds, salt and pepper; cover.
3. Cook on low (190° to 200°) 8 hours, or on high (290° to 300°) 4 hours. Taste and add additional salt and pepper, if you wish. Serve in heated soup bowls with pumpernickel bread and pickled beets.

SAUCY MEATBALLS

Everyone loves meatballs and these are extra moist and flavorful.

Cook on 190° to 200° for 8 hours,
or   on 290° to 300° for 4 hours.
Makes 8 servings.

- 1½ pounds ground chuck
- ½ pound bulk sausage meat
- 1 jar (8 ounces) junior applesauce (baby-pack)
- 1 cup soft whole-wheat bread crumbs (2 slices)
- 8 prunes, pitted and chopped
- 1 teaspoon salt
- ¼ teaspoon pepper
- 1 can condensed tomato soup
- ¼ cup water

1. Mix ground beef and sausage meat lightly with applesauce, bread crumbs, prunes, salt and pepper until well-blended; shape into 24 balls.
2. Place in an electric slow cooker; blend soup and water in a 2-cup measure; pour over meatballs; cover.
3. Cook on low (190° to 200°) 8 hours, or on high (290° to 300°) 4 hours. Serve with thin spaghetti and a crisp salad.

SLOW COOKER TIPS

● Take the time to read the use and care booklet that come with your slow cooker. It is filled with information on all of the special features of your cooker and how to get the most from your appliance. A half hour with this booklet before you start will mean great success in your cooking, right from the beginning. Keep the booklet in a safe place and refer to it occasionally to refresh your memory on all the wonderful ways this appliance can serve you.
● To start your slow cooker after you have left the house, use the automatic time plug on your range, following manufacturer's directions, or you can use an appliance timer. Then plug the slow cooker into the appliance timer that is plugged into the electrical outlet. Set the cooker's heat control to the setting in recipe. Then set the appliance timer, following manufacturer's directions. Dinner is done when you return without you being there to get the slow cooker started.

SLUMGULLION ON A BUN

Sort of a "Sloppy Joe." Everyone can spoon up his serving when he gets home.

Cook on 190° to 200° for 8 hours,
or   on 290° to 300° for 4 hours.
Makes 6 servings.

1½ pounds ground chuck
 1 large onion, chopped (1 cup)
 1 clove garlic, minced
 1 envelope (1½ ounces) spaghetti
     sauce mix
 2 cups tomato juice
 1 cup chopped celery
 1 can (12 or 16 ounces) whole-
     kernel corn
 ¼ cup sliced stuffed olives
 6 split hamburger buns, toasted

1. Shape ground beef into a large patty in a large skillet or an electric slow cooker with a browning unit. Brown 5 minutes on each side, then break up into chunks; push to one side.
2. Add onion and garlic; sauté just until soft. Stir in spaghetti sauce mix and tomato juice, then celery and corn.
3. Spoon mixture into cooker; cover.
4. Cook on low (190° to 200°) 8 hours, stirring after 4 hours if possible, or on high (290° to 300°) 4 hours, stirring after 2 hours, if possible. Add stuffed olives and serve over toasted buns.

BERMUDA LAMB STEW

A delightfully mild-seasoned dish with a springtime flavor.

Cook on 190° to 200° for 8 hours,
or   on 290° to 300° for 4 hours.
Makes 6 servings.

 2 pounds boneless lamb shoulder,
     cubed
 1 Bermuda onion, thinly sliced and
     separated into rings
 2 cups shredded lettuce
 2 medium-size ripe tomatoes,
     chopped
 2 pounds fresh peas, shelled (2 cups)
     OR: 2 cups frozen peas (from a
     1½-pound bag)
 2 medium-size yellow squash, cut into
     2-inch pieces
 2 teaspoons salt
 ½ teaspoon leaf rosemary, crumbled
 ¼ teaspoon freshly ground pepper
 1 envelope or teaspoon instant
     chicken broth
 1 cup hot water
 3 tablespoons cornstarch

1. Trim all excess fat from lamb. Place lamb in the bottom of an electric slow cooker; add onion rings, lettuce, tomatoes, peas, squash, salt, rosemary and pepper to cover lamb.
2. Dissolve instant broth in hot water in a 2-cup measure; pour over meat and vegetables; stir to mix well; cover.

3. Cook on low (190° to 200°) 8 hours, or on high (290° to 300°) 4 hours, or until lamb is tender.
4. Turn heat control to high (290° to 300°). Combine cornstarch and ⅓ cup cold water in a cup; stir into liquid until well-blended. Cover; simmer 15 minutes longer, until bubbly-hot.

BORSCHT

A Russian favorite that is classically served with a dollop of sour cream.

Cook on 190° to 200° for 8 hours,
or   on 290° to 300° for 4 hours.
Makes 8 servings.

 2 cups shredded cabbage
 2 large onions, chopped (2 cups)
 1 cup chopped celery
 4 large beets, pared and shredded
 2 large carrots, pared and shredded
 3 tablespoons butter or margarine
 2 pounds chicken wings
 1 pound boneless chuck, cubed
10 cups water
 1 can (6 ounces) tomato paste
 2 teaspoons salt
 ¼ teaspoon pepper
     Dairy sour cream

1. Sauté cabbage, onions, celery, beets and carrots in butter or margarine in a large skillet or a 5-quart slow cooker with a browning unit.
2. Combine vegetables with chicken wings, cubed beef, water, tomato paste, salt and pepper in a 5-quart slow cooker; cover cooker.
3. Cook on low (190° to 200°) 8 hours, or on high (290° to 300°) 4 hours, or until soup is rich and flavorful. Taste and season with additional salt and pepper, if you wish.
4. Serve in heated soup bowls and top each serving with sour cream.

CHOLENT

This is a traditional Sabbath dish in Jewish households.

Cook on 190° to 200° for 10 to 12 hours.
Makes 6 servings.

 1 cup dried lima beans (from a
     1-pound package)
     Water
 1 beef brisket (about 3 pounds)
 2 tablespoons vegetable oil
 2 large onion, sliced
 1 clove garlic, minced (optional)
 1 cup barley or kasha
 1 marrow bone
 2 teaspoons salt
 ¼ teaspoon pepper
 1 bay leaf

1. Pick over lima beans; rinse under running cold water; place in a glass bowl; cover with cold water; cover bowl with plastic wrap; let soak overnight at room

temperature; drain.
2. Trim excess fat from brisket; brown in oil in a large skillet or an electric slow cooker with a browning unit; remove and reserve. Sauté onion and garlic until soft in pan drippings.
3. Arrange brisket, onions and garlic in slow cooker; add drained lima beans, barley or kasha, marrow bone, salt, pepper and bay leaf; add water just to cover surface of food; cover.
4. Cook on low (190° to 200°) 10 to 12 hours, or until brisket is tender; taste and season with salt and pepper if you wish. *Suggested Variations:* Orthodox Jewish households couldn't turn the stove on or off on the Sabbath, so many of them prepared dishes to cook in a pre-heated oven overnight. Seasonings vary with the country. Many cooks use paprika, ginger, allspice berries, or a little brown sugar. A split calve's foot is often substituted for the marrow bone. A rich dumpling (Kreaidel) is often cooked with the CHOLENT.

SLOW COOKER TIPS

FOR CROCKERY COOKERS:
Crockery and stoneware liners in slow cookers are made of natural clay with particular qualities that require special handling to keep them in perfect condition:
• Do not allow sudden change in temperature, either by pouring boiling liquids into a very cold crockery cooker, or placing a hot cooker on a cold surface.
• Be very careful not to bang your crockery cooker in the sink or on the faucet. A sharp blow could break or chip the crockery lining.
• Never store foods in a crockery slow cooker in the refrigerator. The change in temperature can be harmful to the finish.
• To clean the interior surface of the cooker, fill with hot sudsy water as soon as cooker has cooled down; allow to soak at least 15 minutes, then rub surface with a cloth, nylon net pad or a plastic sponge, but never use a harsh abrasive cleanser, metal pad or steel wool. Rinse well in hot water and wipe dry with a towel.
• To remove mineral stains on crockery, fill cooker with hot water and 1 cup white vinegar; cover. Turn heat control to high (290° to 300°) for 2 hours. Then clean following directions above, without the 15 minute soaking.
• To remove water marks from highly glazed crockery, rub the surface with vegetable oil and allow to stand for 2 hours before cleaning. Clean, following directions above, without the 15 minute soaking.
• Never add frozen foods directly to your crockery slow cooker. Thaw first, then add during the last 30 minutes to 1 hour of cooking.
• Do not place crockery cooker, crockery liners or stoneware pots on electric or gas range-top surface burner, or place under the broiler.

STUFFED GREEN PEPPERS

See how well your slow cooker prepares stuffed vegetables.

Cook on 190° to 200° for 8 hours,
or   on 290° to 300° for 4 hours.
Makes 4 servings.

- 4 large green peppers
- 1 pound ground beef
- 1 can (1 pound) pork and beans in tomato sauce
- 1 can (3 ounces) French fried onion rings
- 1 teaspoon prepared mustard
- 1 can (8 ounces) tomato sauce

1. Cut a thin slice from top of each pepper; scoop out seeds and membrane. Parboil peppers in a small amount of boiling salted water 3 minutes; drain well. Stand peppers in slow cooker.
2. Shape ground beef into a large patty in a skillet; brown 5 minutes on each side, then break up into small chunks.
3. Stir in pork and beans, half of the onion rings and mustard. Spoon into pepper cups, dividing evenly; pour tomato sauce over; cover.
4. Cook on low (190° to 200°) 8 hours, or on high (290° to 300°) 4 hours, or until peppers are tender. Top with remaining French fried onion rings.

AU PORTO CHICKEN

Chicken in wine with a Portuguese touch —white Port is the cooking liquid. If you prefer a less sweet flavor, choose a dry white wine, such as Chablis.

Cook on 190° to 200° for 10 hours,
or   on 290° to 300° for 6 hours.
Makes 4 servings.

- 1 broiler-fryer (about 3 pounds)
- 1½ teaspoons salt
- ½ teaspoon pepper
- 1 large onion, chopped (1 cup)
- 1 clove garlic, minced
- 2 large carrots, pared and chopped
- 2 tablespoons olive oil or vegetable oil
- 1 teaspoon leaf rosemary, crumbled
- 1 cup white Port or dry white wine or chicken broth
- ½ pound fresh mushrooms, quartered
  OR: 1 can (6 ounces) whole mushrooms
- 2 tablespoons all-purpose flour

1. Season chicken with ½ teaspoon of the salt and ¼ teaspoon of the pepper. Skewer neck skin to back and tie legs.
2. Sauté onion, garlic and carrots until soft in oil in a large skillet or 3½-quart electric slow cooker with a browning unit. Stir in remaining 1 teaspoon salt, ¼ teaspoon pepper and rosemary. Spoon into the bottom of electric slow cooker.
3. Place chicken on top of vegetables; pour in wine or chicken broth; cover.

4. Cook on low (190° to 200°) 10 hours, or on high (290° to 300°) 6 hours, or until chicken is tender when pierced with a two-tined fork. Remove chicken to a heated platter and keep warm.
5. Turn heat control to high (290° to 300°). Add mushrooms and cook 15 minutes. Combine flour with ¼ cup cold water in a cup; stir into cooker until well-blended. Cover; simmer 15 minutes. Stir in a few drops bottled gravy coloring, if you wish. Slice chicken and pass sauce in heated gravy boat. Serve with a bottle of chilled dry white wine and a crisp salad of tossed greens with marinated artichokes, if you wish.

WINE BRAISED OXTAILS

Great when the gravy is spooned over mountains of mashed potatoes.

Cook on 290° to 300° for 2 hours,
then   on 190° to 200° for 8 hours.
Makes 6 servings.

- 3½ pounds oxtails, cut up
- ⅓ cup all-purpose flour
- 2 teaspoons salt
- ¼ teaspoon pepper
- 3 tablespoons vegetable shortening
- 12 small white onions, peeled
- 2 small white turnips, pared and cubed
- 2 large carrots, pared and sliced
- 1 large leek, washed and sliced
- ¼ cup chopped parsley
- 4 whole allspice
- ¼ teaspoon leaf thyme, crumbled
- 1 can condensed beef broth
- 1 cup dry red wine
- 1 bay leaf

1. Shake oxtails, a few pieces at a time, in a mixture of flour, salt and pepper in a plastic bag to coat well.
2. Brown in shortening in a large skillet or an electric slow cooker with a browning unit; remove and reserve.
3. Sauté onions, turnips, carrots, leek and parsley in pan drippings 5 minutes; season with allspice and thyme.
4. Combine oxtails and vegetables in slow cooker; pour beef broth and wine over; add bay leaf; cover.
5. Cook on high (290° to 300°) 2 hours. Turn heat control to low (190° to 200°) and cook for 8 hours, or until oxtails are so tender that meat falls from bones.
6. Unplug slow cooker and let mixture cool 5 minutes for fat to rise to the surface; skim off fat. Serve oxtails with a big bowl of mashed potatoes and a coleslaw and apple salad, if you wish.
COOK'S TIP: This recipe can be started the night before and slow cook while you sleep. In the morning, place in a refrigerator container and cover. Refrigerate until evening. Remove fat layer from oxtails and then heat in a large saucepan or place in an 8-cup casserole and bake in moderate oven (350°) for 1 hour, 15 minutes, until bubbly-hot.

BEEF JARDINIÈRE

Jardinière means gardener's style—or presented with a bouquet of vegetables.

Cook on 190° to 200° for 10 hours,
or   on 290° to 300° for 5 hours.
Makes 4 servings.

- 1½ pounds beef chuck, cubed
- 1 can (1 pound) tomatoes
- 1 teaspoon salt
- 1 bay leaf
- ½ teaspoon leaf thyme, crumbled
- ¼ teaspoon pepper
- 4 carrots, pared and cut into 3-inch lengths
- 4 celery stalks, cut into 3-inch lengths

1. Trim excess fat from beef; brown beef quickly in a few melted trimmings in a large skillet or an electric slow cooker with a browning unit.
2. Place meat in slow cooker with tomatoes, salt, bay leaf, thyme and pepper; cover cooker.
3. Cook on low (190° to 200°) for 10 hours, or on high (290° to 300°) 5 hours.
4. Turn heat control to high (290° to 300°); add carrots and celery; cover. Cook 20 minutes longer, or until vegetables are crisply tender. Serve with a light red wine and crusty French bread.

PRESCOTT BEEF BURGOO

Ground beef, rice and vegetables bubble away all day in this Arizona-style dish.

Cook on 190° to 200° for 8 hours,
or   on 290° to 300° for 4 hours.
Makes 8 servings.

- 2 pounds ground beef
- 1 large onion, chopped (1 cup)
- 1 clove garlic, minced
- 1 to 3 tablespoons chili powder
- 1 tablespoon salt
- ¼ teaspoon pepper
- 1 can (46 ounces) tomato juice
- 4 cups shredded cabbage
- 1 cup uncooked rice
- ½ pound green beans, tipped and cut up

1. Shape meat into a large patty in a large skillet or an electric slow cooker with a browning unit; brown 5 minutes on each side, then break up into chunks. Push to one side.
2. Add onion and garlic; sauté 5 minutes, or until soft. Stir in chili powder and cook 2 minutes. Add salt, pepper and tomato juice; bring to boiling.
3. Layer ⅓ each of the cabbage, rice, green beans and meat mixture into slow cooker; repeat to make 2 more layers of each; cover cooker.
4. Cook on low (190° to 200°) 8 hours, or on high (290° to 300°) 4 hours, or until vegetables are tender. Serve with chunks of corn bread and a crisp greens salad.

MINESTRONE

This version of an Italian favorite includes salami and garden vegetables.

Cook on 190° to 200° for 8 hours,
or   on 290° to 300° for 4 hours.
Makes 8 servings.

- 1 cup dried white beans (cannellini), from a 1-pound package
- 8 cups water
- ½ pound salami, diced
- 2 cups chopped celery
- 1 can (1 pound) tomatoes
- 4 cups shredded cabbage
- 2 large zucchini, trimmed and sliced
- 1 cup cubed pared yellow turnip
- ¼ cup chopped parsley
- 1 teaspoon salt
- 1 teaspoon leaf basil, crumbled
- ½ cup elbow macaroni, cooked
  Grated Parmesan cheese

1. Pick over beans and rinse under running water. Combine beans and water in a large saucepan. Bring to boiling; cook 2 minutes; remove from heat; cover; let stand 1 hour. (Or combine beans and water in an electric slow cooker and let stand all night at room temperature.)
2. Combine beans and liquid with salami, celery, tomatoes, cabbage, zucchini, turnip, parsley, salt and basil in slow cooker; cover.
3. Cook on low (190° to 200°) 8 hours, or on high (290° to 300°) 4 hours; stir in cooked macaroni and cook 10 minutes.
4. Ladle into soup bowls; sprinkle with grated Parmesan cheese.

BURGUNDY MEATLOAF

Try our trick with foil for the easy removal of any meat loaf from your deep slow cooker.

Cook on 290° to 300° for 1 hour,
then on 190° to 200° for 4 hours.
Makes 6 servings.

- 2 pounds ground meatloaf mixture
- 1 small onion, chopped (¼ cup)
- 2 eggs
- 1 cup soft white bread crumbs (2 slices)
- ½ cup chopped parsley
- ½ cup dry red Burgundy wine
- 1 tablespoon finely chopped fresh basil
  OR: 1 teaspoon leaf basil, crumbled
- 1½ teaspoons salt
- ¼ teaspoon freshly ground pepper
- 5 slices bacon
- 1 bay leaf
- 1 can (8 ounces) tomato sauce with mushrooms, heated

1. Combine meatloaf mixture, onion, eggs, bread crumbs, parsley, wine, basil, salt and pepper in a large bowl; mix.
2. Crisscross 3 bacon slices on a 12-inch square of aluminum foil; shape meatloaf

mixture into a 6-inch round on top of bacon. Top with remaining bacon slices, halved, and bay leaf. Lift foil with loaf into an electric slow cooker; cover.
3. Cook on high (290° to 300°) 1 hour; turn heat control to low (190° to 200°); cook 4 hours longer, or until meatloaf is well-done.
4. Remove loaf from slow cooker by lifting the foil "ears" as easy-lift handles, tilting fat back into slow cooker. Discard bacon and bay leaf.
5. Serve on heated platter and spoon part of the heated tomato sauce over. Great with buttered noodles and Frenched green beans, if you wish. Beef broth or tomato juice may be substituted for the Burgundy.

SLOW COOKER TIPS

- Slow cookers come in a variety of sizes from 2-quart (8-cup) up to the 8-quart (32-cup) super pots. It is best to choose recipes to use that will at least half fill your slow cooker, so the top surface of the food can be "basted" by the condensed steam under the slow cooker's cover. That's why we have included recipes for various sized slow cookers.
- Be patient the first few times you use your slow cooker. It takes about 2 hours for the temperature to come to 160° so the food may seem to be just sitting there —but please, do not lift the cover at this time, or you'll just lose valuable heat.
- Some slow cookers have heat coils on the bottom. If your model does, it is best to place some of the vegetables at the bottom of the slow cooker and then place the meat on top. The vegetables act as a grid and keep the meat from sticking after many hours of contact with the heated surface.
- If you have an older model of the multi-purpose electric pots, do not try a slow cooker recipe in it for the first time unless you plan to be home while it cooks. Set the control on 200° and cook, following low (190° to 200°) cooking times. Check the pot every few hours. If the liquid seems to be boiling, or if you smell food that is about to scorch, open pot and stir, then reduce temperature on heat control. If your first recipe is a success, you can feel free to use your pot as a slow cooker in the future. Do not try to use the 300° setting. The food will quickly burn and not cook the slow-simmering slow cooker way.

FOR CROCKERY COOKERS:
Here's a kitchen formula for removing stains that may build up on the surface of a crockery slow cooker:

- 1 cup water
- ½ cup chlorine bleach
- 2 tablespoons baking soda

Pour mixture into slow cooker and wipe well over stained area. Cover cooker. Set heat control to high (290° to 300°) for 2 hours. Wash to sudsy hot water, rinse well and wipe with a towel.

IRISH LAMB STEW

Traditionally, the lamb is not browned in making Irish stew. Peas add color and flavor when cooked just before serving.

Cook on 190° to 200° for 8 hours,
or   on 290° to 300° for 4 hours.
Makes 6 servings.

- 2 pounds lean boneless lamb shoulder, cubed
- 18 small white onions, peeled
- 1 pound carrots, pared and cut into 1-inch pieces
- 2 teaspoons salt
- ¼ teaspoon pepper
- 2 envelopes or teaspoons instant chicken broth
- 1 teaspoon leaf basil, crumbled
- ½ teaspoon leaf thyme, crumbled
- 1 clove garlic, minced
- 2 cups water
- 1 package (10 ounces) frozen green peas, thawed
- 1 cup shredded lettuce

1. Layer lamb, onions and carrots in an electric slow cooker; season with salt, pepper, instant chicken broth, basil, thyme and garlic; pour water over; cover slow cooker.
2. Cook on low (190° to 200°) 8 hours, or on high (290° to 300°) 4 hours, or until lamb is tender.
3. Turn heat control to high (290° to 300°). Add peas and lettuce; stir to blend well; cover. Simmer 30 minutes. Serve with slices of brown soda bread.

BEEF BARBECUE

Use the 5-quart slow cooker to make this party-size recipe.

Cook on 190° to 200° for 8 hours,
or   on 290° to 300° for 4 hours.
Makes 12 servings.

- 3 pounds ground chuck
- 1 pound bulk sausage meat
- 2 large onions, chopped (2 cups)
- 1 clove garlic, minced
- 2 cups chopped celery
- 1 small green pepper, halved, seeded and chopped
- 2 to 4 teaspoons chili powder
- 1 bottle (14 ounces) catsup
- 2 tablespoons brown sugar
- 1 tablespoon dry mustard
- 1 tablespoon salt
- 2 teaspoons paprika
- ½ teaspoon pepper
- 3½ cups water
- ¼ cup cider vinegar
- 2 tablespoons Worcestershire sauce

1. Mix ground beef and sausage meat in a bowl; shape into 2 large patties. Brown, 1 at a time, 5 minutes on each side in a large kettle or 5-quart electric slow cooker with a browning unit. Re-

move and reserve.

2. Pour off all but 2 tablespoonfuls of the drippings. Add onions and garlic; sauté just until soft. Stir in celery and green pepper; continue cooking just until celery is soft, then stir in chili powder; cook 2 minutes longer.

3. Combine meat, broken into chunks, and sautéed vegetables in a 5-quart slow cooker. Stir in catsup, brown sugar, mustard, salt, paprika, pepper, water, vinegar and Worcestershire sauce; stir until well-blended; cover.

4. Cook on low (190° to 200°) 8 hours, stirring after 4 hours, if possible, or on high (290° to 300°) 4 hours, stirring after 2 hours, if possible. Spoon over your choice of hot corn bread squares, rice, toast or tamales, if you wish.

CABBAGE CROWN

Seasoned ground beef is stuffed into a hollowed-out cabbage, then your slow cooker does the steaming.

Cook on 190° to 200° for 8 hours,
or   on 290° to 300° for 4 hours.
Makes 6 servings.

     1 pound ground beef
    ⅓ cup all-purpose flour
  1 ½ teaspoons salt
    ¼ teaspoon pepper
     1 egg
     1 cup milk
     2 tablespoons grated onion
     1 large cabbage (about 3 pounds)
     1 cup boiling water

1. Combine ground beef, flour, salt, pepper, and egg in the large bowl of an electric mixer; beat at medium speed until blended, then gradually beat in milk, a tablespoon at a time, until smooth and paste-like; stir in onion.

2. Trim off outside leaves of cabbage. Cut off a slice about an inch thick from core end; set aside. Cut core from cabbage with a sharp knife, then hollow out cabbage to make a shell about ½-inch-thick. (Chop cut-out pieces coarsely and cook as a vegetable for another day.)

3. Spoon meat mixture into shell; fit cut slice back into place; tie tightly with soft kitchen string.

4. Place stuffed cabbage, core-end down, in an electric slow cooker; add boiling water to cooker.

5. Cook on low (190° to 200°) 8 hours, or on high (290° to 300°) 4 hours, or until cabbage is tender; remove; keep warm.

6. Turn heat control to high (290° to 300°). Combine 3 tablespoons all-purpose flour and ⅓ cup cold water in a cup; pour into liquid in slow cooker, cover; cook 15 minutes. Season to taste with salt and pepper; darken with a few drops bottled gravy coloring.

7. Place stuffed cabbage on a heated serving platter; remove string. Pour gravy into a separate bowl. Cut cabbage into wedges; spoon gravy over.

GALA FRUITED CHICKEN

All the flavor of tropical islands come together to sauce plump chicken parts.

Cook on 190° to 200° for 8 hours,
or   on 290° to 300° for 4 hours.
Makes 6 servings.

     1 roasting chicken, cut up (about
          5 pounds)
     2 teaspoons paprika
  1 ½ teaspoons salt
    ¼ teaspoon pepper
         Dash cayenne pepper
     3 tablespoons vegetable oil
     1 can (8 ounces) crushed pineapple
          in pineapple juice
    ½ cup golden raisins
     1 cup orange juice
    ½ cup dry white wine
    ⅛ teaspoon ground cinnamon
    ⅛ teaspoon ground allspice
     2 California oranges, sectioned
    ½ cup toasted slivered almonds

1. Rub chicken pieces with a mixture of paprika, salt, pepper and cayenne. Brown in oil on all sides in a large skillet or an electric slow cooker with a browning unit.

2. Combine chicken pieces with crushed pineapple, raisins, orange juice, wine, cinnamon and allspice in slow cooker; cover cooker.

3. Cook on low (190° to 200°) 8 hours, or on high (290° to 300°) 4 hours, or until chicken is tender.

4. Lay orange sections over chicken and sprinkle with almonds; cook 15 minutes longer, just to heat through. Serve with fluffy rice, if you wish.

COLONIAL HOT POT

The Indians introduced the first settlers to the wonders of squash. Since then, thrifty homemakers have added it to their hearty one pot meals.

Cook on 190° to 200° for 8 hours,
or   on 290° to 300° for 4 hours.
Makes 8 servings.

     2 pounds boneless chuck, cubed
    ¼ cup all-purpose flour
     2 cups tomato juice
     2 envelopes or teaspoons instant
          beef broth
    ¼ cup finely chopped parsley
     2 cloves garlic, minced
     1 tablespoon salt
    ¼ teaspoon pepper
     4 medium-size potatoes, pared and
          thinly sliced
     8 small yellow onions, peeled and
          quartered
     1 acorn squash, split and seeded
     2 tablespoons butter or margarine

1. Trim all excess fat from beef. Shake cubes, part at a time, with flour in a plastic bag to coat well.

2. Combine tomato juice and instant beef broth in a small saucepan; heat just to boiling; remove from heat.

3. Combine parsley, garlic, salt and pepper in a cup.

4. Layer vegetables and meat into an electric slow cooker this way: Half of each of potatoes, onions and beef, sprinkling each layer lightly with seasoning mixture. Repeat with remaining potatoes, onions, beef and seasoning.

5. Cut each squash half into 6 slices; pare; arrange on top. Pour hot tomato juice mixture over; dot with butter or margarine; cover.

6. Cook on low (190° to 200°) 8 hours, or on high (290° to 300°) 4 hours, or until meat and vegetables are tender.

KOENIGSBERGER KLOPS

A classic German meat ball dish garnished with lemon slices and capers.

Cook on 190° to 200° for 5 hours.
Makes 6 servings.

     1 pound ground beef
     1 pound ground pork
     1 medium-size onion, chopped
          (½ cup)
    ½ cup packaged dry bread crumbs
  1 ½ teaspoons salt
    ¼ teaspoon pepper
         Dash ground nutmeg
     4 eggs
     1 can condensed beef broth
     1 cup water
     1 large onion, peeled and quartered
    ¼ cup cider vinegar
     1 tablespoon sugar
     1 teaspoon mixed pickling spices

1. Combine ground beef and pork, chopped onion, crumbs, 1 teaspoon of the salt, pepper and nutmeg in a medium-size bowl until well-blended.

2. Separate eggs, putting whites into a large bowl and yolks into a small bowl; cover and refrigerate. Beat whites until they form soft peaks; fold into meat mixture. Shape into 1-inch balls and place in an electric slow cooker.

3. Combine beef broth, water, onion, vinegar, sugar, mixed pickling spices and remaining ½ teaspoon salt in a small saucepan. Bring to boiling; lower heat and simmer 15 minutes; strain into slow cooker; cover.

4. Cook on low (190° to 200°) 5 hours; remove meat balls to a heated deep serving platter and keep warm.

5. Turn heat control to high (290° to 300°). Combine 1 tablespoon all-purpose flour with 2 tablespoons cold water in a cup; stir into liquid in cooker until smooth; cover. Cook 15 minutes; beat saved egg yolks with a fork; beat in 1 cup of hot sauce; return to cooker; cook 5 minutes; then pour over meat balls. Garnish with lemon slices and capers; serve with boiled parslied potatoes and mugs of dark ale, if you wish.

ZURICH PORK

A German influence is often noted in the cooking of this Swiss city.

Cook on 190° to 200° for 10 hours, or on 290° to 300° for 5 hours. Makes 8 servings.

- 4 to 5 pounds fresh pork shoulder butt
- 2 teaspoons salt
- 1 teaspoon caraway seeds
- ¼ teaspoon pepper
- 2 large onions, peeled and cut into thick slices
- 1 large clove garlic, peeled
- ½ cup beer or water

1. Trim excess fat from pork; brown pork slowly in remaining fat in a heavy skillet or an electric slow cooker with a browning unit; drain off all fat.
2. Place meat in slow cooker. Sprinkle salt, caraway seeds and pepper over; add onions, garlic and beer or water; cover.
3. Cook on low (190° to 200°) 10 hours, or on high (290° to 300°) 5 hours, or until pork is tender when pierced with a fork.
4. Remove to carving board or heated serving platter; discard garlic. Spoon onions around meat. Serve with refrigerated crescent rolls.

SLOW COOKER TIPS

Read the slow cooker's use and care booklet to find out the temperatures for the different settings on your cooker. To cook foods safely, the heat control setting must be at least 180°. If your cooker has a warming setting (140° to 160°) for heating cooked foods, never use the setting for cooking.

Some of these cookers can be totally immersed in water and others can't, so be sure to read the use and care booklet that comes with your slow cooker. To clean:

- Fill cooker with hot sudsy water and allow to stand for a few minutes to loosen stubborn food particles. You can use a soap-filled steel pad.
- Rinse with plenty of hot water and dry completely with a towel.
- To shine up the surface of a metal slow cooker, use a stainless steel-aluminum cleaner; rub with a soft cloth and don't use too much water with the powder; wipe with a sudsy cloth, rinse well and dry with a towel.

FOR NONSTICK COOKERS:

This easy-to-clean surface does need some extra attention to keep it in good condition:

- Before using the slow cooker for the first time, wash in hot sudsy water and rinse well; wipe dry with a towel. Then condition the nonstick finish by rubbing the inside of the slow cooker with a little vegetable oil on a paper towel; allow oil to remain on surface.
- Do not use sharp-edged utensils in slow cooker, such as knives, sharp-edged metal spoons or food choppers.

They will scratch the nonstick surface, but will not affect its nonstick qualities.
- You can put frozen foods in nonstick slow cookers, but allow extra cooking time to compensate.
- To remove the white film that may form on the nonstick surface; soak a paper towel in lemon juice or vinegar and rub over surface until film disappears, then follow directions above for the first-time use of slow cooker.
- If the nonstick surface of the slow cooker discolors, buy one of the non-stick finish cleaners at the supermarket and apply, following label directions.

SLOW COOKER COQ AU VIN

Use a really good red Burgundy to get a great flavor. Flaming the brandy also does something delicious to the dish.

Cook on 190° to 200° for 8 hours, or on 290° to 300° for 4 hours. Makes 4 servings.

- 2 chicken breasts, split (about 12 ounces each)
- 4 chicken legs or thighs
- ⅓ cup butter or margarine
- ¼ cup brandy (optional)
- 12 small white onions, peeled
- 2 cloves garlic, crushed
- ½ pound mushrooms, halved
- 1 cup red Burgundy or dry red wine
- 1 cup chicken broth
- 1 teaspoon salt
- ¼ teaspoon pepper
- 1 tablespoon chopped parsley
  Dash ground cloves
- ¼ teaspoon leaf thyme, crumbled
- 1 bay leaf
- 2 tablespoons cornstarch
- ¼ cup cold water

1. Brown chicken pieces in butter or margarine in a large skillet; warm brandy in a small saucepan; pour over chicken and flame; place in slow cooker.
2. Sauté onions, garlic and mushrooms in pan drippings; remove to slow cooker with a slotted spoon.
3. Stir in Burgundy wine, chicken broth, salt, pepper, parsley, cloves, thyme and bay leaf and bring to boiling, stirring up all the cooked-on bits in the bottom of the skillet; pour over chicken and vegetables; cover.
4. Cook on low (190° to 200°) 8 hours, or on high (290° to 300°) 4 hours, or until chicken is tender when pierced with a two-tined fork. Remove chicken and vegetables to a heated platter and keep warm while making gravy.
5. Turn heat control to high (290° to 300°). Combine cornstarch and cold water in a cup to make a smooth paste; stir into sauce in slow cooker until well-blended. Cover; simmer 15 minutes longer to thicken sauce. Spoon sauce over chicken and serve with a bottle of the same hearty Burgundy used in the casserole and chunks of crusty French bread for soaking up the sauce.

MEAT BALL CHOWDER

Tiny balls of mint-seasoned beef and pork cook in a rich onion broth.

Cook on 190° to 200° for 8 hours, or on 290° to 300° for 4 hours. Makes 6 servings.

- ¾ pound ground chuck
- ¾ pound ground pork
- 1 egg
- 2 teaspoons dried mint leaves, crumbled
- 1½ teaspoons salt
- ¼ teaspoon pepper
- 4 cups boiling water
- 1 envelope (2 to a package) onion soup mix
- 1 can (1 pound) stewed tomatoes
- 1 can (1 pound) red kidney beans
- ¼ cup chopped parsley

1. Mix ground beef and pork with egg, mint leaves, salt and pepper in a bowl; shape into tiny balls.
2. Pour boiling water into an electric slow cooker; stir in onion soup mix, meat balls, stewed tomatoes and kidney beans with liquid; cover.
3. Cook on low (190° to 200°) 8 hours, or on high (290° to 300°) 4 hours; stir parsley into hot soup.
4. Ladle into soup bowls; serve with chowder crackers, if you wish.

CAPE COD CHICKEN

Cranberry and spices are the special flavor secrets of this festive chicken dish.

Cook on 190° to 200° for 8 hours, or on 290° to 300° for 4 hours. Makes 8 servings.

- 2 broiler-fryers, quartered (about 2½ pounds each)
- 2 teaspoons salt
- ¼ cup vegetable oil
- 1 large onion, chopped (1 cup)
- 1 tablespoon grated orange rind
- ½ cup orange juice
- 3 tablespoons lemon juice
- 1 can (1 pound) whole-berry cranberry sauce
- 1½ teaspoons ground cinnamon
- 1½ teaspoons ground ginger

1. Rub chickens with salt to coat well. Brown, a few quarters at a time, in oil in a large skillet or an electric slow cooker with a browning unit; remove.
2. Sauté onion in pan drippings until soft; stir in orange rind and juice, lemon juice, cranberry sauce, cinnamon and ginger; bring to boiling; stir constantly.
3. Combine chicken quarters and sauce in slow cooker; cover.
4. Cook on low (190° to 200°) 8 hours, or on high (290° to 300°) 4 hours, or until chicken is tender. Serve with fluffy rice and buttered peas, if you wish.

DRUMSTICKS DIABLE

Sweet and spicy best describes this chicken treat. A cut-up chicken can be used in place of the drumsticks.

Cook on 190° to 200° for 8 hours, or on 290° to 300° for 4 hours. Makes 4 servings.

    8 drumsticks (about 2 pounds)
    ¼ cup all-purpose flour
    1½ teaspoon salt
       Dash pepper
    3 tablespoons butter or margarine
    1 can (1 pound) tomatoes
    2 tablespoons brown sugar
    2 tablespoons cider vinegar
    2 tablespoons Worcestershire
       sauce
    1 teaspoon chili powder
    1 teaspoon dry mustard
    ½ teaspoon celery seeds
    1 clove garlic, minced
       Few drops bottled red-pepper
       seasoning

1. Shake drumsticks in a plastic bag with flour, ½ teaspoon of the salt and pepper.
2. Brown in butter or margarine in a large skillet or an electric slow cooker with a browning unit; remove.
3. Stir tomatoes, brown sugar, vinegar, Worcestershire sauce, chili powder, dry mustard, celery seeds, garlic and red-pepper seasoning into pan drippings; bring to boiling.
4. Combine drumsticks and sauce in slow cooker; cover.
5. Cook on low (190° to 200°) 8 hours, or on high (290° to 300°) 4 hours, or until chicken is tender. Serve with spaghetti.

CORIANDER CHICKEN

Coriander is an herb that is used extensively in North African cooking for a spicy yet fresh flavor.

Cook on 190° to 200° for 8 hours, or on 290° to 300° for 4 hours. Makes 6 servings.

    3 chicken breasts, split (about 12
       ounces each)
    ¼ cup (½ stick) butter or margarine,
       melted
    1 small onion, grated
    1 tablespoon ground coriander
    1½ teaspoons salt
    ½ cup chicken broth
    1 tablespoon lemon juice
    1 container (8 ounces) plain yogurt
    2 tablespoons all-purpose flour

1. Roll chicken breasts in a mixture of melted butter or margarine, grated onion, coriander and salt in a pie plate.
2. Place in a 2½-quart electric slow cooker; pour chicken broth and lemon juice over.
3. Cook on low (190° to 200°) 8 hours, or on high (290° to 300°) 4 hours, or until

chicken is tender. Stir yogurt and flour together until well-blended in a small bowl. Stir into chicken, just before serving. Serve with rice pilaf and top with sliced green onions, if you wish.

LOUISIANA HOT POT

One pot cooking takes on a Southern flavor with ham and sweet potatoes in a mild curry broth.

Cook on 190° to 200° for 8 hours, or on 290° to 300° for 4 hours. Makes 8 servings.

    1 can (2 pounds) ham, cubed
    ¼ cup all-purpose flour
    2 teaspoons salt
    1 teaspoon curry powder
    ¼ teaspoon pepper
    6 medium-size sweet potatoes, pared
       and cut into ¼-inch thick slices
    2 medium-size onions, sliced
    1 package (10 ounces) frozen green
       peas, thawed
    ¼ cup sliced stuffed olives
    2 cups boiling water
    2 tablespoons butter or margarine

1. Trim excess fat from ham. Shake cubes, part at a time, with flour in a plastic bag to coat well.
2. Mix salt, curry powder and pepper in a cup until well-blended.
3. Layer vegetables and meat into an electric slow cooker this way: Half each of sweet potatoes, onions, ham, peas and olives, sprinkling each layer lightly with seasoning mixture. Repeat with remaining vegetables, ham and seasoning.
4. Pour boiling water over; dot with butter or margarine; cover.
5. Cook on low (190° to 200°) 8 hours, or on high (290° to 300°) 4 hours, or until meat and vegetables are tender.

POT AU FEU

Serve this very French soup in deep bowls with toasted French bread and a big salad. Great meal!

Cook on 190° to 200° for 8 hours, or on 290° to 300° for 4 hours. Makes 8 servings.

    1 bottom round roast (about 3 pounds)
    1 marrow bone, cracked
    4 cups cold water
    4 large carrots, pared and sliced
    4 medium-size onions, peeled and
       sliced
    3 potatoes, pared and diced
    3 white turnips, pared and diced
    2 cups sliced celery
    1 small parsnip, pared and diced
    ¼ cup chopped parsley
    2 teaspoons salt

1. Trim excess fat from beef; cut into 3 or 4 pieces. Place in electric slow cooker

with marrow bone and water.
2. Add carrots, onions, potatoes, turnips, celery, parsnip, parsley and salt; cover slow cooker.
3. Cook on low (190° to 200°) 8 hours, or on high (290° to 300°) 4 hours, or until beef and vegetables are very tender. Remove beef and marrow bone from slow cooker; disconnect cooker; drop a few ice cubes into broth. (If your slow cooker is crockery, you might prefer to pour broth into a large metal bowl before adding ice cubes to avoid damage due to temperature change.)
4. Cut beef into small pieces; skim fat from top of broth; return beef and broth (if removed from cooker) to cooker; taste and season with salt and pepper.
5. Turn heat control to high (290° to 300°); cover; heat 30 minutes or until soup is steamy-hot. Ladle into heated deep bowls and serve at once.
Suggested Variations: Try substituting leeks for the onion in this recipe; peeled tomatoes add a new touch; green beans and peas give a springtime flavor to the soup. Note: If you are in a hurry at dinner time, reheat soup in a metal saucepan on top of the range. Soup also freezes well.

SLOW COOKER TIPS

If you are in a real hurry at mealtime and want to thicken the cooking liquid, pour liquid into a saucepan and bring to boiling; add the thickening called for in the recipe and cook, stirring constantly, until gravy thickens and bubbles 3 minutes.

Wine in cooking adds the gourmet touch. Everyday stew becomes ragoût, and pot roast turns into Beef a la Mode. Wine rounds out the flavors, tenderizes tougher cuts of meat and gives distinction to your cooking. Here are a few tips for successful casserole cooking with wines:
• Dry sherry and Madiera go well in shellfish and creamed dishes.
• Dry white wines are for poultry and veal casseroles.
• Hearty red wines are best for beef, game and some fish, chicken and duck dishes.
• Dry vermouth can be used in place of white wine, and stores for months.
• Use the same wines you drink for cooking.
• Pour a few drops of olive oil over the surface of a dry wine you plan to use just for cooking, if you must keep it for more than a few days. This prevents the air from destroying the wine.

The Pot's a Crock

SLOW COOKERS

Here's a collection of some of the newest
slow cookers, and other appliances that can be
used for slow cooking. Of course, the kind
you choose will depend on your cooking needs.
The littler ones are best for small families,
or those who do less cooking. The large ones fit
the needs of big families, and those who like
to cook in quantity for the freezer.

The tiny 2-quart stoneware pot, above, sits on a separate electric base or can go into the oven as a baking dish.

The giant multipurpose 8-quart cooker/fryer, below, with a nonstick cooking surface that can also roast.

An all-purpose pot with a 5½ quart capacity that can also be used for deep fat frying.

The latest addition to slow cookery is the removable stoneware bowl. It's designed to go into dishwashers, and can withstand the change of temperature from refrigerator to cooker.

The heat control is the power center of the slow cooker. For about 5¢ worth of electricity, it will slowly simmer dinner at a constant temperature with perfect safety, all through the day.

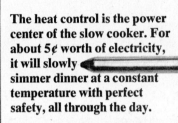

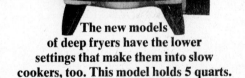

The new models of deep fryers have the lower settings that make them into slow cookers, too. This model holds 5 quarts.

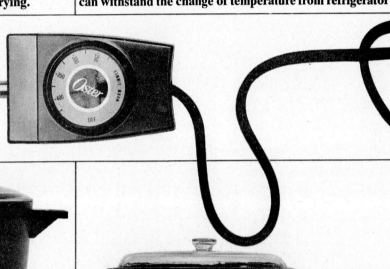

A 6-quart roaster/ slow cooker with a removable porcelain enamel cooking well.

This electric frypan has a 2½-quart crockery insert. The heat control setting is 280° to 300°.

A glass-ceramic casserole heats on its ceramic cooking surface.

Your electric frypan can also be used as a slow cooker. Simply follow the special directions on page 34.

Slow cookers are often attractive enough to use as servers. This one has a colonial motif.

For all cookers, see Buyer's Guide, page 112.

TWIN POT ROASTS

Would you believe pork and beef together? Try it, you'll love it!

Cook on 190° to 200° for 10 hours,
or   on 290° to 300° for 5 hours.
Makes 8 servings.

    1 rib-end loin of pork (about 2
        pounds)
    1 boneless chuck or round roast
        (about 2 pounds)
    1 large onion, chopped (1 cup)
   18 small white onions, peeled
    8 medium-size carrots, pared and
        halved
    1 cup dry red wine or water
    1 tablespoon seasoned salt
   ¼ teaspoon pepper
    1 bay leaf
    3 tablespoons all-purpose flour

1. Trim excess fat from meats; brown
meats in their remaining fat in a large
skillet or an electric slow cooker with a
browning unit; remove.
2. Pour off all but 2 tablespoons fat; add
chopped onion; sauté 5 minutes.
3. Place meats in slow cooker with sautéed onion; add small white onions, carrots, wine or water, seasoned salt, pepper and bay leaf; cover.
4. Cook on low (190° to 200°) 10 hours,
or on high (290° to 300°) 5 hours, or until
meats are tender. Place meats on carving
board to slice; arrange slices on heated
platter with vegetables around them;
keep hot while making gravy.
5. Let fat rise to top of juices in slow
cooker; skim carefully. Turn heat control to high (290° to 300°). Combine flour
and ⅓ cup water in a cup; stir into liquid
in slow cooker; cover; cook 15 minutes.
Pass in heated gravy boat.

KUN KOKI POT ROAST

*Plan ahead when serving this savory
beef dish, as meat seasons in a special
soy marinade overnight before cooking.*

Cook on 190° to 200° for 10 hours,
or   on 290° to 300° for 6 hours.
Makes 8 servings.

    2 tablespoons sesame seeds
    1 cup water
   ¼ cup soy sauce
    2 tablespoons light molasses
    2 tablespoons wine vinegar or cider
        vinegar
    2 green onions, sliced
    1 teaspoon garlic powder
   ⅛ teaspoon cayenne pepper
    1 boneless shoulder or chuck pot
        roast (about 4 pounds)
    2 tablespoons cornstarch

1. Toast sesame seeds in a small skillet
over low heat, shaking pan often, just
until golden-brown.
2. Combine seeds with water, soy
sauce, molasses, vinegar, green onions,

garlic powder and cayenne in a 2-cup
measure. Trim excess fat from beef;
place in a large glass bowl; pour
marinade over; cover. Refrigerate, turning meat several times to season evenly,
overnight, in marinade.
3. When ready to cook, remove meat
from the marinade, then pat dry with
paper towels. Brown pot roast in a large
skillet or an electric slow cooker with a
browning unit. Place meat in slow
cooker; pour marinade over; cover.
4. Cook on low (190° to 200°) 10 hours,
or on high (290° to 300°) 6 hours, or until
beef is tender when pierced with a two-
tined fork. Remove beef to a heated
platter to keep warm.
5. Turn heat control to high (290° to
300°). Combine cornstarch with ¼ cup
cold water in a cup; stir into liquid in
slow cooker until well-blended. Cover;
simmer 15 minutes.
6. Carve meat into ¼-inch-thick slices;
serve with gravy.
Suggested Variation: Pork is equally
delicious in this recipe. Use a fresh
picnic shoulder (about 5 pounds).

SLOW COOKER TIPS

• To stir or not to stir, that is the
question. In most cases it is not necessary to stir foods in the slow cooker, but
in developing some special recipes for
this book, we found that stirring at the
halfway point in the cooking time helped
to distribute the food more evenly and
keep the heavier foods from all going to
the bottom. The heat loss from opening
the slow cooker added 30 minutes to the
cooking time, so if you do not stir these
recipes, you can expect these dishes to
be ready a little sooner.
• Use long-handled wooden spoons
when stirring foods in your slow cooker.
This will protect the inside surface of the
cooker and keep your hands from getting
too close to the hot food and cooker.
• If your slow cooker has the new removable stoneware bowl, you can prepare the food to be cooked the night
before and refrigerate in the stoneware
bowl. Then in the morning, place in
cooker and follow manufacturer's directions for heating.

THE FRYPAN CROCKERY INSERT:

This is the special crockery insert that
comes with an electric frypan. As it is
made of crockery, it should be treated
with the same care as other crockery
slow cookers. A few other points should
be noted:
• Set the frypan heat control to 280° to
300°. Follow cooking times for low (190°
to 200°) directions in these recipes. (Do
not set the frypan heat control below
280°, or the internal temperature of the
food will not reach the 180° necessary
for cooking raw food safely.)
• Use pot holders when removing the
crockery insert from frypan before serving and place on a heat-proof pad before
setting on table.

BONUS BEEF SOUP

*Never let beef bones go to waste. Pack
in plastic bags and freeze until you have
enough to make this delicious soup.*

Cook on 190° to 200° for 10 hours,
or   on 290° to 300° for 5 hours.
Makes 6 servings.

    4 to 6 beef bones
    8 cups water
    1 can (1 pound) tomatoes
    2 medium-size carrots, pared and
        chopped
    1 white turnip, pared and chopped
    1 large onion, chopped (1 cup)
    1 cup chopped celery
    1 bay leaf
  2½ teaspoons salt
    1 teaspoon leaf thyme, crumbled
   ¼ teaspoon pepper
    1 cup elbow macaroni, cooked
    1 cup chopped raw spinach

1. Combine beef bones, water, tomatoes, carrots, turnip, onion, celery, bay
leaf, salt, thyme and pepper in an electric
slow cooker; cover.
2. Cook on low (190° to 200°) 10 hours,
or on high (290° to 300°) 5 hours.
3. Turn heat control to high (290° to
300°); stir in cooked macaroni and
spinach; cook 10 minutes; taste and
season with salt and pepper. Serve with
rye bread and a Waldorf salad.

AUSTRALIAN LAMB "ROASTS"

*Lamb shanks are a meaty treat. Look for
them on special, especially in the spring.*

Cook on 190° to 200° for 8 hours,
or   on 290° to 300° for 4 hours.
Makes 4 servings.

    4 lamb shanks (about 3 pounds)
    1 large onion, chopped (1 cup)
    1 clove garlic, minced
    1 cup dry white wine
    2 teaspoons salt
   ½ teaspoon pepper
    1 bay leaf
    2 tablespoons all-purpose flour
   ¼ cup water

1. Trim excess fat from lamb shanks.
Brown lamb in its remaining fat in a large
skillet or an electric slow cooker with a
browning unit; remove and reserve.
2. Add onion and garlic to pan; sauté
just until soft. Stir in wine, salt, pepper
and bay leaf; remove from heat.
3. Combine lamb shanks and wine mixture in slow cooker; cover.
4. Cook on low (190° to 200°) 8 hours,
or on high (290° to 300°) 4 hours, or until
lamb shanks are tender. Remove to a
heated serving platter and keep warm.
5. Turn heat control to high (290° to
300°). Combine flour and water in a cup.
Stir into liquid in slow cooker; cover.
Cook 15 minutes. Pass in gravy boat.

POTAGE PARMENTIER

This potato soup is named in honor of Antoine Parmentier who worked to make potatoes popular among the French.

Cook on 190° to 200° for 8 hours, or on 290° to 300° for 4 hours. Makes 8 servings.

- 4 leeks, trimmed and sliced
- 1 large onion, chopped (1 cup)
- ¼ cup (½ stick) butter or margarine
- 4 large potatoes, pared and diced
- 6 cups Classic Chicken Broth (recipe on page 36)
  OR: 6 envelopes or teaspoons instant chicken broth and 6 cups water
- 1 teaspoon salt
- 1 bay leaf
- ¼ teaspoon white pepper
- 2 cups light cream

1. Sauté leeks and onion in butter or margarine in a large skillet or 5-quart electric slow cooker with a browning unit until soft.
2. Combine with potatoes, CLASSIC CHICKEN BROTH or instant chicken broth and water, salt, bay leaf and pepper in a 5-quart slow cooker; cover.
3. Cook on low (190° to 200°) 8 hours, or on high (290° to 300°) 4 hours. Stir in cream; taste and add additional salt and pepper, if desired. Heat 15 minutes before serving.

HOSTESS TIP: This is the origin of VICHYSSOISE. To make VICHYSSOISE: Cool soup slightly; then process, a few cups at a time, in an electric blender container until smooth. Pour into a glass bowl and chill thoroughly. Serve in chilled bowls with a sprinkling of chopped chives.

SEVILLE POT ROAST

Colorful stuffed-olive rings dot each slice of this savory roast.

Cook on 190° to 200° for 10 hours, or on 290° to 300° for 6 hours. Makes 8 servings.

- 1 round, rump or boneless chuck roast (about 4 pounds)
- 1 jar (about 5 ounces) stuffed green olives
- 1 medium-size onion, chopped (½ cup)
- 1 jar (about 5 ounces) junior strained carrots (baby-pack)
- 1 cup water
- 1 tablespoon instant coffee powder
- 1 tablespoon sugar
- 1 teaspoon salt
- ¼ teaspoon pepper
- ½ cup light cream
- 2 tablespoons all-purpose flour

1. Trim excess fat from beef; make slashes about 1½ inches deep and 2 inches apart all the way around meat with a sharp knife; push an olive deep into each cut.
2. Brown beef in a large skillet or an electric slow cooker with a browning unit; remove and reserve.
3. Sauté onion until soft in same pan; stir in carrots, water, instant coffee, sugar, salt and pepper. Place beef with onion mixture in slow cooker; cover.
4. Cook on low (190° to 200°) 10 hours, or on high (290° to 300°) 6 hours, or until beef is tender when pierced with a two-tined fork. Remove beef to serving platter and keep warm.
5. Turn heat control to high (290° to 300°). Combine cream and flour in a cup. Stir into liquid until well-blended; cover; simmer 15 minutes.
6. Carve meat into ¼-inch-thick slices and pass gravy separately. Serve with saffron rice, if you wish.

HOSTESS TIP: To prepare saffron rice, crush about 3 strands of saffron and stir into cooking water for rice. For 8 servings of 1 cup each, you will need 2 cups uncooked rice.

SLOW COOKER TIPS

Your electric slow cooker can be one of the most useful appliances in your kitchen , but there are a few precautions that you should take for the safest use:

- Choose a flat moisture-free surface that is in easy reach of a 120 volt AC wall outlet, and out of the reach of young children.
- Turn the heat control of the cooker to OFF; then insert into slow cooker.
- Fill slow cooker with recipe ingredients, then cover slow cooker.
- Plug cord into electric outlet, being sure that the cord does not touch the slow cooker. Turn heat control to setting in recipe.
- When cooking is completed, turn heat control to OFF, then pull plug from electrical outlet. Do not touch the outside surface of the cooker, unless cooker is insulated.
- If heat control is hot and you must touch it, always use a pot holder. Do not pull heat control out of slow cooker until it has cooled down.
- Never immerse the heat control in water.
- Read your use and care booklet and immerse your slow cooker in water only if booklet advises it.
- Use an extension cord with a slow cooker only if its electrical rating is equal to or greater than the electrical rating of your cooker. (Most slow cookers use 70 watts on low (190° to 200°) and 140 watts on high (290° to 300°), so be sure that you use a heavy-duty extension cord. Do not let the cord drape over the counter or get entangled with other cords on counter.
- Never operate your slow cooker with a damaged cord. Bring cooker to the authorized service department for proper repair.
- Never handle a slow cooker or any electrical appliance with wet hands or on a wet surface.

BURGER BURGOO

Meat and rice simmer in an herbed tomato sauce. Easy, yet delicious.

Cook on 190° to 200° for 8 hours, or on 290° to 300° for 4 hours. Makes 6 servings.

- 2 pounds ground beef
- 1 large onion, chopped (1 cup)
- 1 cup sliced celery
- 1 clove garlic, minced
- 1 tablespoon sugar
- 1 tablespoon leaf basil, crumbled
- 2 teaspoons salt
- ⅛ teaspoon pepper
- 1 bay leaf
- 1 can (46 ounces) mixed vegetable juice
- 1 cup uncooked rice

1. Shape ground beef into large patty; brown in a large skillet or an electric slow cooker with a browning unit 5 minutes on each side, then break up into chunks. Push to one side.
2. Add onion, celery and garlic; sauté 5 minutes, or until soft.
3. Stir in sugar, basil, salt, pepper, bay leaf, vegetable juice and rice; bring to boiling; remove from heat.
4. Place mixture in slow cooker; cover.
5. Cook on low (190° to 200°) 8 hours, or on high (290° to 300°) 4 hours, or until liquid is absorbed and rice is very tender.

FRENCH POT ROAST

Flavorful beef simmers fork-tender in canned onion soup.

Cook on 190° to 200° for 10 hours, or on 290° to 300° for 5 hours. Makes 8 servings.

- 1 boneless round or chuck roast (about 4 pounds)
- 2 tablespoons all-purpose flour
- 2 tablespoons vegetable oil
- 1 can condensed onion soup
- 1 green pepper, seeded and cut into rings

1. Trim excess fat from roast; rub beef well with flour; brown in oil in a large skillet or an electric slow cooker with a browning unit.
2. Place meat in slow cooker; pour onion soup over; cover cooker.
3. Cook on low (190° to 200°) 10 hours, or on high (290° to 300°) 5 hours, or until meat is tender when pierced with a two-tined fork. Place green pepper rings on roast to steam during last 10 minutes of cooking. Remove meat and pepper rings to heated serving platter; keep hot while making gravy from cooker juices.
4. Turn heat control to high (290° to 300°). Combine ¼ cup all-purpose flour and ½ cup cold water in a cup to make a smooth paste. Stir into slow cooker; cover; cook 15 minutes; taste and season with salt and pepper, if you wish.

MISSISSIPPI CHICKEN DINNER

Lima beans and green beans bubble along in the slow cooker with ripe olives and slices of tomato—so good, yet easy to prepare.

Cook on 190° to 200° for 8 hours,
or　　on 290° to 300° for 4 hours.
Makes 8 servings.

 2　broiler-fryers, quartered (about 2½ pounds each)
¼　cup all-purpose flour
 2　teaspoons salt
 1　teaspoon leaf basil, crumbled
¼　cup vegetable oil
 1　clove garlic, minced
 2　cans (1 pound each) cooked dried lima beans
 1　can (1 pound) cut green beans, drained
½　cup sliced pitted ripe olives
 4　medium-size firm ripe tomatoes, sliced ½-inch thick
½　cup dry white wine or water

1. Shake chicken pieces with a mixture of flour, salt and basil in a plastic bag to coat evenly.
2. Brown slowly in vegetable oil in a large skillet; remove and reserve. Sauté garlic in pan drippings until soft.
3. Stir in lima beans, green beans and ripe olives until well-blended.
4. Layer half the tomato slices, all of bean mixture and chicken in an electric slow cooker; top with remaining tomato slices; pour wine or water over; cover.
5. Cook on low (190° to 200°) 8 hours, or on high (290° to 300°) 4 hours, or until chicken is tender.

SWISS CABBAGE ROLLS

Try serving these delicious rolls with a dollop of sour cream on top.

Cook on 190° to 200° for 8 hours,
or　　on 290° to 300° for 4 hours.
Makes 6 servings.

12　large cabbage leaves
 1　pound ground meatloaf mixture
 2　cups cooked rice
 1　small onion, chopped (¼ cup)
 1　egg
 1　teaspoon salt
¼　teaspoon pepper
　　Dash ground nutmeg
¼　cup all-purpose flour
 2　tablespoons vegetable shortening
 1　can condensed tomato soup
 1　teaspoon cider vinegar
 1　teaspoon Worcestershire sauce

1. Trim base of cabbage and carefully break off 12 whole leaves. (Save remaining cabbage for another day.)
2. Place leaves in a large saucepan; pour in boiling water and cover; let stand 5 minutes; drain on paper towels; trim off the coarse rib on the back of each leaf

with a sharp paring knife.
3. Combine meatloaf mixture, rice, onion, egg, salt, pepper and nutmeg in a medium-size bowl; mix.
4. Lay cabbage leaves flat on a wooden board; spoon meat mixture into the middle of each, dividing evenly. Fold edges of each leaf over filling and roll up; fasten with wooden picks.
5. Coat cabbage rolls with flour on wax paper. Sauté rolls, a few at a time, in shortening in a large skillet or an electric slow cooker with a browning unit.
6. Place cabbage rolls in slow cooker; pour tomato soup, vinegar and Worcestershire sauce over; cover.
7. Cook on low (190° to 200°) 8 hours, or on high (290° to 300°) 4 hours. Serve with a topping of dairy sour cream.
Suggested Variations: Cooked brown rice or kasha can be substituted for the cooked rice. Ground beef or pork can be used in place of the meatloaf mixture.

MEMPHIS BURGOO

Burgoo is another name for stew. This one is filled with chicken, ham hocks, limas and okra.

Cook on 190° to 200° for 8 hours,
or　　on 290° to 300° for 4 hours.
Makes 8 servings.

 1　broiler-fryer (about 3 pounds)
 2　smoked ham hocks (about 1 pound each)
 4　cups water
 2　large potatoes, pared and diced
 2　large carrots, pared and diced
 1　large onion, chopped (1 cup)
 1　package (10 ounces) frozen Fordhook lima beans
 2　cups shredded cabbage
 1　cup sliced celery
 1　large green pepper, halved, seeded and chopped
 1　tablespoon Worcestershire sauce
 2　teaspoons salt
½　teaspoon cayenne pepper
 1　package (10 ounces) frozen whole okra, thawed
　　Chopped parsley

1. Place chicken and ham hocks in a 5-quart slow cooker; add water, potatoes, carrots, onion, lima beans, cabbage, celery, green pepper, Worcestershire sauce, salt and cayenne; cover.
2. Cook on low (190° to 200°) 8 hours, or on high (290° to 300°) 4 hours, or until chicken is tender. Remove chicken and ham hocks from slow cooker. Cool.
3. Turn heat control to high (290° to 300°). Stir in okra and parsley; cover and cook 15 minutes.
4. While okra cooks, remove skin from chicken and ham hocks; take meat from bones, discarding fat; dice meat; return to slow cooker; cover.
5. Cook 10 minutes; ladle into heated soup bowls. Serve with corn bread or crusty hard rolls, if you wish.

PETITE MARMITE HENRY IV

Marmite is French for stock pot. Henry IV was the French king who promised a chicken in every pot.

Cook on 190° to 200° for 10 hours,
or　　on 290° to 300° for 5 hours.
Makes 8 servings.

 1　stewing chicken (about 5 pounds)
 1　pound boneless chuck
½　pound chicken wings
 1　pound beef bones
12　cups cold water
 2　large carrots, pared and sliced
 3　leeks, trimmed and sliced
 2　stalks celery, chopped
 1　white turnip, pared and diced
 1　large onion stuck with 6 cloves
 1　tablespoon salt
　　Handful parsley
 2　cloves garlic, peeled
 5　peppercorns
 1　bay leaf

1. Place chicken, beef, chicken wings, and beef bones in a 5-quart electric slow cooker; add water, carrots, leeks, celery, turnip, onion and salt. Tie parsley, garlic, peppercorns and bay leaf in cheesecloth; add to cooker; cover.
2. Cook on low (190° to 200°) 10 hours, or on high (290° to 300°) 5 hours, or until chicken is tender. Remove chicken and beef. Let cool enough to handle, then slice or cut in julienne pieces; reserve.
3. Strain broth through cheesecloth into a heated soup tureen; add meat and freshly cooked carrot and turnip slices, if you wish. Taste and season with additional salt and pepper.

LAMB SHANKS AND VEGETABLES

Dried rosemary leaves give lamb an especially lovely flavor and slow cooking develops that flavor.

Cook on 190° to 200° for 8 hours,
or　　on 290° to 300° for 4 hours.
Makes 4 servings.

 4　lamb shanks (about 3 pounds)
¼　cup all-purpose flour
 2　teaspoons salt
¼　teaspoon pepper
 3　tablespoons vegetable oil
 4　medium-size onions, peeled and halved
 4　large carrots, pared and cut in 1-inch pieces
½　cup chicken broth
½　cup dry white wine or water
 1　clove garlic, minced
½　teaspoon leaf rosemary, crumbled
¼　teaspoon leaf thyme, crumbled
⅛　teaspoon celery powder

1. Trim excess fat from lamb shanks. Shake in a plastic bag with flour, 1 teaspoon of the salt and pepper.
2. Brown in oil on all sides in a large

skillet or an electric slow cooker with a browning unit.

3. Place lamb shanks in slow cooker; arrange onions and carrots around meat; add chicken broth, wine or water, garlic, rosemary, thyme and celery powder; cover cooker.

4. Cook on low (190° to 200°) 8 hours, or on high (290° to 300°) 4 hours, or until lamb shanks are tender when pierced with a two-tined fork. Remove shanks and vegetables to a heated serving platter and keep warm.

5. Turn heat control to high (290° to 300°). Pour liquid from cooker into a 2-cup measure; let fat rise to the top; skim off; return liquid to cooker. Combine 2 tablespoons flour and ¼ cup cold water in a cup; stir into liquid until well-blended; flavor with a few drops bottled gravy coloring; cover; cook 15 minutes. Spoon over shanks and serve with wheat pilaf, if you wish.

BLACK FOREST BEEF PLATTER

Pot roasts are more flavorful and tender when treated to slow, gentle cooking.

Cook on 190° to 200° for 10 hours, or on 290° to 300° for 5 hours. Makes 8 servings.

- 1 boneless chuck roast (about 4 pounds)
- 1 cup water
- ¼ cup chili sauce
- 1 envelope (2 to a package) onion soup mix
- 1 tablespoon caraway seeds, crushed
- 1 tablespoon paprika
- ¼ teaspoon pepper
- 1 can (1 pound, 11 ounces) sauerkraut, drained
- ¼ cup firmly packed brown sugar
- 1 container (8 ounces) dairy sour cream

1. Trim excess fat from roast; brown in its remaining fat in a large skillet or an electric slow cooker with a browning unit; remove and reserve.

2. Stir in water, chili sauce, onion soup mix, caraway seeds, paprika and pepper; bring to boiling.

3. Place meat with sauce in slow cooker; mix sauerkraut and brown sugar in a medium-size bowl; stir into liquid around meat; cover.

4. Cook on low (190° to 200°) 10 hours, or on high (290° to 300°) 5 hours, or until meat is very tender. Remove to a carving board; keep hot while finishing sauce for the sauerkraut.

5. Stir about ½ cup of the hot sauerkraut mixture into sour cream in a medium-size bowl; then stir back into remaining sauerkraut mixture in slow cooker. Heat just until hot, about 5 minutes.

6. Spoon sauerkraut into a deep serving platter. Carve meat into ¼-inch thick slices; place on top of sauerkraut. Serve with buttered noodles, if you wish.

OLD FARM BEAN SOUP

Mothers have known for generations that a bubbling pot of rich bean soup makes hearty family eating that's easy on the budget.

Cook on 190° to 200° for 8 hours, then on 290° to 300° for 4 hours. Makes 8 servings.

- 1 package (1 pound) dried navy or pea beans
- 6 cups water
- ¼ pound salt pork
- 1 large onion, chopped (1 cup)
- 1 large carrot, pared and chopped
- 4 smokie sausage links, scored (from a 12-ounce package)
- 1 bay leaf
- 1½ teaspoons salt
- ½ teaspoon pepper
- ¼ teaspoon leaf thyme, crumbled

1. Pick over beans and rinse under running water. Combine beans and water in a large kettle. Bring to boiling; cover; cook 10 minutes. Remove from heat; let stand 1 hour; pour into an electric slow cooker. (Or soak beans in water in slow cooker overnight.)

2. Place beans and liquid in slow cooker; score salt pork, almost to rind; push down into beans; stir in onion, carrot, sausage links, bay leaf, salt, pepper and leaf thyme; cover.

3. Cook on low (190° to 200°) 8 hours; stir beans; turn heat control to high (290° to 300°) and cook for 4 hours; stir beans with a wooden spoon and mash some of them against the side of the cooker to thicken soup. Taste beans; season with additional salt and pepper, if desired.

OLD-FASHIONED BRUNSWICK STEW

In Colonial days, rabbit, rather than stewing chicken would have gone into the pot, but the long slow cooking flavor of 1776 is still there.

Cook on 190° to 200° for 10 hours, or on 290° to 300° for 5 hours. Makes 8 servings.

- 1 stewing chicken, cut up (about 5 pounds)
- 2 large onions, peeled and sliced
- 1 large green pepper, seeded and sliced
- ¼ cup chopped parsley
- 1 tablespoon salt
- 1 tablespoon Worcestershire sauce Few drops bottled red-pepper seasoning
- 1 package (10 ounces) frozen whole-kernel corn, thawed
- 1 package (10 ounces) frozen speckled butter beans or lima beans, thawed
- 1 can (1 pound) tomatoes, broken up
- 2 tablespoons cornstarch

1. Arrange half the chicken parts in the

bottom of an electric slow cooker; sprinkle with onion and green pepper slices and parsley.

2. Layer remaining chicken parts in cooker; season with salt, Worcestershire sauce and red-pepper seasoning; top with thawed corn, beans and tomatoes; cover slow cooker.

3. Cook on low (190° to 200°) 10 hours, or on high (290° to 300°) 5 hours, or until chicken is tender when pierced with a two-tined fork.

4. Turn heat control to high (290° to 300°). Combine cornstarch with ¼ cup cold water in a cup; stir into liquid in slow cooker until well-blended; cover; simmer 15 minutes. Serve with hot cornbread or baking powder biscuits.

Suggested Variations: A tablespoon of chopped fresh oregano or marjoram leaves or a teaspoon of dried oregano or marjoram can be added for a more aromatic flavor.

CANNELLINI ALLA CATANIA

This Sicilian-style main dish feeds big appetites on a small budget.

Cook on 190° to 200° for 10 hours, or on 290° to 300° for 5 hours. Makes 6 servings.

- 1 package (1 pound) dried cannellini beans (white kidney beans) or dried Great Northern beans
- 6 cups water
- 2 hot Italian sausages, sliced
- 1 large onion, chopped (1 cup)
- 1 large clove garlic, crushed
- 2 large ripe tomatoes, peeled and coarsely chopped
- 1 bay leaf, crumbled
- ½ teaspoon leaf thyme, crumbled
- ½ teaspoon leaf basil, crumbled
- 3 one-inch strips orange rind
- 1 teaspoon salt
- ¼ teaspoon pepper
- 1 envelope or teaspoon instant beef broth

1. Pick over beans and rinse. Cover beans with water in a large kettle; bring to boiling; cover; cook 2 minutes; remove from heat; let stand 1 hour. Pour into an electric slow cooker. (Or cover beans with water in slow cooker and soak overnight at room temperature.)

2. Brown sausages in a small skillet; push to one side; sauté onion and garlic in same pan until soft; stir in tomato, bay leaf, thyme, basil, orange strips, salt, pepper and instant beef broth; bring to boiling; stir into beans; cover.

3. Cook on low (190° to 200°) for 10 hours, or on high (290° to 300°) 5 hours, or until beans are tender. For a classic Italian dessert, serve an assortment of fruits and cheeses.

Suggested Variations: Dried lima beans can be substituted for the cannellini beans. Sweet Italian sausage, ¼ pound salami or 1 cup sliced pepperoni can be used instead of the hot Italian sausages.

BRAZILIAN FEIJOADA

Black bean soup is a favorite in all Latin American countries. This is the slow cook method of preparing it.

Cook on 190° to 200° for 8 hours, or on 290° to 300° for 4 hours. Makes 12 servings.

- 2 bags (1 pound each) dried black beans
- 10 cups water
- 1 boneless smoked pork butt (about 2 pounds)
- ½ pound pepperoni, cut into ½-inch pieces
- 3 large onions, sliced
- 2 cups dry red wine or beef broth
- 2 teaspoons salt
- 3 oranges, peeled and sectioned
- ¼ cup chopped parsley

1. Pick over beans and rinse under running water. Combine beans with water in a large kettle or a 5-quart electric slow cooker; bring to boiling and boil 2 minutes; cover. Remove from heat; let stand 1 hour.
2. Place beans and liquid in a 5-quart electric slow cooker; add pork butt, pepperoni, onions, wine or beef broth and salt; cover.
3. Cook on low (190° to 200°) 8 hours, stirring after 4 hours, if possible, or on high (290° to 300°) 4 hours, stirring after 2 hours, if possible, or until beans and meat are tender.
4. Remove pork butt; press beans against the side of the slow cooker with a wooden spoon to mash some of them. Serve with orange sections and chopped parsley arranged atop beans.
5. Slice pork butt thinly and pass it around, on a separate plate, with mustard and whole-wheat bread.

SLOW COOKER TIPS

There are several ways to thicken liquids in your slow cooker:
- Blend flour or cornstarch into a smooth paste with cold water, then stir into cooker at the end of the cooking time; cover. Cook on high (290° to 300°) for 15 minutes. (See individual recipes for exact amounts.)
- Combine 2 tablespoons softened butter or margarine and 2 tablespoons all-purpose flour until smooth for each cup of liquid in cooker. Drop by bit into liquid and stir to blend well; cover cooker. Cook on high (290° to 300°) 15 minutes, or until thickened.
- Add 2 teaspoons quick-cooking tapioca for each cup of liquid in the recipe at the start of cooking.

When washing a slow cooker that does not have a detachable heat control, place the cooker in an empty sink and clean, following the general directions for its interior surface, but take care not to allow water to get onto the heat control.

RIBS AND LENTIL STEW

Seasoned just right for most tastes, you can add more thyme if your family prefers more pungent food.

Cook on 290° to 300° for 2 hours, then on 190° to 200° for 8 hours. Makes 6 servings.

- 3 pounds short ribs, cut up
- 2 cups water
- 1 cup dry red wine
- 1 teaspoon salt
- 1 bay leaf
- ¼ teaspoon leaf thyme, crumbled
- ¼ teaspoon celery seeds, crushed
- 1 large onion, chopped (1 cup)
- 1 clove garlic, minced
- 1 cup dried lentils (from a 1-pound package)
- 1 tablespoon quick-cooking tapioca
- 1 cup small shells or elbow macaroni, cooked

1. Trim away as much fat as possible from short ribs. Place in an electric slow cooker; combine water, wine, salt, bay leaf, thyme and celery seeds in a 4-cup measure; pour over ribs.
2. Stir in onion, garlic, lentils and tapioca; cover.
3. Cook on high (290° to 300°) 2 hours; turn heat control to low (190° to 200°) and cook 8 hours longer, or until lentils are tender. Unplug slow cooker; remove cover; let fat rise to surface and skim off. Stir in hot cooked pasta and top with chopped parsley, if you wish.

"VERY BRITISH" CASSEROLE

It's sort of steak and kidney pie in a pot! You could top it with dumplings, but mashed potatoes are more British.

Cook on 290° to 300° for 2 hours, then on 190° to 200° for 5 hours. Makes 12 servings.

- 3 pounds boneless chuck, cubed
- 1 pound boneless veal shoulder, cubed
- ¼ cup all-purpose flour
- 1 teaspoon salt
- ¼ teaspoon pepper
- ¼ cup (½ stick) butter or margarine
- ¼ cup vegetable shortening
- 2 veal kidneys
- 2 tablespoons white vinegar
- 2 Bermuda onions, sliced
- 3 large tomatoes, peeled, cored and sliced
- 1 can condensed beef broth
- ½ cup dry red wine
- 1 teaspoon Worcestershire sauce
- 1 teaspoon seasoned salt
- ½ teaspoon leaf thyme, crumbled
- ¼ teaspoon seasoned pepper

1. Shake beef and veal cubes, part at a time, in a mixture of flour, salt and pepper in a plastic bag to coat evenly.
2. Brown meat cubes in a mixture of

butter or margarine and shortening in a large skillet or an electric slow cooker with a browning unit; remove with a slotted spoon and reserve.
3. While cubed meats brown, cover veal kidneys with water in a medium-size saucepan; add vinegar; bring to boiling; lower heat; simmer 4 to 5 minutes; drain on paper towels; cut into thin slices.
4. Sauté veal kidneys in pan drippings; remove and reserve.
5. Place meats in slow cooker; place onion and tomato slices over; combine beef broth, wine, Worcestershire sauce, seasoned salt, thyme and seasoned pepper in a medium-size bowl; pour into slow cooker; cover.
6. Cook on high (290° to 300°) 2 hours. Turn heat control to low (190° to 200°) for 5 hours, or until meats are tender. Taste and season with salt and pepper, if desired. If you wish to thicken the gravy, turn heat control to high (290° to 300°); combine 2 tablespoons cornstarch and ¼ cup cold water; stir into cooker; cover; cook 15 minutes. Serve with mashed potatoes.

NEW-STYLE SAUERBRATEN STEW

If you like your stew on the spicy side, simmer the spice bag in the cooker. Otherwise, discard after marinating.

Cook on 190° to 200° for 8 hours, then on 290° to 300° for 1½ hours. Makes 8 servings.

- 1 envelope (about 1 ounce) instant meat marinade
- ⅔ cup white vinegar
- 6 whole cloves
- 6 peppercorns
- 6 whole allspice
- 1 bay leaf
- ½ teaspoon celery seeds
- 1 cross rib beef pot roast (about 3 pounds)
- ½ cup all-purpose flour
- 2 tablespoons sugar
- 3 tablespoons vegetable shortening
- 6 small yellow onions, peeled and halved
- 4 large carrots, pared and sliced
- ½ cup dry red wine
- ⅓ cup crushed gingersnaps
- Ginger Dumplings (recipe follows)

1. Combine meat marinade and vinegar in a small saucepan; tie cloves, peppercorns, allspice, bay leaf and celery seeds in cheesecloth and add to saucepan. Bring to boiling; let cool.
2. Trim excess fat from meat; pierce all over with a two-tined fork. Place in a glass or earthenware bowl. Pour marinade over and let stand 20 minutes, basting several times with marinade.
3. Remove meat from marinade; reserve marinade. Cube meat and roll in a mixture of flour and sugar on wax paper.
4. Brown meat in vegetable shortening in a large skillet or an electric slow

cooker with a browning unit; remove and reserve. Sauté onions and carrots until soft in pan drippings; stir in wine.

5. Combine meat with onions and carrots in slow cooker; add reserved marinade and spice bag, if you wish; cover cooker.

6. Cook on low (190° to 200°) 8 hours; turn heat control to high (290° to 300°); stir in gingersnap crumbs.

7. Cook 1 hour longer, stirring several times. Drop GINGER DUMPLINGS onto surface; cover; cook 30 minutes longer, or until dumplings are light and fluffy. Serve at once.

GINGER DUMPLINGS—Sift 1½ cups sifted all-purpose flour, 2 teaspoons baking powder and ½ teaspoon salt into a medium-size bowl. Stir in ¼ cup crushed gingersnap crumbs. Blend in 1 tablespoon vegetable shortening with a fork until crumbly. Stir in ¾ cup milk, just until mixture is moist. Drop onto hot food in slow cooker. Cook on high (290° to 300°) 30 minutes, or until puffy and light. (No peeking, or the dumplings won't puff up.)

ARIZONA CHUCK WAGON BEANS

Use whatever cut of beef is on special. This is a delicious bean dish, simple and economical.

Cook on 190° to 200° for 10 hours,
or   on 290° to 300° for 6 hours.
Makes 8 servings

- 1 package (1 pound) dried navy, pinto or cranberry beans
- 6 cups water
- ¼ pound salt pork, diced
- 1 large onion, chopped (1 cup)
- 1 clove garlic, minced
- 1 large green pepper, halved, seeded and chopped
- 1½ pounds boneless chuck, cubed
- 1½ teaspoons salt
- ½ teaspoon leaf oregano, crumbled
- ¼ teaspoon crushed red pepper
- ¼ teaspoon ground cumin
- 1 can (8 ounces) tomato sauce

1. Pick over beans and rinse well. Combine beans and water in a large kettle. Bring to boiling; cover; cook 2 minutes. Remove from heat; let stand 1 hour; pour into an electric slow cooker. (Or soak beans in water in cooker overnight at room temperature.)

2. Brown salt pork in a large skillet; remove with a slotted spoon to cooker; sauté onion, garlic and green pepper in pan drippings; remove with slotted spoon to cooker. Brown beef, a few pieces at a time in pan drippings; remove to cooker with slotted spoon; stir in salt, oregano, red pepper, cumin and tomato sauce. (Add more water, if necessary, to bring liquid level above beans.) Cover.

3. Cook on low (190° to 200°) 10 hours, or on high (290° to 300°) 6 hours, or until beans are tender.

LAMB CHOPS POLYNESIAN

Thrifty pork shoulder chops can also be used in this recipe.

Cook on 190° to 200° for 8 hours,
or   on 290° to 300° for 4 hours.
Makes 6 servings.

- 6 shoulder lamb chops, cut ¾-inch thick
- 2 teaspoons curry powder
- 2 tablespoons vegetable oil
- 1 large onion, chopped (1 cup)
- 1 clove garlic, minced
- 1½ teaspoons salt
- 1 teaspoon ground allspice
- 1 cup water
- ¼ cup lemon juice
- 1 jar (about 8 ounces) junior prunes (baby-pack)
- 1 jar (about 8 ounces) junior applesauce-and-apricots (baby-pack)

1. Trim excess fat from chops. Rub lamb with curry powder. Brown slowly in oil in a large skillet or slow cooker with a browning unit; remove.

2. Sauté onion and garlic until soft in same pan; stir in salt, allspice, water and lemon juice. Bring to boiling; stir in junior fruits.

3. Place lamb chops in slow cooker with fruit sauce; cover.

4. Cook on low (190° to 200°) 8 hours, or on high (290° to 300°) 4 hours, or until tender. Serve with fried rice and sautéed bananas, if you wish.

MACARONI STUFFED PEPPERS

An American favorite for luncheon or supper.

Cook on 190° to 200° for 8 hours,
or   on 290° to 300° for 4 hours.
Makes 4 servings.

- 4 large green peppers
- ½ pound ground beef
- 1 small can evaporated milk
- ½ cup shredded process American cheese
- 1 cup cooked elbow macaroni
- 1 can condensed cream of onion soup

1. Cut a slice from top of each pepper; scoop out seeds and membrane. Chop slices and set aside for filling. Parboil peppers in a small amount of boiling water 3 minutes; drain well. Stand peppers in an electric slow cooker.

2. Shape ground beef into a large patty in a skillet; brown with chopped green pepper 5 minutes on each side, then break up into small chunks. Stir in evaporated milk, and cheese; stir in macaroni. Spoon into pepper cups. Add soup to slow cooker; cover.

3. Cook on low (190° to 200°) 8 hours, or on high (290° to 300°) 4 hours, or until peppers are tender.

ENGLISH HOT POT

British cooks have made these one-pot specialities for generations.

Cook on 190° to 200° for 8 hours,
or   on 290° to 300° for 4 hours.
Makes 8 servings.

- 2 pounds boneless lamb shoulder, cubed
- ¼ cup all-purpose flour
- 2 envelopes or teaspoons instant chicken broth
- 2 teaspoons salt
- 1 teaspoon leaf oregano, crumbled
- ½ teaspoon leaf rosemary, crumbled
- ¼ teaspoon pepper
- 1 large onion, sliced and separated into rings
- 3 small yellow squash, cut into 2-inch pieces
- 12 small potatoes, pared and halved
- 1 cup boiling water
- 2 tablespoons butter or margarine, melted

1. Trim all excess fat from lamb. Shake cubes, part at a time, in flour in a plastic bag to coat well.

2. Mix instant chicken broth, salt, oregano, rosemary and pepper in a cup.

3. Layer meat and vegetables into an electric slow cooker this way: Half of each of lamb, onion and squash, sprinkling each layer with seasoning mixture. Repeat with remaining lamb, vegetables and seasoning mixture.

4. Lay potatoes, rounded side up, on top; pour boiling water over. Brush potatoes with butter; cover.

5. Cook on low (190° to 200°) 8 hours, or on high (290° to 300°) 4 hours, or until meat and vegetables are tender. Serve with hearts of lettuce and cold apple cider, if you wish.

QUICK TIPS

- For sand-free fresh vegetables, place trimmed broccoli, cauliflower, asparagus or spinach in a large pan of salted warm water. Soak 5 minutes, then lift the vegetables out. Rinse in cold water, if vegetables are extra sandy.
- If you want to keep the bright color of fresh green vegetables, it's best to cook them in a saucepan at meal time and add to slow cooker, just before serving.
- To peel tomatoes easily, lower each tomato on a slotted spoon into a pan of boiling water for 30 seconds; remove and peel immediately.

LIMA BEANS IN BROTH

A dish so hearty-rich, no one will suspect that it isn't packed with meat.

Cook on 190° to 200° for 10 hours, or on 290° to 300° for 5 hours. Makes 8 servings.

- 1 **package (1 pound) dried lima beans**
- 8 **cups water**
- 1 **large onion, chopped (1 cup)**
- 1 **clove garlic, minced**
- 2 **tablespoons vegetable oil**
- 1 **can condensed beef broth**
- 2 **large green peppers, halved, seeded and chopped**
- 2 **teaspoons salt**
- 1 **teaspoon mixed Italian herbs, crumbled**
- ¼ **teaspoon pepper**
- 1 **package (6 ounces) sliced Provolone cheese, diced**

1. Pick over beans and rinse under running water. Combine beans and water in a large kettle. Bring to boiling; cover kettle. Boil 2 minutes; remove from heat; let stand 1 hour; pour into an electric slow cooker. (Or soak beans in water in cooker overnight.)
2. Sauté onion and garlic in oil in a medium-size skillet until soft; stir in beef broth, green peppers, salt, mixed Italian herbs and pepper; cook 2 minutes; add to beans in slow cooker. (Add more water, if necessary, to bring liquid level above beans.) Cover.
3. Cook on low (190° to 200°) 10 hours, or on high (290° to 300°) 5 hours, or until beans are tender. Stir cheese into beans.

DUTCH HOT POT

Coriander seeds and leaf thyme add the distinctive touch to this Amsterdam dish.

Cook on 190° to 200° for 8 hours, or on 290° to 300° for 4 hours. Makes 8 servings.

- 2 **pounds boneless pork shoulder, cubed**
- ¼ **cup all-purpose flour**
- 1 **tablespoon salt**
- 1 **teaspoon leaf thyme, crumbled**
- 1 **teaspoon coriander seeds, crushed**
- ¼ **teaspoon pepper**
- 1 **can (1 pound) red kidney beans Boiling water**
- 4 **medium-size potatoes, pared and cut into ¼-inch thick slices**
- 4 **medium-size onions, sliced and separated into rings**
- 8 **carrots, pared and cut in 4-inch lengths**
- 2 **tablespoons butter or margarine**

1. Trim excess fat from pork. Shake cubes, part at a time, with flour in a plastic bag to coat well.
2. Mix salt, thyme, coriander seeds and pepper in a cup; reserve.

3. Drain liquid from kidney beans into a 2-cup measure; add boiling water to make 1½ cups.
4. Layer vegetables and meat into an electric slow cooker this way: Half each of potatoes, onions, pork, kidney beans and carrots, sprinkling each layer lightly with seasoning mixture. Repeat with remaining vegetables, pork and seasoning mixture for a second layer.
5. Pour liquid over; dot with butter or margarine; cover.
6. Cook on low (190° to 200°) 8 hours, or on high (290° to 300°) 4 hours, or until meat and vegetables are tender. Serve with dark beer, if you wish.

LAREDO BARBECUED POT ROAST

Try the rich flavor of barbecued beef, Texas-style, with a crown of Cornmeal Dumplings.

Cook on 190° to 200° for 10 hours, or on 290° to 300° for 6 hours. Makes 8 servings.

- 1 **cross rib beef pot roast, (about 3 pounds)**
- 1 **large onion, chopped (1 cup)**
- 1 **clove garlic, minced**
- 1 **can (8 ounces) tomato sauce**
- ¼ **cup firmly packed brown sugar**
- 3 **tablespoons cider vinegar**
- 1 **tablespoon prepared mustard**
- 1 **tablespoon Worcestershire sauce**
- 2 **teaspoons salt**
- 1 **teaspoon mixed Italian herbs, crumbled**
- ¼ **teaspoon pepper Cornmeal Dumplings (recipe follows)**

1. Trim excess fat from beef; brown in a large skillet or an electric slow cooker with a browning unit; remove and reserve. Sauté onion and garlic until soft in pan drippings.
2. Place pot roast in slow cooker with onion and garlic. Combine tomato sauce, brown sugar, vinegar, mustard, Worcestershire sauce, salt, Italian herbs and pepper in a small bowl; pour over beef; cover.
3. Cook on low (190° to 200°) 10 hours, or on high (290° to 300°) 6 hours, or until beef is tender when pierced with a two-tined fork. Remove beef to a heated platter and keep warm.
4. Turn heat control to high (290° to 300°) while making dumplings.
5. Drop CORNMEAL DUMPLINGS into cooker by tablespoons; cover. Cook without peeking 30 minutes. Carve beef into thin slices and serve with sauce and dumplings from slow cooker.
CORNMEAL DUMPLINGS—Combine ⅔ cup milk and 2 tablespoons vegetable oil in a medium-size bowl. Sift ¾ cup sifted all-purpose flour, ½ cup yellow cornmeal, 2 teaspoons baking powder and 1 teaspoon salt over. Stir just until mixture is moist. (Dough will be soft.)

Drop onto hot food in slow cooker. Cook on high (290° to 300°) 30 minutes, or until puffy light. (No peeking, or the dumplings won't puff up.)

CATTLEMAN'S BEEF AND BEANS

Since the days of the cowboys in the Golden West, kettles of beef and richly flavored beans have been he-man food.

Cook on 290° to 300° for 2 hours, then on 190° to 200° for 8 hours. Makes 8 servings.

- 1 **package (1 pound) dried pinto, small lima or pea beans**
- 6 **cups water**
- 1 **boneless beef brisket or round roast (about 3 pounds)**
- 1 **large onion, chopped (1 cup)**
- ⅓ **cup dark molasses**
- 2 **teaspoons salt**
- ½ **teaspoon ground ginger**
- ½ **teaspoon dry mustard**
- ¼ **teaspoon pepper**
- 1 **bay leaf**

1. Rinse beans under running water; place in a large kettle with water; bring to boiling; cover kettle; lower heat; cook 15 minutes; let stand 1 hour.
2. Trim all excess fat from beef; brown meat on all sides in remaining fat in a large skillet or an electric slow cooker with a browning unit.
3. Place meat in the bottom of slow cooker; add beans and liquid, onion, molasses, salt, ginger, mustard, pepper and bay leaf. Add more water, if needed, to cover meat and beans; cover.
4. Cook on high (290° to 300°) 2 hours; stir beans, adding more liquid, if needed, to keep beans and meat covered.
5. Turn heat control to low (190° to 200°) and cook for 8 hours, or until beans are very tender and liquid is absorbed. Taste and season with a spoonful of hot prepared mustard, if you wish.
6. Remove meat to a carving board and cut into slices; spoon beans around beef on a platter; serve with crusty bread.

SLOW COOKER TIPS

Dumplings can be made successfully in your slow cooker if you follow these directions:
- Use a recipe that has at least 1 teaspoon baking powder to each cup of sifted all-purpose flour.
- The slow cooker should be at least ¾ full and the level of the liquid should not be above the level of the food. If the liquid is above the food, remove excess liquid from cooker with a bulb baster before dropping dumpling batter onto food. (Excess liquid can prevent dumplings from cooking completely.)
- Dumplings can either be cooked for 30 minutes on high (290° to 300°) with the cooker covered, or cooked on high (290° to 300°) 15 minutes uncovered, then 15

minutes covered.

● You can follow the recipe for dumplings on the biscuit mix label and have successful slow cooker dumplings.

ALDILLA

Try this south-of-the-border steak dish with chili powder and hot chili pepper for a dish with a dash.

Cook on 190° to 200° for 8 hours, or on 290° to 300° for 4 hours. Makes 6 servings.

- 1 flank steak (about 1½ pounds)
- 2 to 4 teaspoons chili powder
- ½ cup all-purpose flour
- 1½ teaspoons salt
- ½ teaspoon seasoned pepper
- 3 tablespoons vegetable oil
- 1 large onion, chopped (1 cup)
- 1 large carrot, pared and chopped
- 1 large green pepper, halved, seeded and chopped
- 2 large ripe tomatoes, peeled and chopped
- ¼ cup dry red wine
- 1 hot chili pepper, seeded (from a 4-ounce can)

1. Score steak and rub with chili powder; coat with a mixture of flour, ½ teaspoon salt and ¼ teaspoon of the seasoned pepper; pound steak on both sides with a wooden mallet or the edge of a plate to tenderize; cut into 6 pieces.
2. Brown steak in hot oil in a large skillet or an electric slow cooker with a browning unit; remove and reserve. Sauté onion, carrot, green pepper and tomato in pan drippings; add remaining 1 teaspoon salt and ¼ teaspoon seasoned pepper; remove from heat.
3. Combine steak and sautéed vegetables in slow cooker; add wine and hot chili pepper; cover.
4. Cook on low (190° to 200°) 8 hours, or on high (290° to 300°) 4 hours, or until meat is tender. Serve with cornbread and an avocado, ripe olive and shredded lettuce salad, if you wish.

LAMB STEW WITH MINT DUMPLINGS

Tender lamb, colorful vegetables and mint-seasoned dumplings make a perfect main dish for a spring dinner.

Cook on 190° to 200° for 8 hours, or on 290° to 300° for 4 hours. Makes 6 servings.

- 2 pounds boneless lamb shoulder, cubed
- 2 cups boiling water
  Handful celery leaves, chopped
- 2 teaspoons salt
- ¼ teaspoon pepper
- 18 small white onions, peeled
- 6 large carrots, pared and cut into 1-inch lengths
- 1 cup sliced celery
- 2 cups biscuit mix
- 1 tablespoon chopped fresh mint
- ¾ cup milk

1. Trim excess fat from lamb; place in an electric slow cooker; pour boiling water over. Top with celery leaves, salt and pepper; stir in onions, carrots and celery; cover cooker.
2. Cook on low (190° to 200°) 8 hours, or on high (290° to 300°) 4 hours, or until lamb is tender.
3. Turn heat control to high (290° to 300°) while making dumplings.
4. Combine biscuit mix and mint in small bowl; stir in milk just until dumpling mixture is moistened.
5. Drop by tablespoons on top of steaming stew; cover. Cook, without peeking, 30 minutes longer.

DUTCH SPARERIBS

Country-style spareribs are simmered with sauerkraut and topped with caraway flavored dumplings.

Cook on 190° to 200° for 8 hours, then on 290° to 300° for 30 minutes. Makes 6 servings.

Meat
- 3 pounds country-style spareribs, cut up
- 1 can (1 pound, 13 ounces) sauerkraut
- 2 tart apples, cored and cut into wedges
- 1 large onion, chopped (1 cup)
- 2 teaspoons seasoned salt
- ½ teaspoon seasoned pepper
- ¼ teaspoon caraway seeds, crushed

Dumplings
- 2 cups sifted all-purpose flour
- 2 teaspoons baking powder
- 1 teaspoon salt
- ½ teaspoon caraway seeds
- 1 egg
- ¾ cup milk

1. Trim excess fat from spareribs; place in an electric slow cooker. Wash sauerkraut under running water; drain very well; place over ribs with apple wedges and onion; sprinkle with seasoned salt, seasoned pepper and caraway seeds; cover.
2. Cook on low (190° to 200°) 8 hours, or until ribs are very tender when pierced with a two-tined fork.
3. Make dumplings: Turn heat control to high (290° to 300°). Sift flour, baking powder and salt into a large bowl; stir in caraway seeds. Beat egg in a cup with a fork; beat in milk; pour, all at once, into dry mixture. Stir until blended.
4. Uncover slow cooker. (If there is a level of liquid above the sauerkraut; remove some of the liquid with a bulb baster.) Drop dumplings by spoonfuls on top of sauerkraut; cover. Cook 30 minutes, or until dumplings are fluffy.

EL RANCHO ROAST

Ripe olives and cinnamon give this roast its tantalizing flavor.

Cook on 190° to 200° for 10 hours, or on 290° to 300° for 6 hours. Makes 8 servings.

- 1 round, rump, sirloin tip or boneless chuck roast (about 4 pounds)
- 1 can (6 ounces) tomato paste
- 1 cup sliced pitted ripe olives
- ¼ cup water
- 2 tablespoons lemon juice
- 1 tablespoon sugar
- 2 teaspoons salt
- 1 teaspoon ground cinnamon
- ½ teaspoon pepper
- 3 tablespoons all-purpose flour

1. Trim excess fat from beef; brown meat in a large skillet or an electric slow cooker with a browning unit.
2. Place beef in slow cooker. Combine tomato paste, olives, water, lemon juice, sugar, salt, cinnamon and pepper in a small bowl; pour over meat; cover.
3. Cook on low (190° to 200°) 10 hours, or on high (290° to 300°) 6 hours, or until beef is tender when pierced with a two-tined fork. Remove beef to a heated platter and keep warm.
4. Turn heat control to high (290° to 300°). Combine flour and ⅓ cup cold water in a cup; stir into liquid until well-blended; cover; simmer 15 minutes. Slice meat; serve with gravy.
Suggested Variations: Use a boned and rolled lamb shoulder or shank-half of a leg of lamb for the beef. Serve with saffron rice, if you wish.

COUNTY KERRY PORK ROAST

Fresh pork shoulder makes an especially delicious gravy to spoon over fluffy, buttered mashed potatoes.

Cook on 190° to 200° for 10 hours, or on 290° to 300° for 5 hours. Makes 8 servings.

- 1 fresh picnic or shoulder butt (about 5 pounds)
- 1 large onion, chopped (1 cup)
- 1 teaspoon leaf marjoram, crumbled
- ¾ cup bottled barbecue sauce
- ¾ cup water

1. Trim excess fat from pork; place in an electric slow cooker; sprinkle with onion and marjoram; pour mixture of barbecue sauce and water over; cover.
2. Cook on low (190° to 200°) 10 hours, or on high (290° to 300°) 5 hours, or until pork is tender when pierced with a fork.
3. Slice hot and serve with mashed potatoes, steamed cabbage and horse-radish mustard, if you wish.
Suggested Variations: Fresh ham, pork loin or lamb shoulder can be substituted for the pork shoulder in this recipe. Also, use leaf savory instead of marjoram.

ENGLISH GIBLET SOUP

Frugal British cooks have always known how to get the most from a chicken.

Cook on 190° to 200° for 10 hours, or on 290° to 300° for 5 hours. Makes 6 servings.

- 1 pound chicken giblets
- 3 tablespoons butter or margarine
- ½ cup all-purpose flour
- 8 cups Classic Chicken Broth (recipe on page 36)
  OR: 8 envelopes or teaspoons instant chicken broth and 8 cups water
- 2 teaspoons salt
- ¼ teaspoon pepper
- 1 bay leaf
- 2 cups cooked rice
- ½ cup chopped celery

1. Sauté chicken giblets in butter or margarine in a large skillet or an electric slow cooker with a browning unit.
2. Stir in flour and cook, stirring constantly, 5 minutes, or until flour browns.
3. Combine chicken giblets with CLASSIC CHICKEN BROTH or instant chicken broth and water, salt, pepper and bay leaf in an electric slow cooker; cover.
4. Cook on low (190° to 200°) 10 hours, or on high (290° to 300°) 5 hours, or until giblets are tender.
5. Stir in rice and celery and cook 15 minutes to heat rice. Serve in heated soup bowls topped with chopped parsley, if you wish.

ENSENADA CHILI POT

There's South-of-the-border flavor in this no-watch special.

Cook on 190° to 200° for 8 hours, or on 290° to 300° for 4 hours. Makes 8 servings.

- 2 pounds lean boneless chuck, cubed
- ¼ cup all-purpose flour
- 1 to 2 tablespoons chili powder
- 2 teaspoons salt
- ¼ teaspoon pepper
- ¼ cup vegetable shortening
- 1 large onion, chopped (1 cup)
- 2 cans (1 pound each) red kidney beans
- 1 can (1 pound, 13 ounces) tomatoes
- 1 can (12 or 16 ounces) whole-kernel corn
- 1 can (4 ounces) pimiento, sliced
- 1 can (4 ounces) green chili peppers, seeded and chopped
  Hot cooked rice
  Shredded Cheddar cheese

1. Trim excess fat from beef; shake beef cubes with flour, chili powder, salt and pepper in a plastic bag to coat well.
2. Brown, a few at a time, in shortening in a large skillet or an electric slow cooker with a browning unit; remove and reserve. Stir in onion; sauté 5 minutes, or until onion is soft. Spoon off any excess drippings; stir any remaining flour-seasoning mixture into pan.
3. Drain liquid from kidney beans and add to pan; stir in tomatoes; bring to boiling; remove from heat.
4. Place beef in slow cooker with tomato mixture; stir in kidney beans and corn; cover cooker.
5. Cook on low (190° to 200°) 8 hours, or on high (290° to 300°) 4 hours; stir in pimiento and green chili peppers.
6. Spoon chili over rice in soup bowls. Top with shredded Cheddar cheese.

MEMPHIS PORK SUPPER

Pork, apples, onion and sweet potatoes make this Southern-style main dish.

Cook on 190° to 200° for 8 hours, or on 290° to 300° for 4 hours. Makes 8 servings.

- 8 medium-size sweet potatoes (about 3 pounds)
- 3 pounds boneless pork shoulder, cubed
- 3 medium-size onions, sliced
- 4 medium-size tart red apples, cored and sliced into rings
- 2 tablespoons brown sugar
- 2 cups apple juice
- 2 teaspoons salt
- 1 teaspoon leaf marjoram, crumbled
- ¼ teaspoon pepper
  Chopped parsley

1. Pare and quarter sweet potatoes.
2. Trim all fat from pork; brown, a few pieces at a time, in a little of the trimmed fat in a large skillet or an electric slow cooker with a browning unit; remove with a slotted spoon and reserve.
3. Arrange potatoes around edge of an electric slow cooker; place half of meat in middle. Top with layer each of half of the onion slices and apple rings; sprinkle with half the brown sugar. Repeat to make a second layer of meat and onion; overlap remaining apple rings around edge; sprinkle remaining brown sugar over. Combine apple juice, salt, marjoram and pepper in a 2-cup measure; pour over apple rings; cover.
4. Cook on low (190° to 200°) 8 hours, or on high (290° to 300°) 4 hours, or until pork is tender. Sprinkle with chopped parsley, just before serving.

SLOW COOKER TIPS

For a quicker start in assembling your slow cooker recipe in the morning, brown meat or poultry and sauté vegetables the night before. Store in a covered bowl overnight, then place in slow cooker with other ingredients in the morning. (Don't refrigerate browned food in cooker unless it is one of the new removable stoneware bowls that come in some slow cookers.)

FOOD SAFETY TEMPERATURES

The USDA has set up this chart as a guide to the safest temperatures for holding various foods:

0°	Safest temperature to store frozen foods. Do not store foods above 10°.
32° to 40°	The best temperature for holding foods in refrigerator.
60° to 125°	DANGER ZONE for all perishable foods.
140° to 165°	This is the temperature at which bacteria begin to be destroyed in cooking. Foods can be warmed at 140°, but not cooked.
212°	This is the temperature that a water-bath canner reaches and is safe for most jams, jellies, pickles and high-acid tomatoes.
240°	This is the temperature at which to process all low-acid vegetable, meats and poultry in a home-size pressure canner.

LANCASHIRE HOT POT

Lancashire, a county in northwestern England, is the home of hot-pot cooking. This is one of their best.

Cook on 190° to 200° for 8 hours, or on 290° to 300° for 4 hours. Makes 8 servings.

- 1½ pounds boneless beef chuck, cubed
- 2 veal kidneys
- ¼ cup all-purpose flour
- 2 envelopes or teaspoons instant beef broth
- 2 cups boiling water
- 1 tablespoon Worcestershire sauce
- 6 medium-size potatoes, pared and thinly sliced
- 3 large onions, sliced
- 2 teaspoons salt
- ¼ teaspoon pepper
- 2 tablespoons butter or margarine

1. Trim excess fat from beef. Halve kidneys; cut out tubes and white membrane, then cut kidneys into ½-inch cubes. Shake meats, part at a time, with flour in a plastic bag to coat well.
2. Dissolve instant beef broth in boiling water in a 2-cup measure; stir in Worcestershire sauce.
3. Layer vegetables and meats into an electric slow cooker this way: Half of each of potatoes, onions and meats, sprinkling each layer lightly with salt and pepper. Repeat with remaining vegetables, meats, salt and pepper.
4. Pour broth mixture over; dot with butter or margarine; cover.
5. Cook on low (190° to 200°) 8 hours, or on high (290° to 300°) 4 hours, or until meats are tender. A baked apple cobbler with pour cream makes a good dessert.

CHICKEN QUEBEC

Serving chicken flavored with bacon is a cooking secret French Canadians brought from France centuries ago.

Cook on 190° to 200° for 10 hours,
or   on 290° to 300° for 5 hours.
Makes 6 servings.

- 1 stewing chicken, cut up (about 5 pounds)
- 6 slices bacon
- 1 medium-size onion, chopped (½ cup)
- 1 teaspoon salt
- ½ teaspoon freshly ground pepper
- 4 cups water
- 1 package (8 ounces) elbow macaroni, cooked
- 1 tablespoon parsley flakes, crumbled

1. Trim fat from chicken; melt fat in a large skillet or an electric slow cooker with a browning unit. Brown chicken, a few pieces at a time in fat; drain.
2. Fry bacon lightly in same pan; remove and set aside; pour off all fat.
3. Place chicken and bacon in slow cooker; add onion, salt, pepper and water; cover cooker.
4. Cook on low (190° to 200°) 10 hours, or on high (290° to 300°) 5 hours, or until chicken is tender.
5. Turn heat control to high (290° to 300°); add macaroni and parsley flakes. Cook 10 minutes; taste and season with additional salt and pepper, if you wish.

POACHED CHICKEN

When chickens are on special, poach one or two and keep on hand for salads, sandwiches or casseroles.

Cook on 190° to 200° for 8 hours,
or   on 290° to 300° for 4 hours.
Makes 4 servings.

- 1 broiler-fryer (about 3 pounds)
- 1 small onion studded with 4 whole cloves
- 1 medium-size carrot, pared and diced
- 1 stalk celery with leaves, chopped
- 1 leek, trimmed and sliced (optional)
- ½ cup dry white wine
- ½ cup water
- 2 slices lemon
- 1 teaspoon salt
- ¼ teaspoon white pepper
- 1 bay leaf
- 3 whole allspice

1. Place chicken in an electric slow cooker with giblets, but not liver. Add onion, carrot, celery, leek, wine, water, lemon slices, salt, pepper, bay leaf and allspice; cover.
2. Cook on low (190° to 200°) 8 hours, or on high (290° to 300°) 4 hours, or until

chicken is tender when pierced with a two-tined fork; remove chicken from broth and let cool.
3. Strain broth through cheesecloth into a bowl; chill and use within 3 days or soften 1 envelope unflavored gelatin in ¼ cup cold water; stir into hot broth until dissolved; pour into a 2-cup mold or 8x8x2-inch pan; chill until firm. Serve as a chicken aspic, if you wish.
4. Slip skin from cooled chicken and pull meat from bones in large pieces. Refrigerate and use within 3 days or pack in plastic freezer containers; seal; label and date. Freeze; use within 3 months.

KENTUCKY CHICKEN

Even folks who think they don't like lima beans will be sending their plates back for seconds.

Cook on 190° to 200° for 10 hours,
or   on 290° to 300° for 5 hours.
Makes 8 servings.

- 1 stewing chicken, cut up (about 5 pounds)
- ½ cup all-purpose flour
- 1 envelope (about 1 ounce) herb salad dressing mix
- 3 tablespoons peanut oil
- 1 large onion, chopped (1 cup)
- 1 can (1 pound) tomatoes
- 2 cups diced celery
- 1 can (about 1 pound) lima beans
- 1 can (12 or 16 ounces) whole-kernel corn
- 1 package (10 ounces) frozen whole okra, thawed
- 1 can (4 ounces) pimiento, drained and chopped
- ¼ cup chopped parsley

1. Shake chicken with flour and salad dressing mix in plastic bag to coat evenly. Brown chicken in oil in a large skillet or an electric slow cooker with a browning unit; remove and reserve.
2. Sauté onion until soft in pan drippings; stir in tomatoes, celery, lima beans and corn; cover. (If using a skillet, place chicken and vegetables in slow cooker; cover.)
3. Cook on low (190° to 200°) 10 hours, or on high (290° to 300°) 5 hours, or until chicken is tender when pierced with a two-tined fork. Stir in okra and pimiento; cover and cook 15 minutes. Sprinkle with parsley just before serving.

SLOW COOKER TIPS

As with most cooking at altitudes above 4,000 feet, foods take longer to cook, so as a rule of thumb, increase the cooking time 1 hour on low (190° to 200°) for every 1,000 feet of altitude above 4,000 feet. Dried beans will be tender if you pre-cook in a pressure cooker before adding to slow cooker. (For directions on pre-cooking dried beans in a pressure cooker, see page 58.)

DENVER LAMB STEW

Lamb lovers will enjoy this hearty dish for a cold winter's dinner.

Cook on 190° to 200° for 8 hours,
or   on 290° to 300° for 4 hours.
Makes 6 servings.

- 2 pounds boneless lamb shoulder, cubed
- 1 clove garlic, peeled and halved
- 1 pound green beans, tipped and cut into 1-inch pieces
- 12 small white onions, peeled
- 6 small potatoes, pared
- 1 can (1 pound) tomatoes
- 1 teaspoon salt
- 1 teaspoon leaf marjoram, crumbled

1. Trim excess fat from lamb; rub lamb on all sides with garlic; place in an electric slow cooker.
2. Add green beans, onions, potatoes, tomatoes, salt and marjoram; cover.
3. Cook on low (190° to 200°) 8 hours, or on high (290° to 300°) 4 hours, or until meat is tender. Serve with chunks of crusty French bread.
Suggested Variations: Omit tomatoes and add 2 cups dry red wine. Acorn squash slices and zucchini sticks can be substituted for the potatoes and green beans in this stew.

DODGE CITY SHORT RIBS

Hefty chunks of beef simmer in a pungent sauce with lots of vegetables.

Cook on 190° to 200° for 10 hours,
or   on 290° to 300° for 5 hours.
Makes 6 servings.

- 3 pounds short ribs, cut up
- 1 large onion chopped (1 cup)
- 1 can (1 pound, 4 ounces) tomatoes
- 3 whole cloves
- 1 bay leaf
- 1 teaspoon dry mustard
- 1 teaspoon salt
- 1 small yellow turnip, pared and cubed
- 3 large potatoes, pared and quartered
- 1 package (10 ounces) frozen peas, thawed

1. Trim excess fat from short ribs; brown, a few at a time, in their own fat in large skillet or an electric slow cooker with a browning unit; remove and reserve. Stir onions into pan drippings; sauté until golden. Add tomatoes, cloves, bay leaf, mustard and salt.
2. Place short ribs with tomato mixture in slow cooker; add turnip, potatoes and peas; cover.
3. Cook on low (190° to 200°) 10 hours, or on high (290° to 300°) 5 hours, or until short ribs are tender. Unplug slow cooker; remove cover; let fat rise to surface and skim off. Serve ribs with chunks of sour dough bread and canned pears topped with chocolate sauce.

SACRAMENTO BEEF POT

Red wine gives beef a hearty flavor.

Cook on 190° to 200° for 10 hours,
or on 290° to 300° for 5 hours.
Makes 8 servings.

- 1 beef blade or round-bone chuck roast (about 4 pounds)
- 1 medium-size onion, sliced
- 6 medium-size potatoes, pared and halved
- 6 small zucchini, sliced
- 1 red pepper, sliced in rings
- 1 cup dry red wine or beef broth
- 2 teaspoons salt
- ¼ teaspoon pepper
- 1 bay leaf
- 3 tablespoons all-purpose flour
- ⅓ cup cold water

1. Trim all excess fat from meat. Brown beef in its own fat in a large skillet or an electric slow cooker with a browning unit; remove and set aside. Drain all but 2 tablespoons fat from skillet. Sauté onion until soft in fat.
2. Place meat, sautéed onion, potatoes, zucchini, red pepper rings, wine or broth, salt, pepper and bay leaf in slow cooker; cover.
3. Cook on low (190° to 200°) 10 hours, or on high (290° to 300°) 5 hours, or until meat is tender when pierced with a two-tined fork. Place meat and vegetables on heated platter and keep warm.
4. Turn heat control to high (290° to 300°). Combine flour and water in a cup; pour into liquid in slow cooker; cover. Cook 15 minutes; pass sauce separately in heated gravy boat.

PERSIAN STEAK ROLL

Wheat pilaf and spinach are the special ingredients that takes this casserole out of the ordinary.

Cook on 190° to 200° for 10 hours,
or on 290° to 300° for 5 hours.
Makes 6 servings.

- 1 flank steak (about 1½ pounds)
- 1 small onion, chopped (¼ cup)
- 4 tablespoons vegetable oil
- ½ cup wheat pilaf (from a 12-ounce package)
- 1 teaspoon curry powder
- 1 cup water
- 1 package (10 ounces) frozen chopped spinach, thawed
- 1 can (1 pound) red kidney beans
- ½ teaspoon cardamom seeds, crushed
- 1½ teaspoons salt
- ¼ teaspoon pepper
- 1 can (1 pound) stewed tomatoes
- 1 tablespoon lemon juice

1. Ask your meatman to split flank steak, butterfly fashion. Or, at home, split it yourself, working slowly with a sharp long-blade knife and cutting with a sawing motion as evenly as possible. Pound steak with a mallet or rolling pin to make it evenly thin.
2. Sauté onion in 2 tablespoons of the oil until soft in a large skillet. Stir in wheat pilaf; cook 2 minutes, or until lightly browned. Stir in curry powder and water; cover skillet.
3. Bring to boiling, then simmer 15 minutes, or until liquid is absorbed. Cool slightly; spread over meat in a thin layer.
4. Drain spinach, then pat as dry as possible between paper towels.
5. Drain kidney beans, saving liquid. Mix beans, spinach, cardamom seeds and ½ teaspoon of the salt in a medium-size bowl; spread over pilaf layer.
6. Starting at one long side, roll up tightly, tucking in any loose stuffing; tie with string every 2 inches. Sprinkle with remaining 1 teaspoon salt and pepper.
7. Brown roll in remaining 2 tablespoons oil in the large skillet or in an electric slow cooker with a browning unit; remove and reserve.
8. Stir tomatoes, lemon juice and saved bean liquid into pan until well-blended.
9. Place the stuffed meat roll and sauce in slow cooker; cover.
10. Cook on low (190° to 200°) 10 hours, turning meat after 5 hours, if possible, or on high (290° to 300°) 5 hours, turning meat after 3 hours, if possible. Place meat on heated serving platter and remove strings. Cut into 1-inch slices and serve with pan sauce.

SCANDINAVIAN SUPPER SOUP

In the land of the Midnight Sun, families appreciate steaming bowls of thick pea soup. Your family will, too.

Cook on 190° to 200° for 10 hours,
or on 290° to 300° for 5 hours.
Makes 8 servings.

- 1 package (1 pound) dried yellow split peas
- 6 cups boiling water
- ½ pound lean salt pork
- 3 large carrots, pared and sliced
- 1 large leek, trimmed and sliced
- 1 large onion, chopped (1 cup)
- 1 teaspoon salt
- 1 teaspoon leaf thyme, crumbled
- ¼ teaspoon pepper
- 1 pound frankfurters, scored
  Chopped parsley

1. Pick over peas and rinse under running water; place peas in an electric slow cooker; pour in boiling water; cover. Let stand 1 hour.
2. Score salt pork and push down into peas; add carrots, leek, onion, salt, thyme, pepper and frankfurters; cover.
3. Cook on low (190° to 200°) 10 hours, stirring after 5 hours, if possible, or on high (290° to 300°) 5 hours, stirring after 3 hours, if possible.
4. Ladle soup into soup bowls; sprinkle with chopped parsley.

HARVEST PORK CHOPS

Pork chops are extra moist and juicy when made the slow-cooking way.

Cook on 190° to 200° for 8 hours,
or on 290° to 300° for 4 hours.
Makes 6 servings.

- 1 can (6 ounces) frozen concentrate for pineapple-orange juice
- 3 tablespoons soy sauce
- 2 teaspoons ground ginger
- 1 teaspoon salt
- ½ teaspoon leaf marjoram, crumbled
- 6 loin, rib or shoulder pork chops, cut ¾-inch thick
- 2 acorn squashes
- 3 pickled sweet red peppers, halved

1. Combine unthawed fruit juice, soy sauce, ginger, salt and marjoram in 2-cup measure; let stand.
2. Trim excess fat from chops; brown chops well in remaining fat in a large skillet or an electric slow cooker with a browning unit; remove and reserve. Drain all fat from pan. Stir in fruit juice mixture; bring to boiling, stirring up all the cooked-on bits in bottom of pan.
3. Wash and slice squash into 1-inch thick rings; remove seeds; halve rings.
4. Arrange browned chops and squash rings in slow cooker; pour fruit juice mixture over; cover.
5. Cook on low (190° to 200°) 8 hours, or on high (290° to 300°) 4 hours, or until pork is tender.
6. Put pickled red peppers into slow cooker 5 minutes before serving. Serve with frozen Italian vegetables in cream sauce.

YANKEE BEEF PLATTER

Pot roast on special? Try slow cooking it and notice how much less shrinkage you'll have.

Cook on 190° to 200° for 10 hours,
or on 290° to 300° for 6 hours.
Makes 8 servings.

- 1 boneless rolled chuck roast (about 4 pounds)
- 1 tablespoon minced dried onion
- 2 teaspoons salt
- ½ teaspoon freshly ground pepper
- ⅛ teaspoon ground cloves
- 1 bay leaf
- 1 cup dry red wine
- 1 cup thinly sliced celery
- 2 cloves garlic, sliced
- 1 can condensed onion soup
- 2 tablespoons all-purpose flour
  Braised Leeks (recipe follows)

1. Trim excess fat from beef; pierce meat all over with a fork; place in a large glass or earthenware bowl.
2. Sprinkle with onion, salt, pepper and cloves. Add bay leaf and wine to bowl. Refrigerate, turning meat several times, overnight to marinate.

3. When ready to cook meat, remove from marinade; pat dry with paper towels. Brown in a large skillet or an electric slow cooker with a browning unit.
4. Place beef in slow cooker; stir in marinade, plus celery, garlic and onion soup; cover.
5. Cook on low (190° to 200°) 10 hours, or on high (290° to 300°) 6 hours, or until beef is tender when pierced with a two-tined fork. Remove beef to a heated platter and keep warm.
6. Turn heat control to high (290° to 300°). Combine flour and ¼ cup cold water in a cup; stir into liquid in slow cooker until well-blended; cover; simmer 15 minutes.
7. Carve part of the roast into ¼-inch-thick slices. Arrange slices with rest of roast and BRAISED LEEKS on a large serving platter. Add parsley potatoes and steamed whole carrots, if you wish. Serve gravy separately to spoon over all.
BRAISED LEEKS—Trim roots and about half of the green tops from 1 bunch leeks; split each leek lengthwise; wash well. Arrange pieces, cut-side down, in a large skillet. Add just enough water to cover; bring to boiling; cover. Simmer 5 minutes; drain; return to pan. Add 3 tablespoons butter or margarine and sprinkle with ½ teaspoon each salt and celery salt. Cook slowly, 5 minutes longer, or until leeks are tender.
Suggested Variation: Green onions can be substituted for the leeks; use 2 bunches sliced in 3-inch pieces and cook a total of 6 minutes.

QUICK TIPS

• Garlic is the most powerful of the onion family and gives character to many international dishes. The whole bulb or bud is made up of individual cloves that fit together like orange sections. It is one or a few of these cloves that are listed as ingredients in our recipes. The following are garlic substitutions:
 1 teaspoon garlic salt = 1 clove
 ⅛ teaspoon garlic powder = 1 clove
 5 drops liquid garlic = 1 clove
• For the subtle flavor of garlic in your cooking, place a few halved cloves of garlic in a cup of olive oil or vegetable oil; allow to stand overnight; remove garlic and store flavored oil in a glass jar with a screw top.
• When the recipe calls for just a little chopped onion, cut deep crisscrosses over cut surface of an onion, then slice. Cover remaining onion with plastic wrap and refrigerate.

COUNTRY BAKED BEANS

This is a recipe for the 5-quart slow cookers. If yours is 3½-quart, follow directions for a smaller version below.

Cook on 190° to 200° for 10 hours,
or   on 290° to 300° for 6 hours.
Makes 12 servings.

 1 package (2 pounds) dried pea beans
    Water
 2 medium-size onions, peeled
 8 whole cloves
 ¾ cup light molasses
 2 tablespoons sugar
 1 tablespoon salt
 1 tablespoon dry mustard
 ½ pound lean salt pork

1. Pick over beans and rinse under running water. Cover beans with water in a large kettle. Bring to boiling; cover kettle. Boil 2 minutes; remove from heat; let stand 1 hour; pour into a 5-quart electric slow cooker. (Or soak beans in water in slow cooker overnight.)
2. Stud onions with cloves and hide deep in beans. Stir in molasses, sugar, salt and mustard. Cut salt pork into 8 pieces; lay on top. Pour boiling water over just until it shows above beans; cover.
3. Cook on low (190° to 200°) 10 hours, or on high (290° to 300°) 6 hours, or until beans are very tender.
Suggested Variation: For a 6-serving recipe, use 1 pound beans, 1 medium-size onion, ⅓ cup molasses, 1 tablespoon sugar, 1½ teaspoons each salt and dry mustard and ¼ pound salt pork. The cooking times will be the same.

BEEF AND SPANISH RICE

This is the perfect recipe for a 2½-quart slow cooker.

Cook on 190° to 200° for 8 hours,
or   on 290° to 300° for 4 hours.
Makes 4 servings.

 4 slices bacon, diced
 1 pound ground chuck
 1 egg
 ½ cup soft white bread crumbs (1 slice)
 2 teaspoons salt
 1 large onion, chopped (1 cup)
 ½ cup chopped celery
 1 large green pepper, halved, seeded and chopped
 1 to 3 teaspoons chili powder
 1 cup uncooked rice
 1 can (1 pound) tomatoes
 1 cup water

1. Sauté bacon until crisp in a large skillet; remove and drain on paper towels; reserve for garnish.
2. Mix ground beef lightly with egg, bread crumbs, and 1 teaspoon of the salt until well-blended; shape into 16 balls.
3. Brown in drippings in same pan.

4. Stir onion, celery, green pepper and chili powder into pan; sauté just until vegetables are soft.
5. Stir in rice, tomatoes, water and remaining salt; bring to boiling, stirring lightly to blend well.
6. Place mixture in a 2½-quart electric slow cooker; cover.
7. Cook on low (190° to 200°) 8 hours, or on high (290° to 300°) 4 hours, stirring, if possible halfway through cooking, or until rice is tender and liquid is almost absorbed. Top with cooked bacon. Serve with an avocado and grapefruit section salad, if you wish.

BROWN OCTOBER STEW

Have you ever tried beef and lamb combined? It is delicious in this specially seasoned sauce.

Cook on 190° to 200° for 8 hours,
or   on 290° to 300° for 4 hours.
Makes 8 servings.

 1½ pounds boneless beef chuck, cubed
 1½ pounds boneless lamb shoulder, cubed
  3 tablespoons all-purpose flour
  2 teaspoons salt
  ½ teaspoon pepper
  ¼ teaspoon ground ginger
  3 tablespoons olive oil or vegetable oil
  1 large onion, chopped (1 cup)
  2 cloves garlic, minced
  2 cups mixed vegetable juice (from a 46-ounce can)
  1 one-inch stick cinnamon
  1 medium-size eggplant, cut in large cubes (do not pare)
  4 medium-size carrots, pared and quartered
  4 stalks celery, cut in 3-inch pieces
  8 large dried prunes
  8 large dried apricot halves

1. Trim all excess fat from beef and lamb; shake beef and lamb cubes in a mixture of flour, salt, pepper and ginger in a plastic bag to coat evenly; brown quickly in oil in a large skillet or an electric slow cooker with a browning unit; remove and reserve; sauté onion and garlic in pan drippings until soft.
2. Place meat in slow cooker with onion and garlic. Pour mixed vegetable juice over; add cinnamon stick; arrange eggplant, carrots and celery around meat; cover cooker.
3. Cook on low (190° to 200°) 8 hours, or on high (290° to 300°) 4 hours, or until meats and vegetables are tender. Stir in prunes and apricots; cook 15 minutes longer. Serve with fluffy baked potatoes, if you wish, to soak up all the delicious gravy. A crisp Waldorf salad with green celery and chopped walnuts would make a perfect accompaniment.
COOK'S TIP: Use your toaster oven to bake potatoes or any go-along vegetable.

RAGOÛT OF LAMB

When you add quick-cooking tapioca to your slow cooker recipe at the beginning, you have a thickened gravy or sauce at the end with no additional work.

Cook on 190° to 200° for 7 hours,
or   on 290° to 300° for 4 hours.
Makes 6 servings.

- 2 pounds lean boneless lamb, cubed
- ¼ cup all-purpose flour
- 2 teaspoons salt
- ½ teaspoon pepper
- 2 tablespoons butter or margarine
- 2 tablespoons olive oil or vegetable oil
- 1 can condensed chicken broth
- ¼ cup dry white wine
- 4 large carrots, pared and cut into sticks
- 4 medium-size onions, peeled and quartered
- 3 tomatoes, peeled and chopped
- 1 clove garlic, minced
- 2 tablespoons chopped parsley
- 1 tablespoon quick-cooking tapioca
- 1 bay leaf
- ½ teaspoon caraway seeds, crushed

1. Trim excess fat from lamb; shake in a plastic bag with flour, 1 teaspoon of the salt and ¼ teaspoon of the pepper.
2. Heat butter or margarine and oil in a large skillet or an electric slow cooker with a browning unit; brown lamb, a few pieces at a time, in hot fat.
3. Combine browned lamb, chicken broth, wine, carrots, onions, tomatoes, garlic, parsley, tapioca, bay leaf, caraway seeds and remaining 1 teaspoon salt and ¼ teaspoon pepper in slow cooker; cover.
4. Cook on low (190° to 200°) for 7 hours, or on high (290° to 300°) for 4 hours, or until lamb is tender. Taste and season with additional salt and pepper, if you wish. Serve with mashed potatoes and a crisp salad with a mint-lemon dressing, if you wish.

CHICKEN ORLÉANS

This suberb dish is named for the Ile d'Orléans near Quebec City, which is noted for its apple orchards.

Cook on 190° to 200° for 8 hours,
or   on 290° to 300° for 4 hours.
Makes 4 servings.

- 1 broiler-fryer (about 3 pounds)
  Apple brandy or Cognac
- 1 teaspoon salt
- ¼ teaspoon freshly ground pepper
- 2 cups diced white bread (4 slices)
- ½ cup chopped celery
- ½ cup chopped apple
- ¼ cup raisins
- 3 tablespoons butter or margarine, melted
- 1 tablespoon chopped parsley
- ½ teaspoon leaf thyme, crumbled

- 3 slices thickly-sliced bacon
- 6 medium-size apples
- 1 cup light cream

1. Rub chicken inside and out with brandy or Cognac, then with salt and pepper.
2. Combine bread cubes, celery, chopped apple, raisins, butter or margarine, parsley and thyme in a bowl.
3. Stuff chicken with dressing, packing lightly, Skewer neck skin to back; twist the wing tips flat against skewered neck skin; tie legs to tail with kitchen string.
4. Place bacon in a saucepan; cover with water. Bring to boiling; lower heat and simmer 10 minutes. Dry on paper towels.
5. Fry bacon lightly in an electric slow cooker with a browning unit or a large kettle. Remove bacon and reserve. Brown chicken on all sides in bacon drippings; remove and keep warm.
6. Quarter, core and thickly slice apples; brown lightly in pan drippings. Place chicken on top of apple slices in slow cooker; lay bacon slices over chicken; cover cooker.
7. Cook on low (190° to 200°) 8 hours, or on high (290° to 300°) 4 hours, or until chicken is tender. Pour cream and 2 tablespoons apple brandy or Cognac over, just before serving.

QUICK TIPS

PRESSURE COOKING DRIED BEANS AND LENTILS:
When making casseroles, you may wish to cut down on cooking time by precooking dried beans in a 4- to 6-quart pressure cooker. To do so, soak 1 package (1 pound) dried beans overnight in a large bowl with ¼ cup vegetable oil, 1 tablespoon salt and enough water to cover beans. In the morning, drain beans; place in pressure cooker with enough water to cover. (Important: Never fill pressure cooker more than half way; the beans will gain bulk as they absorb water.) Cover cooker securely; set pressure regulator on vent pipe; cook, according to the table below:

Black Beans	35 minutes
Blackeyed Peas	20 minutes
Great Northern Beans	30 minutes
Kidney Beans	25 minutes
Lentils	20 minutes
Lima Beans	25 minutes
Navy Beans	30 minutes
Pinto Beans	25 minutes

HUNGARIAN LAMB

Eggplant and sour cream give the distinctive flavors to this dish.

Cook on 190° to 200° for 8 hours,
or   on 290° to 300° for 4 hours.
Makes 6 servings.

- 1½ pounds lean lamb shoulder, cubed
- ¼ cup all-purpose flour
- 1 teaspoon salt
- ¼ teaspoon pepper
- 3 tablespoons vegetable oil
- 2 envelopes instant beef broth
- 1½ cups water
- 12 small white onions, peeled
- 1 small eggplant, pared and diced
- 1 cup dairy sour cream
- 1 teaspoon paprika

1. Shake lamb with flour, salt and pepper in a plastic bag to coat well.
2. Brown quickly in oil in an electric slow cooker with a browning unit, or a large skillet; stir in instant beef broth and water; bring to boiling.
3. Combine lamb mixture, onions and eggplant in slow cooker; cover.
4. Cook on low (190° to 200°) 8 hours, or on high (290° to 300°) 4 hours, or until lamb and onions are tender.
5. Stir 1 cup of hot mixture into sour cream and paprika in a medium-size bowl; return to cooker and stir to blend.

INDIANA BEAN BAKE

Midwest USA contributes this hearty favorite with its big mealy lima beans.

Cook on 190° to 200° for 10 hours,
or   on 290° to 300° for 5 hours.
Makes 8 servings.

- 1 package (1 pound) dried lima, navy or Great Northern beans
- 6 cups water
- 2 teaspoons salt
- 2 tablespoons vegetable oil
- 1 large onion, chopped (1 cup)
- ½ cup light molasses
- ½ cup chili sauce
- ¼ cup prepared mustard

1. Pick over beans and rinse under running water. Combine beans and water in a large kettle. Bring to boiling; cover kettle; boil 2 minutes; remove from heat; let stand 1 hour; add salt. (Or soak beans in water in an electric slow cooker overnight at room temperature.)
2. Heat oil in a medium-size skillet; sauté onion until soft; stir in molasses, chili sauce and mustard; bring to boiling.
3. Drain beans, reserving liquid. Combine beans and onion mixture in an electric slow cooker; add enough reserved liquid to just cover the beans; cover cooker.
4. Cook on low (190° to 200°) 10 hours, or on high (290° to 300°) 5 hours, or until beans are very tender. Serve with slices of sharp cheese on homemade bread.

BOSTON BAKED BEANS

Every Bostonian has a favorite bean recipe. This is ours.

Cook on 190° to 200° for 10 hours,
or   on 290° to 300° for 5 hours.
Makes 8 servings.

  1 **package (1 pound) dried pea beans**
  6 **cups water**
  1 **large onion, chopped (1 cup)**
 ½ **cup firmly-packed dark brown sugar**
 ½ **cup light molasses**
  2 **tablespoons prepared mustard**
  1 **teaspoon salt**
 ½ **pound lean salt pork, thinly sliced**

1. Pick over beans and rinse. Place in a large kettle and add water. Bring to boiling; boil 2 minutes; remove kettle from heat and cover. Allow to stand 1 hour. (Or soak beans in water in an electric slow cooker overnight at room temperature.)
2. Place beans and liquid in slow cooker with onion, brown sugar, molasses, mustard and salt. Stir to blend well; push salt pork slices into mixture; cover.
3. Cook on low (190° to 200°) 10 hours, stirring after 4 hours, if possible, or on high (290° to 300°) 5 hours, stirring after 3 hours, if possible, or until beans are tender. Serve with coleslaw.

SOUTH PACIFIC POT ROAST

It's the subtle flavor of lemon juice that gives this beef dish a distinctive flavor.

Cook on 190° to 200° for 10 hours,
or   on 290° to 300° for 5 hours.
Makes 8 servings.

    1 **blade-bone chuck beef roast**
        (about 4 pounds)
    2 **tablespoons lemon juice**
    6 **slices bacon, diced**
    1 **medium-size onion, chopped**
        (½ cup)
    1 **clove garlic, minced**
 1½ **cups orange juice**
    1 **large tomato, peeled and chopped**
        OR:1 can (8 ounces) tomatoes
    1 **tablespoon salt**
    1 **teaspoon leaf thyme, crumbled**
   ½ **teaspoon ground nutmeg**
   ¼ **teaspoon pepper**
    1 **bay leaf**
    3 **tablespoons cornstarch**
   ⅓ **cup cold water**

1. Trim excess fat from roast. Brush beef all over with lemon juice; let stand about 5 minutes.
2. Sauté bacon with onion and garlic until bacon is crisp in a large skillet or an electric slow cooker with a browning unit; remove and reserve.
3. Brown beef in bacon drippings in same pan on all sides.
4. Place beef in slow cooker; add bacon

and onion mixture, orange juice, tomato, salt, thyme, nutmeg, pepper and bay leaf; cover cooker.
5. Cook on low (190° to 200°) 10 hours, or on high (290° to 300°) 5 hours, or until meat is tender when pierced with a two-tined fork; remove to heated platter and keep warm while making gravy.
6. Turn heat control to high (290° to 300°). Combine cornstarch and cold water in a cup; stir into liquid in slow cooker; cover; cook 15 minutes. Pass in heated gravy boat. Serve meat with steamed acorn squash, if you wish.

OSSOBUCO

From Milan comes this recipe for veal shanks braised in a rich tomato sauce. Can't find veal shanks? Why not try well-trimmed lamb shanks?

Cook on 190° to 200° for 8 hours,
or   on 290° to 300° for 4 hours.
Makes 6 servings.

  4 **pounds meaty veal shanks, cut into**
     3-inch pieces
  2 **teaspoons salt**
 ½ **teaspoon freshly ground pepper**
     Flour
 ¼ **cup olive oil or vegetable oil**
     Soffrito
  2 **tablespoons butter or margarine**
  1 **large onion, finely chopped (1 cup)**
  1 **leek, washed and sliced**
  1 **large carrot, pared and finely**
     chopped
  1 **stalk celery, finely chopped**
  1 **clove garlic, finely minced**
  1 **can (1 pound, 1 ounce) Italian**
     tomatoes
  1 **cup dry red wine**
  1 **tablespoon chopped fresh basil**
     OR: 1 teaspoon leaf basil, crumbled
  2 **bay leaves**
     Gremolata (recipe follows)

1. Tie veal shanks around the middle with kitchen string to hold the meat in place. Rub with salt and pepper; coat well with flour on wax paper, shaking off excess.
2. Heat oil until almost smoking in a large skillet or an electric slow cooker with a browning unit; brown shanks, a few at a time until golden-brown; remove from cooker and keep warm.
3. Make Soffrito: Add butter or margarine to drippings in pan; sauté onion, leek, carrot, celery and garlic until soft; stir in Italian tomatoes, breaking up with the back of the spoon, add wine, basil and bay leaves, bring to boiling. Lower heat and simmer 5 minutes.
4. Stand veal shanks upright in slow cooker and spoon Soffrito over, if using a skillet. Cover slow cooker.
5. Cook on low (190° to 200°) 8 hours, or on high (290° to 300°) 4 hours, or until meat is very tender and almost falling off bones. Taste sauce and add more salt and pepper, if desired. Sprinkle GREMOLATA

on top and serve with Risotto, if you wish.
GREMOLATA (The traditional topping for OSSOBUCO)—Combine 1 tablespoon finely chopped Italian parsley, 1 teaspoon grated lemon peel (just the zest, not the white part) and 1 small clove garlic, finely minced. Sprinkle over OSSOBUCO. just as casserole is removed from the oven.
HOSTESS TIP: OSSOBUCO can be made the day ahead and baked. Cool; cover and refrigerate. One hour before serving, remove from refrigerator; skim any fat on the surface of the sauce; cover casserole. Place in oven; turn oven control to moderate (350°) and bake 55 minutes, or until bubbly-hot. Make GREMOLATA while the casserole bakes, and sprinkle over top just before serving.

NANTUCKET PORK PLATTER

Smoked pork boneless butt or cottage roll simmers with winter vegetables for a new twist on New England Boiled Dinner.

Cook on 190° to 200° for 10 hours,
or   on 290° to 300° for 5 hours.
Makes 6 servings.

  1 **smoked boneless shoulder butt or**
     cottage roll (about 2 pounds)
  4 **large boiling potatoes, pared and**
     quartered
  1 **pound Brussel sprouts, washed and**
     trimmed
     OR: 1 package (10 ounces) frozen
     Brussel sprouts, thawed
  6 **medium-size carrots, pared and cut**
     into 2-inch pieces
  1 **large onion, chopped (1 cup)**
  6 **whole cloves**
  1 **bay leaf**
  3 **cups water**
     Raisin Sauce (recipe follows)

1. Place meat, potatoes, Brussel sprouts, carrots, onion, cloves and bay leaf in an electric slow cooker; pour water over; cover.
2. Cook on low (190° to 200°) 10 hours, or on high (290° to 300°) 5 hours, or until meat and vegetables are tender when pierced with a two-tined fork.
3. Lift meat from broth, saving 1 cup of the broth; place meat on a heated serving platter. Arrange vegetables around edge; keep hot while making sauce. An apple cobbler with pour cream would make a perfect ending to this Yankee meal.
RAISIN SAUCE: Makes 1½ cups. Combine 3 tablespoons brown sugar, 1 tablespoon cornstarch, ⅛ teaspoon cinnamon, and ⅛ teaspoon ground allspice in a small saucepan; stir in the 1 cup saved broth, 1 tablespoon bottled lemon juice and ¼ cup raisins. Cook, stirring constantly, until sauce thickens and bubbles 1 minute; stir in 1 tablespoon butter or margarine until melted. Serve hot in heated gravy boat.

CHILI CHICKEN

Serve this chili in deep soup bowls, but add forks as well as spoons. A salad of shredded lettuce and toasted corn chips are the perfect accompaniment.

Cook on 290° to 300° for 2 hours, then on 190° to 200° for 6 hours. Makes 4 servings.

    1 broiler-fryer, cut up
          (about 3 pounds)
    ¼ cup all-purpose flour
    2½ teaspoons salt
    ¼ teaspoon pepper
    ¼ cup vegetable shortening
    1 large onion, chopped (1 cup)
    1 clove garlic, minced
    1 green pepper, halved, seeded and
          chopped
    1 can (1 pound) tomatoes
    1 can condensed chicken broth
    1 cup chopped ripe olives
    ½ cup yellow cornmeal
    ¼ cup tomato paste
    1 to 3 tablespoons chili powder
    1 teaspoon sugar

1. Shake chicken pieces in a mixture of flour, 1½ teaspoons of the salt and pepper in a plastic bag to coat evenly.
2. Brown chicken pieces in shortening in a large skillet or an electric slow cooker with a browning unit; remove and reserve. Pour off all but 2 tablespoons of the pan drippings. Sauté onion, garlic and green pepper in drippings until soft.
3. Place chicken pieces and onion mixture in slow cooker. Combine tomatoes, chicken broth, olives, cornmeal, tomato paste, chili powder, remaining 1 teaspoon salt and sugar in a medium size bowl, pour over chicken; cover.
4. Cook on high (290° to 300°) for 2 hours. Stir at this point. Turn heat control to low (190° to 200°) and cook 6 hours longer, or until chicken is tender.

SOUTHAMPTON VEAL ROLL

An elegant choice when veal is on special at the market.

Cook on 190° to 200° for 8 hours, or on 290° to 300° for 4 hours. Makes 8 servings.

    1 rolled boned veal
          shoulder, (about 3 to 4 pounds)
    2 tablespoons all-purpose flour
    1 tablespoon dry mustard
    1 tablespoon brown sugar
    2 teaspoons salt
    1 teaspoon poultry seasoning
    ⅛ teaspoon pepper
    2 tablespoons vegetable oil
    1 large onion, chopped (1 cup)
    ¼ cup chopped celery
    2 tablespoons chopped parsley
    ½ cup dry white wine or water
    2 teaspoons prepared horseradish

1. Trim excess fat from veal; rub well with mixture of flour, mustard, brown sugar, salt, poultry seasoning and pepper to coat evenly.
2. Brown meat slowly in oil in a large skillet or an electric slow cooker with a browning unit.
3. Place veal in slow cooker with onion, celery, parsley and wine or water; cover.
4. Cook on low (190° to 200°) 8 hours, or on high (290° to 300°) 4 hours, or until veal is tender when pierced with a two-tined fork; place on heated serving platter and keep warm.
5. Turn heat control to high (290° to 300°). Combine ¼ cup all-purpose flour and ½ cup cold water in a cup; stir into liquid in slow cooker; cover; cook 15 minutes. Stir in horseradish and serve in heated gravy boat. Serve veal with asparagus spears and potato balls.

QUICK TIPS

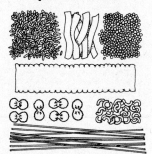

POPULAR PASTAS: There is an immense variety of pastas suitable for use in casserole cooking. Here are a few:
Pastina—Tiny pasta bits good for use in soups or as baby food.
Spaghetti—The long, round, thin favorite perfect with many kinds of sauces.
Spaghettini—A thinner version of spaghetti most prefered in Italy.
Ziti—Thicker hollow tubes of pasta that can be served in baked dishes.
Elbow Macaroni—Curved hollow tubes most widely used in cold salads, casseroles and macaroni and cheese combinations.
Fettuccine—The Romans call it Tagliatelle. Excellent with clam sauce or just butter and grated cheese.
Linguine—Long flattened macaroni served with cheese, clam or pesto sauces and grated Parmesan.
Alphabets—Letters made of pasta used mainly in soups.
Lasagna—Flat, wide ribbons of pasta that come plain, or with a ruffled edge, in white or spinach-flavored green.
Macaroni Wheels—Pasta shaped like tiny wagon wheels, used in soups and casseroles, and a favorite with children.
Ravioli—Pillow-shaped pasta filled with either meat or cheese. They are first boiled, then combined with a tomato or cheese sauce.
Farfalle—Pasta shaped like small bows, used in soups, casseroles, or served alone with sauce.
Shells—This pasta comes in small, medium and large sizes. The small ones can be sauced, the larger ones can be stuffed with meat or cheese and baked.
Manicotti—Large pasta tubes, first filled with meat or cheese, then baked in a tomato sauce.
Cannelloni—Fat, ridged tubes of pasta also suitable for stuffing.
Vermicelli—Called 'angel hair' for its fine delicate texture, this spaghetti is best when served with a clam sauce.
Rigati—Tubes of pasta more finely ridged than Cannelloni, usually stuffed and baked in tomato sauce.
Tortellini—These small pasta rings are filled with meat and dished up in clear consommé, or with a creamy cheese sauce, and topped with Parmesan.
Noodles—Flat strands of pasta rich in eggs, and often served as an accompaniment to casserole main dishes such as Beef Stroganoff. Available in plain (white) and spinach (green).

PHILADELPHIA PEPPER POT

A tripe soup that is said to go back to the time of George Washington.

Cook on 190° to 200° for 8 hours, or on 290° to 300° for 4 hours. Makes 8 servings.

    ½ cup diced salt pork
    3 leeks, trimmed and chopped
    1 medium-size onion, chopped
          (½ cup)
    3 green peppers, halved, seeded and
          chopped
    1 cup chopped celery
    1 tablespoon all-purpose flour
    1 cup diced parboiled tripe
    2 medium-size potatoes, pared
          and diced
    3 small tomatoes, peeled and
          chopped
    8 cups Classic Beef Broth (recipe
          page 36)
       OR: 8 envelopes or teaspoons
          instant beef broth and 8 cups
          water
    1 tablespoon salt
    ½ teaspoon freshly ground pepper
    1 bay leaf
    ¼ teaspoon leaf thyme, crumbled

1. Brown salt pork in a large skillet or an electric slow cooker with a browning unit; remove and reserve.
2. Sauté leeks, onion and green peppers in pan drippings until soft; stir in flour and cook 2 minutes.
3. Combine mixture with salt pork and tripe in an electric slow cooker. Add potatoes, tomatoes, CLASSIC BEEF BROTH or instant beef broth and water, salt, pepper, bay leaf and thyme; cover.
4. Cook on low (190° to 200°) 8 hours, or on high (290° to 300°) 4 hours, or until broth is rich and flavorful. Taste and season with salt and pepper, if you wish. Serve with refrigerated flaky biscuits and a hearty Burgundy, if you wish.

CASSOULET

A classic lamb and dried bean dish from the Languedoc region of France.

Cook on 190° to 200° for 10 hours, or on 290° to 300° for 5 hours. Makes 6 servings.

1 package (1 pound) large dried lima beans
4 cups water
1 pound lean boneless lamb shoulder, cubed
2 tablespoons vegetable oil
1 large onion, chopped (1 cup)
1 clove garlic, minced
1 can (1 pound) tomatoes
¼ cup light molasses
2 teaspoons salt
1 cup grated raw carrot
4 slices bacon

1. Pick over beans and rinse. Cover lima beans with water in a large kettle; bring to boiling; cover; cook 2 minutes. Remove from heat; let stand 1 hour.
2. While beans cook, brown lamb in oil in an electric slow cooker with a browning unit, or a large skillet. Push to one side of pan and sauté onion and garlic lightly; stir in tomatoes and molasses; cover; simmer 15 minutes.
3. Combine beans and liquid with lamb mixture in kettle; add salt, grated carrot and bacon (do not cut slices); cover; cook 1 hour, or until skins of beans burst when you blow on a few in a spoon; place in cooker; cover.
4. Cook on low (190° to 200°) 10 hours, or on high (290° to 300°) 5 hours, or until beans are tender. Serve with a platter of cold marinated vegetables and a fresh fruit dessert for a truly French meal.

SPAGHETTI TAORMINA

Slow cookers are great for making spaghetti sauce because the longer they cook, the better the flavor. Try this sauce on lasagna, too.

Cook on 190° to 200° for 8 hours, or on 290° to 300° for 4 hours. Makes 6 servings.

1 medium-size onion, chopped (½ cup)
1 medium-size green pepper, halved, seeded and chopped
½ clove garlic, crushed
3 tablespoons olive oil or vegetable oil
½ pound lean chuck, cubed
¼ pound beef liver, cut in ½-inch cubes
1 can (2 pounds, 3 ounces) Italian tomatoes
1 can (6 ounces) tomato paste
3 cups water
2 teaspoons salt
2 teaspoons mixed Italian herbs, crumbled
¼ teaspoon pepper

1 package (1 pound) linguini or thin spaghetti
Grated Parmesan cheese

1. Sauté onion, green pepper and garlic lightly in oil in a large skillet or an electric slow cooker with a browning unit. Push to one side; add beef and brown lightly, then add and brown liver.
2. Stir in tomatoes, tomato paste, water, salt, Italian herbs and pepper. Ladle into slow cooker; cover.
3. Cook on low (190° to 200°) 8 hours, or on high (290° to 300°) 4 hours. Remove cover and turn heat control to high (290° to 300°). Simmer while cooking pasta.
4. Cook pasta following label directions; drain; place in a deep heated platter. Spoon sauce over and toss just before serving; sprinkle with freshly grated Parmesan cheese. Pass any extra sauce in a heated gravy boat.

QUICK TIPS

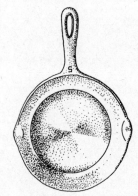

A chef's tricks for browning meat:
• Choose a large heavy skillet, if you haven't a heavy flame-proof casserole.
• Wipe meat on paper towels before hand. If using seasoned flour, coat just before cooking.
• Heat fat or oil in pan until almost smoking. Add just enough of the meat to cover the bottom of the pan, leaving a little space around each piece.
• Brown one side until beads of blood show around the bone or on the upper surface, then turn with tongs; repeat until evenly brown on all sides.
• Remove meat with tongs to a bowl or the lid of the casserole while browning remaining pieces; then add browned meat and any juices to casserole.
• For an extra meaty-flavor, pour all fat from pan and add a little water, wine or broth; heat and stir to get all the cooked-on juices from the bottom of pan; add the liquid in casserole.
• For quicker clean-ups:
To remove rust build-up on a cast iron casserole. Wash it in sudsy water; scrub with a steel wool pad, then rub with vegetable oil. Place on a cooky sheet in a warm oven, turn off oven and keep in overnight. In the morning, rub off the excess oil. Repeat as needed.

ELDORADO LAMB PILAF

Try lamb baked with bulgur wheat and rice, Conquistador-style.

Cook on 190° to 200° for 8 hours, or on 290° to 300° for 4 hours. Makes 6 servings.

1 pound ground lamb
1 large onion, chopped (1 cup)
1 clove garlic, minced
1 teaspoon curry powder
1 teaspoon leaf rosemary, crumbled
2 envelopes or teaspoons instant chicken broth
2 teaspoons salt
4 cups water
1 cup bulgur wheat (from a 1-pound package)
¾ cup uncooked long-grain rice
Chopped fresh mint or parsley

1. Brown lamb in an 8-cup flame-proof casserole or a large skillet; break into chunks; remove with a slotted spoon; reserve. Pour off all but 3 tablespoons of the pan drippings.
2. Sauté onion and garlic in drippings until soft; stir in curry powder and rosemary; cook 2 minutes; add instant chicken broth, salt and water. Bring to boiling; stir in bulgur wheat and rice. Spoon mixture into slow cooker; cover.
3. Cook on low (190° to 200°) 8 hours, stirring after 4 hours, if possible or on high (290° to 300°) 4 hours, stirring after 3 hours, if possible, or until liquid is absorbed and rice is tender. Sprinkle with chopped mint or parsley, just before serving.

NORTHWEST PEARS AND BEANS

West Coast women have been adding fruit to their bean pots for years.

Cook on 190° to 200° 8 hours, or on 290° to 300° 4 hours. Makes 4 servings.

2 cans (1 pound each) lima beans OR: 2 cans (1 pound, 4 ounces each) white kidney beans (cannellini)
1 can (1 pound) sliced pears
3 tablespoons brown sugar
1 tablespoon minced dried onion
1 tablespoon chili sauce
1 package (8 ounces) heat-and-serve sausage links

1. Spoon beans into a 2½ quart electric slow cooker; add pear slices, ¼ cup pear syrup, brown sugar, onion and chili sauce; stir gently, just to blend. Arrange sausage links on top; cover.
2. Cook on low (190° to 200°) 8 hours, or on high (290° to 300°) 4 hours, or until you are ready to serve dinner.
COOK'S TIP: The electric slow cooker is a perfect way to add extra flavor to canned beans by slowing cooking with extras such as mustard, brown sugar and chili sauce.

CLAY POT COOKERY

Besides the modern electric slow cooker method, there is another, quite ancient, yet modern way to cook foods, using an unglazed terra cotta clay pot. Clay pot cooking dates back to the ancient Etruscans, who discovered the advantages of using the readily available Roman terra cotta in very hot earthen ovens. Clay pots must first be soaked in water 10 to 15 minutes before cooking time to allow the porous material to absorb a good amount of water. Once in the oven, the moisture from the pot walls provides a constant self-basting for the food within. The food is permeated with savory cooking juices, and the natural food value is preserved as well. Twentieth century calorie-counters will also appreciate yet another clay pot feature; you can cook completely fat-free, without losing an ounce of flavor.

To try wet-clay cooking, start with an unglazed terra cotta pot with a lid. Note: You must use an unglazed terra cotta pot that has been manufactured as a cooking utensil. Other unglazed terra cotta containers are made of clay with a high lead content. If you were to use one of these containers, your family could suffer from lead poisoning. (Many suitable clay pots are imported from Germany and France in a variety of shapes and sizes.) Choose one that is quite porous, and has been fired at a very high temperature.

In preparing the recipes on these two pages, follow these basic steps for flavorful, self-basting casseroles:

PREPARATION
• Invest in a good meat thermometer (the flat dial type is best). The thermometer will be a much better guide to the internal temperature of the cooking meat or poultry, than a cooking time.
• First, soak the pot, top and bottom, in water for 10 to 15 minutes before adding food.
• Place the food in the pot; cover. Then set the pot in the center of the rack in a cold oven (do not preheat).

COOKING
• Since the cooking time can vary according to the size of the pot and the type and amount of food being cooked, place the meat thermometer inside the meat for an accurate reading. Cooking time should end just before the thermometer reaches the desired temperature.
• Use heavy oven mitts when handling the pot after cooking, as oven temperature in clay pot cooking averages about 450°.
• Place hot clay pot and top on a dry, room temperature heat-proof surface. Never set a hot pot on a cold or wet surface, as it may crack.

• For sauces, simply drain juices from the clay pot into a pitcher, and follow directions on page 74 for making sauces. If you wish to brown meat, slide the uncovered pot with meat back into the oven while making sauce, and cook 10 minutes longer, or until slightly browned.
• Clay pot cooking requires more than the usual amount of salt. However, you may omit salt if cooking corned beef or seasoning with soy sauce, as both have high salt contents to begin with.

CLAY POT CARE
• Always clean a clay pot with hot water and a stiff wire brush. Never use soap or detergent as they may clog the pores and give food a soapy taste.
• Store the pot with its lid upside down in the base in a place where air circulates freely. Stuffy, closed-in storage areas may cause the pot to retain odors that might affect the taste of foods cooked in the clay pot.
• Repair cracks and chips in clay pots with household epoxy, and dry the mend in a warm (100°) oven for 3 to 4 hours.

FLOUNDER AND EGGPLANT BAKE

Delicate fish fillets are layered with eggplant and sauce for a delectable and decidedly Continental treat.

Bake at 450° for 45 minutes.
Makes 6 servings.

---

1 large eggplant, sliced and pared
⅓ cup olive oil or vegetable oil
1 large green pepper, halved, seeded and sliced
2 cloves garlic, minced
1 teaspoon leaf oregano, crumbled
1 teaspoon salt
¼ teaspoon freshly ground pepper
1 can (8 ounces) tomato sauce
2 pounds fresh flounder fillets
OR: 2 packages (1 pound each) frozen flounder fillets, thawed
⅓ cup grated Parmesan cheese
3 tablespoons packaged fine dry bread crumbs
2 tablespoons butter or margarine

1. Do not preheat oven.
2. Soak a 2- to 6-serving-size unglazed clay pot, top and bottom, in water for 15 minutes before using.
3. Brown eggplant slices in part of the oil in a large skillet, adding half to drained clay pot; sauté green pepper slices and garlic in remaining oil; place over eggplant in pot.
4. Season with half of a mixture of oregano, salt and pepper; drizzle half the tomato sauce over; place fish fillets in clay pot; top with remaining eggplant slices, tomato sauce and seasoning mixture for another layer.
5. Combine cheese and crumbs in a cup; sprinkle over top and dot with butter or margarine; cover with drained top.
6. Place covered clay pot in the center

of the rack in a cold oven.
7. Turn oven control to very hot (450°). Bake 45 minutes, or until eggplant is tender. Serve with French bread to soak up fish and vegetable juices.

BOMBAY CHICKEN IN A POT

This is a curry with a difference—the roasting chicken is kept whole, but the clay pot allows the flavor to penetrate into the bird.

Bake at 450° for 1 hour, 45 minutes.
Makes 6 servings.

---

1 roasting chicken (about 5 pounds)
1 large apple, quartered
1 large onion, quartered
¼ cup raisins
3 tablespoons softened butter or margarine
2 to 3 tablespoons curry powder
1 tablespoon all-purpose flour
1 teaspoon salt
2 tablespoons vegetable oil
6 large carrots, pared and cut into sticks
1 large green pepper, halved, seeded and cut into strips
½ cup frozen chopped onion
½ cup cocktail sherry
¼ cup chicken broth

1. Do not preheat oven.
2. Soak a 2-to 6-serving-size unglazed clay pot, top and bottom, in water for 15 minutes before using.
3. Stuff chicken with quartered apple and onion and raisins. Skewer neck skin to back; twist the wing tips flat against skewered neck skin; tie the legs to tail with kitchen string.
4. Combine butter or margarine, curry powder, flour and salt in a cup. Rub mixture all over chicken. Insert a flat dial meat thermometer, if you wish.
5. Sauté carrots, green pepper and onion in oil in a large skillet; spoon into bottom of drained clay pot; place coated chicken on vegetables; add sherry and broth; cover with drained top.
6. Place covered clay pot in the center of the rack in a cold oven.
7. Turn oven control to very hot (450°). Bake 1 hour, 30 minutes, or until meat thermometer registers 180°. Remove top; baste chicken with juices in bottom.
8. Bake 15 minutes longer, basting several times, or until chicken is golden brown. Remove chicken from clay pot; cut off string and place in the center of a heated platter lined with fluffy rice; keep warm.
9. Strain juices in clay pot into a large saucepan; bring to boiling. Combine 3 tablespoons cornstarch and ⅓ cup cold water in a cup until smooth; stir into bubbling liquid; cook, stirring constantly, until mixture thickens and bubbles 1 minute; pour into a gravy boat.
10. Serve chicken with gravy and an assortment of curry condiments.

CLAY POT BAKED FISH

This is a delicious way to cook a whole piece of fish—and the sauce is superb.

Bake at 450° for 45 minutes.
Makes 6 servings.

- 1 large lemon, thinly sliced
- 1 piece fresh swordfish, salmon or bass (about 3 pounds)
- 3 tablespoons olive oil or vegetable oil
- 1 tablespoon chopped fresh dill OR: 1 teaspoon dillweed
- 1 tablespoon chopped parsley
- 1 teaspoon seasoned salt Freshly ground pepper
- 1 large onion, thinly sliced
- 1 large tomato, thinly sliced
- 12 small new potatoes, parboiled
- 3 tablespoons dry white wine

1. <u>Do not</u> preheat oven.
2. Soak a 2- to 6-serving-size unglazed clay pot, top and bottom, in water for 15 minutes before using.
3. Arrange lemon slices in drained clay pot to cover bottom; lay fish over lemon slices; brush with oil; sprinkle with dill, parsley, seasoned salt and pepper; cover with a layer of onion slices, then tomato slices. Arrange potatoes around edge of clay pot and drizzle wine over; cover with drained top.
4. Place covered clay pot in the center of the rack in a cold oven.
5. Turn oven control to very hot (450°). Bake 45 minutes, or just until fish is done. Remove fish and vegetables to a heated serving platter. Pour juices into a small bowl and stir in ¼ cup dairy sour cream; sprinkle top with chopped fresh dill, if you wish.

SWEET AND SPICY CORNED BEEF

This is corned beef with a difference. The clay pot cooking adds special flavor and moisture to the meat.

Bake at 450° for 2 hours, 20 minutes, then at 400° for 20 minutes.
Makes 8 servings.

- 1 "mild cure" corned beef brisket (about 4 pounds)
- 1 large onion, sliced
- 1 large carrot, pared and sliced
- 1 clove garlic, minced
- 1 tablespoon mixed pickling spices
- 1 cup boiling water
- ⅓ cup firmly packed brown sugar
- ¼ cup wine vinegar
- ¼ cup catsup
- 1 tablespoon butter or margarine
- 1 tablespoon hot prepared mustard Whole cloves

1. <u>Do not</u> preheat oven.
2. Soak a 2- to 6-serving size unglazed clay pot, top and bottom, in water for 15 minutes before using.
3. Place corned beef in drained clay pot

bottom and insert a flat dial meat thermometer, if you wish. Top with onion and carrot slices and garlic; sprinkle with mixed pickling spices; pour boiling water over; cover.
4. Place covered clay pot in the center of the rack in a cold oven.
5. Turn oven control to very hot (450°). Bake 2 hours, 20 minutes, or until meat thermometer registers 160°; lower oven temperature to hot (400°).
6. While meat cooks, combine brown sugar, wine vinegar, catsup, butter or margarine and mustard in a small saucepan; bring to boiling; reduce heat and simmer 5 minutes to blend flavors.
7. Remove corned beef from clay pot; drain liquid from pot; remove any vegetables or spices adhering to meat and stud the top of corned beef with cloves.
8. Return corned beef to clay pot; pour sauce over; do not cover pot.
9. Bake in hot oven (400°) 20 minutes, basting several times with sauce. Carve meat on a wooden carving board; place on heated serving platter and spoon sauce over; serve immediately.

HAWAIIAN BARBECUED SPARERIBS

If you like very crisp ribs, you can place the glazed ribs on a broiler pan and broil for 8 to 10 minutes at the end of the clay pot cooking time.

Bake at 450° for 2 hours.
Makes 8 servings.

Sauce
- 1 cup cider vinegar
- 1 cup sugar
- 1 cup orange juice
- ½ cup soy sauce
- ½ cup catsup
- 1 tablespoon minced dried onion
- 1 clove garlic, minced Few drops bottled red-pepper seasoning
- 3 tablespoons cornstarch

Meat
- 4 pounds spareribs
- 1 teaspoon salt
- ½ teaspoon coarsely ground pepper
- 1 can (13¼ ounces) pineapple chunks, drained
- 1 large green pepper, halved, seeded and chopped
- 1 tomato, cut into eighths
- 1 California orange, chopped

1. <u>Do not</u> preheat oven.
2. Soak a 2- to 6-serving-size unglazed clay pot, top and bottom, in water for 15 minutes before using.
3. Combine vinegar, sugar, ¾ cup of the orange juice, soy sauce, catsup, onion, garlic and red-pepper seasoning in a medium-size saucepan; bring to boiling; simmer 10 minutes. Stir cornstarch into remaining ¼ cup orange juice until smooth; pour into saucepan; cook, stirring constantly, until sauce thickens and bubbles 1 minute.

4. Trim excess fat from spareribs and cut into serving-size pieces; season with salt and pepper; brush well with sauce; place in the bottom of drained clay pot; pour over about 1 cup of the remaining sauce; cover with drained top.
5. Place covered clay pot in the center of the rack in a cold oven.
6. Turn oven control to very hot (450°). Bake 1 hour; remove cover, arrange pineapple chunks, green pepper, tomato and orange over ribs; cover.
7. Bake 45 minutes longer, or until ribs are tender; uncover; bake 15 minutes longer, or until top is golden. Place ribs on heated serving platter. Combine pot juices with remaining sauce in pan and heat until bubbly. Pass with spareribs. Serve with OVEN BAKED RICE PILAF (recipe, page 84), if you wish.

PARTY RAGOÛT

No need to brown the meats for this party-size lamb and veal dish.

Bake at 450° for 1 hour, 30 minutes.
Makes 12 servings.

- 2 pounds lean boneless lamb shoulder, cubed
- 2 pounds lean boneless veal shoulder, cubed
- 18 small new potatoes, pared
- 1 Bermuda onion, sliced thin
- 4 cups shredded lettuce
- 1 tablespoon salt
- ¼ teaspoon pepper
- 1 teaspoon leaf rosemary, crumbled
- 3 envelopes instant chicken broth
- 4 cups hot water
- 3 cups frozen peas, cooked (from a 1½-pound bag)
- 4 medium-size yellow squash, tipped, sliced and cooked
- ⅓ cup cornstarch
- ¾ cup water

1. <u>Do not</u> preheat oven.
2. Soak a 6- to 8-serving size unglazed clay pot, top and bottom, in water for 15 minutes before using.
3. Combine meats with potatoes, onion, lettuce, salt, pepper and rosemary in clay pot.
4. Dissolve instant chicken broth in hot water in 4-cup measure; pour over meats and vegetables; cover with drained top.
5. Place covered clay pot in the center of the rack in a cold oven.
6. Turn oven control to very hot (450°). Bake 1 hour, 30 minutes, or until meat and vegetables are tender; remove meats and vegetables with a slotted spoon to the center of a heated serving platter; arrange cooked peas and squash in piles; keep warm while making sauce.
7. Strain juices in clay pot into a large saucepan; bring to boiling. Combine cornstarch and ¾ cup water in a cup; stir in bubbling liquid; cook, stirring constantly, until mixture thickens and bubbles 1 minute; spoon over platter.

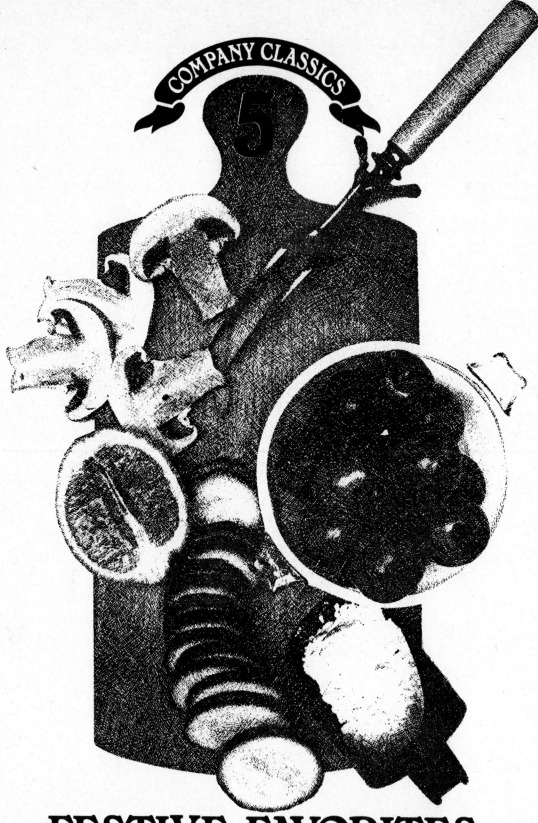

FESTIVE FAVORITES

Entertaining is supposed to be just that—entertaining. And in this chapter, it's practically guaranteed, because we've taken some of the world's classic dishes and adapted them to the company casserole in festive new ways. So relax, and visit with your guests—there's nothing last-minute to do but enjoy yourself.

The French taught the
world the way to cook
'en casserole'. Beef
Burgundy is a classic
example of this type
of cooking. Presented
with a bouquet of
fresh vegetables,
it is on page 67.

Once a basic cook-
ing technique is
learned, you can
apply it to other
foods. Lamb Burgundy
(Recipe is on Page 67.)
is a variation of Beef
Burgundy with a
different variety of
garden vegetables.

BRUNSWICK STEW

Meaty pieces of chicken bake lazily with corn and limas in a peppy tomato sauce. Pictured on page 2.

Bake at 350° for 1 hour.
Makes 8 servings.

- 2 broiler-fryers, cut up (about 2½ pounds each)
- ½ cup all-purpose flour
- 1 envelope (about 1 ounce) herb salad dressing mix
- ¼ cup vegetable shortening
- 1 large onion, chopped (1 cup)
- 1 can (1 pound, 12 ounces) tomatoes Few drops bottled red-pepper seasoning
- 4 ears corn, husked and with silks removed, cut into 1-inch pieces OR: 1 package (10 ounces) frozen whole-kernel corn
- 1 package (10 ounces) frozen Fordhook lima beans
- 1 pound okra, washed (optional)

1. Shake chicken in mixture of flour and salad dressing mix in a plastic bag to coat well; reserve any remaining flour.
2. Brown chicken, a few pieces at a time, in vegetable shortening in a 12-cup flame-proof casserole or a large skillet; remove and reserve.
3. Sauté onion in same casserole; blend in reserved seasoned flour; stir in tomatoes and red-pepper seasoning. Bring to boiling, stirring constantly.
4. Return chicken to casserole; add corn, lima beans and okra. Spoon sauce over; cover. (If using a skillet, place browned chicken, corn, limas and okra in 12-cup casserole; add sauce; cover.)
5. Bake in moderate oven (350°) 1 hour, or until chicken is tender.

CHICKEN CACCIATORE

This is the Italian version of Chicken Hunter-style, with pieces of chicken and green pepper in wine-tomato sauce.

Bake at 350° for 1 hour.
Makes 6 servings.

- 2 broiler-fryers, cut up (about 2½ pounds each)
- ⅓ cup all-purpose flour
- 2 teaspoons salt
- ¼ teaspoon freshly ground pepper
- 1 large onion, chopped (1 cup)
- 2 cloves garlic, minced
- ¼ cup olive oil or vegetable oil
- 2 large green peppers, halved, seeded and cut into chunks
- 1 cup dry white wine
- 1 can (1 pound, 1 ounce) Italian tomatoes
  Hot linguini or thin spaghetti

1. Shake chicken pieces in a mixture of flour, salt and pepper in a plastic bag.
2. Sauté onion and garlic in 2 table-spoons of the oil until soft in a 12-cup flame-proof casserole or a large skillet. Remove with slotted spoon and reserve.
3. Brown chicken, a few pieces at a time, adding remaining oil as needed; remove and reserve. Sauté peppers in drippings until soft; stir in wine; bring to boiling, stirring constantly. Return onion and garlic to casserole; stir in tomatoes.
4. Return chicken to casserole; spoon sauce over chicken; cover. (If using a skillet, arrange chicken in a 12-cup casserole and spoon sauce over; cover.)
5. Bake in moderate oven (350°) 1 hour, or until chicken is tender. Sprinkle with chopped parsley, if you wish. Serve with linguini or thin spaghetti.

Suggested Variation: CHICKEN CHAS-SEUR: This is the French version of chicken Hunter-style. It is named in honor of the famous Chasseur cavalry regiments who hunted for their food. Follow the recipe for CHICKEN CAC-CIATORE. except use ½ cup chopped shallots or green onions instead of the yellow onions. Substitute 1 cup brown gravy for the wine and ½ pound sliced fresh mushrooms or 1 can (6 ounces) sliced mushrooms for the green peppers. Sprinkle with chopped parsley and serve with boiled potatoes.

BEEF BURGUNDY

This recipe takes a little time, but the resulting dish will make your reputation as a cook. Shown on page 65.

Bake at 325° for 1 hour, 30 minutes.
Makes 8 servings.

- ½ pound thickly sliced bacon
- 2 pounds lean boneless beef chuck, cubed
- 1 large onion, chopped (1 cup)
- 1 cup finely chopped carrot
- 1 cup finely chopped celery
- 2 cloves garlic, minced
- 2 teaspoons salt
- 1 teaspoon leaf thyme, crumbled
- 1 bay leaf
- ¼ teaspoon pepper
- 2 cups dry red wine
- ¼ cup all-purpose flour
- 1 pound mushrooms
- 1 bunch leeks
- 1 bunch carrots
- ¼ cup (½ stick) butter or margarine
- 1 envelope or teaspoon instant chicken broth
- ½ cup water

1. Cut bacon into 1-inch pieces; place in a saucepan; cover with water. Bring to boiling; lower heat and simmer 10 minutes. Dry bacon on paper towels. Fry bacon until crisp in a 12-cup flame-proof casserole or a large kettle. Remove bacon and reserve; pour off all but 2 tablespoons of the bacon fat into a cup.
2. Brown beef, a few pieces at a time, in casserole; remove and reserve. Sau-té onion, carrot, celery and garlic in pan drippings, adding more bacon fat, if needed; stir in salt, thyme, bay leaf and pepper; return beef to casserole; add wine; bring slowly to boiling; cover. (If using a kettle; spoon mixture into a 12-cup casserole; cover.)
3. Bake in slow oven (325°) 1 hour, 30 minutes, or until beef is very tender; remove bay leaf. Remove beef from liquid with slotted spoon; keep warm.
4. Pour liquid, half at a time, into an electric blender container; add flour, half at a time; cover container; whirl at high speed 1 minute. (Or press liquid through a sieve with a wooden spoon into a bowl; cool slightly; stir in flour until well-blended.) Return liquid to flame-proof casserole or a large saucepan; bring to boiling. Cook, stirring constant-ly, until sauce thickens and bubbles 3 minutes longer.
5. While beef cooks, wipe mushrooms with damp paper towel; flute mushrooms by marking the center of each cap with a small, sharp paring knife. Starting there, make a curved cut, about ⅛-inch deep, to edge. Repeat around to make 8 even cuts. Now make a second cut just behind each line, angling knife so you can lift out a narrow strip; set mush-rooms aside. Cut leeks into 5-inch pieces and halve; wash well to remove all sand; pare and cut carrots into 5-inch pieces.
6. Sauté mushrooms in butter or marga-rine in a large skillet; remove; sauté leeks lightly in skillet; remove; add carrots and sauté 5 minutes; add instant chicken broth and water to skillet; cover and simmer 15 minutes, or until carrots are almost tender; push to one side. Return mushrooms and leeks to skillet. Cover; simmer 10 minutes, or until vegetables are tender.
7. Return beef and sauce to casserole. Surround with vegetables; sprinkle beef with cooked bacon. Pour vegetable liq-uid in skillet over and serve.

HOSTESS TIP: The finished dish can be held in a very slow oven (275°) for 1 hour before serving. Beef can be cooked and sauce made the day before. Cool, then cover and refrigerate. One hour before serving, place casserole in oven. Set oven control on moderate (350°) and bake 1 hour, or until bubbly-hot, while preparing vegetables.

Suggested Variation: For LAMB BURGUN-DY (shown on page 66): Use 2 pounds cubed lamb shoulder instead of beef. Use leaf rosemary instead of thyme. You may wish to choose a lighter dry red wine, such as a California Grenache or a Grenache Noir. Substitute 2 bunches green onion, 1 package (10 ounces) frozen wax beans and 1 package (10 ounces) frozen asparagus spears for the leeks and carrots in the recipe. Canned sliced mushrooms can be used for the fresh. Sauté trimmed green onions in butter; in a large skillet 2 minutes; push to one side; add wax beans and asparagus in separate piles; add instant chicken broth and water; cover; simmer 5 minutes longer.

MOUSSAKA A LA GRECQUE

A classic Greek dish of lamb and eggplant with a velvety sauce topping.

Bake at 350° for 45 minutes.
Makes 8 servings.

- **2** medium-size eggplants (about 1 pound each)
- **⅓** cup olive oil or vegetable oil
- **1** pound ground lamb
- **1** large onion, chopped (1 cup)
- **1** clove garlic, minced
- **1** can (8 ounces) tomato sauce
- **1** teaspoon salt
  Dash ground cinnamon
  Rich Cheese Sauce (recipe follows)

1. Trim eggplants; cut into ¼-inch slices; pare slices. Sauté, part at a time, until soft, in part of the oil in a large skillet. Drain on paper towels; reserve. Repeat with remaining eggplant and oil.
2. Brown lamb in same skillet; remove from skillet with a slotted spoon and crumble into a medium-size bowl. Drain all but 2 tablespoons drippings from skillet. Add onion and garlic; sauté until soft, but not browned.
3. Return crumbled lamb to skillet; stir in tomato sauce, salt and cinnamon. Bring to boiling; reduce heat; cover. Simmer 5 minutes to blend flavors.
4. Spread ⅓ of tomato sauce on bottom of a 12-cup shallow casserole; layer eggplant slices and remaining sauce. Top with RICH CHEESE SAUCE.
5. Bake in moderate oven (350°) 45 minutes, or until sauce is light brown. Let stand 10 minutes before cutting.
HOSTESS TIP: Eggplant and lamb sauce can be made ahead and layered in casserole, covered and refrigerated. About 1½ hours before serving, remove cover; spoon RICH CHEESE SAUCE over. Place casserole in oven. Turn oven control to moderate (350°) and bake 1 hour, 30 minutes, or until bubbly-hot.

RICH CHEESE SAUCE

Makes about 4 cups.

- **¼** cup (½ stick) butter or margarine
- **¼** cup all-purpose flour
  Dash ground nutmeg
- **1** tall can evaporated milk
- **½** cup water
- **1** envelope or teaspoon instant chicken broth
- **2** eggs, beaten
- **1** container (15 ounces) ricotta cheese
  OR: 1 container (1 pound) cream-style cottage cheese
- **½** cup grated Parmesan cheese

1. Melt butter or margarine in a medium-size saucepan; stir in flour and nutmeg. Cook, stirring constantly, just until bubbly. Stir in evaporated milk, water and instant chicken broth; continue cooking and stirring until mixture thickens and bubbles 3 minutes.
2. Slowly beat half of the hot mixture into beaten eggs in a small bowl, then beat back into hot mixture in saucepan. Cook, stirring constantly, 1 minute. Remove from heat; stir in cheeses until well-blended.

NAVARIN PRINTANIER

A savory lamb stew that's abundant with spring vegetables.

Bake at 350° for 1 hour, 45 minutes.
Makes 8 servings.

- **3** tablespoons olive oil or vegetable oil
- **2** pounds lean boneless lamb, cubed
- **3** tablespoons finely chopped shallots
  OR: 1 small onion, chopped (¼ cup)
- **1** clove garlic, minced
- **3** tablespoons all-purpose flour
- **1** can condensed beef broth
- **1** can (1 pound) tomatoes
  OR: 2 large tomatoes, peeled and chopped
- **2** teaspoons salt
- **1** teaspoon leaf thyme, crumbled
- **2** tablespoons butter or margarine
- **12** small white onions, peeled
- **4** small white turnips, pared and quartered
- **4** large carrots, pared and cut into 2-inch lengths
- **12** small new potatoes, peeled
- **1** cup frozen peas (from a 1½-pound bag)
- **2** tablespoons chopped parsley

1. Heat oil in a 16-cup flame-proof casserole or a large skillet; brown lamb, a few pieces at a time. Remove pieces, as they brown, and keep warm.
2. Pour off all but 1 tablespoon fat from casserole; add shallots or onion and garlic; sauté, stirring often, 5 minutes, or until golden-brown. Return lamb to pan. Sprinkle flour over meat; cook over moderate heat, stirring and tossing meat with wooden spoon until evenly coated, about 5 minutes. (This browns the flour slightly.) Stir in beef broth and tomatoes; bring to boiling, stirring constantly to loosen browned bits. Stir in salt and thyme. Bring to boiling; cover. (If using a skillet, spoon mixture into a 16-cup casserole; cover.)
3. Bake in moderate oven (350°) 1 hour; skim off fat, if any.
4. While lamb simmers, heat butter or margarine in a skillet; add onions, turnips and carrots. Sauté, stirring 10 minutes, or until vegetables are browned and glazed.
5. Add glazed vegetables and potatoes to lamb, pushing them down under liquid; cover; simmer for 40 minutes longer, or until lamb and vegetables are tender. Stir in peas and parsley; cover; simmer 5 minutes longer. Sprinkle with additional parsley, if you wish.

POULET EN CASSEROLE

This chicken dish is a standard on the menus of many gourmet restaurants.

Bake at 350° for 1 hour.
Makes 4 servings.

- **1** broiler-fryer (about 3 pounds)
- **2** tablespoons vegetable oil
- **2** tablespoons butter or margarine
- **2** cloves garlic, minced
- **12** whole white onions, peeled
- **12** small white potatoes, pared
- **4** large carrots, pared and quartered
- **1** cup dry white wine
- **2** teaspoons salt
- **1** teaspoon leaf rosemary, crumbled
- **½** teaspoon freshly ground pepper
- **1** can condensed chicken broth

1. Wash and dry chicken; skewer neck skin to back; twist the wing tips flat against skewered neck skin; tie the legs to tail with kitchen string.
2. Heat oil and butter or margarine with the minced garlic in a 12-cup flame-proof casserole or a large kettle. Brown chicken in the hot fat; remove.
3. Sauté onions, potatoes and carrots in drippings; remove and reserve. Stir wine, salt, rosemary and pepper into casserole and bring to boiling, scraping up all the cooked-on juices from bottom of casserole; stir in chicken broth; return chicken to casserole; surround with browned vegetables; cover. (If using a kettle, place chicken in a 12-cup casserole; surround with browned vegetables; pour sauce over; cover.)
5. Bake in moderate oven (350°) 1 hour, basting several times with casserole juices, or until chicken is tender. Garnish with a bouquet of parsley and serve with a chilled dry white wine, such as a Chablis, and chunks of crusty French bread, if you wish.

CURRIED HAM SOUFFLÉ

Here's an ideal way to use bits and pieces of cooked ham.

Bake at 350° for 1 hour.
Makes 6 servings.

- **¼** cup (½ stick) butter or margarine
- **1** small onion, grated
- **¼** cup all-purpose flour
- **1** teaspoon curry powder
- **¼** teaspoon salt
  Dash pepper
- **2** cups milk
- **½** cup soft white bread crumbs (1 slice)
- **2** cups ground cooked ham (about 1 pound)
- **4** eggs, separated

1. Melt butter or margarine in a large saucepan. Sauté onion until soft; blend in flour, curry powder, salt and pepper; cook, stirring constantly, just until mixture bubbles.

2. Stir in milk; continue cooking and stirring until sauce thickens and bubbles 3 minutes. Beat in bread crumbs until well-blended; remove from heat; stir in ground ham.

3. Beat egg yolks slightly with a fork in a small bowl; blend in a few spoonfuls of the hot ham mixture, then quickly stir back into saucepan, blending well.

4. Beat egg whites until they form soft peaks in a large bowl; pour ham mixture over and gently fold in with a wire whip until no streaks of white remain.

5. Spoon into an ungreased 6-cup soufflé dish or straight-sided casserole. Set dish in a shallow baking pan; place on oven shelf; pour boiling water into pan to a depth of 1 inch.

6. Bake in moderate oven (350°) 1 hour, or until soufflé is puffy-light and firm in center. Serve at once with a crisp tossed greens salad.

OXTAIL RAGOÛT

Oxtails simmer in a hearty sauce. Good eating at moderate cost.

Bake at 375° for 2 hours.
Makes 8 servings.

- 4 pounds oxtails, cut up
- ½ cup all-purpose flour
- 1 teaspoon salt
- 1 teaspcon leaf savory, crumbled
- ¼ teaspoon freshly ground pepper
- ¼ cup vegetable oil
- 1 large onion, chopped (1 cup)
- 1 clove garlic, minced
- 1 can (12 ounces) carrot juice
- 1½ cups water
- ½ cup dry red wine
- 1 bay leaf

1. Shake oxtail pieces in a mixture of flour, salt, savory and pepper in a plastic bag to coat well; reserve remaining seasoned flour.

2. Brown oxtails, a few pieces at a time, in oil in a 10-cup flame-proof casserole or a large skillet; remove and keep warm.

3. Stir onion and garlic into drippings; sauté until soft. Stir in reserved seasoned flour; cook, stirring just until bubbly. Stir in carrot juice, water and wine; continue cooking and stirring, until gravy thickens and bubbles 3 minutes. Return oxtails to casserole; add bay leaf; cover. (If using a skillet, place browned oxtails in a 10-cup casserole; pour sauce over; add bay leaf; cover.)

4. Bake in moderate oven (375°) 2 hours, or until meat separates easily from bones. Remove bay leaf.

5. Ladle ragoût into soup plates; serve with French bread, if you wish.
HOSTESS TIP: OXTAIL RAGOUT is more delicious if made the day ahead. Cook, then cover and refrigerate. About 1 hour before serving, remove any fat from surface of sauce. Place in oven. Turn oven control to moderate (350°); bake 1 hour, or until bubbly-hot.

CHICKEN TETRAZZINI

This glamorous dish was created in honor of the famous opera singer, Madame Tetrazzini.

Bake at 400° for 20 minutes.
Makes 8 servings.

- 1 package (1 pound) linguini or spaghetti
- 4 cups diced cooked chicken
- 6 tablespoons (¾ stick) butter or margarine
- ½ pound mushrooms, sliced
  OR: 1 can (3 or 4 ounces) sliced mushrooms
- ¼ cup all-purpose flour
- 1 teaspoon salt
- 1½ cups light cream
  OR: 1 tall can evaporated milk
- 1 envelope or teaspoon instant chicken broth
- 1⅓ cups water
- ½ cup grated Romano cheese

1. Cook pasta in a kettle, following label directions; drain; return to kettle.

2. While pasta cooks, sauté chicken slightly in butter or margarine in a large saucepan; remove with a slotted spoon to a large bowl.

3. Sauté sliced mushrooms in same pan until soft; remove to a large metal second bowl. (If using canned sliced mushrooms, drain liquid into a cup.)

4. Blend flour and salt into drippings in saucepan; cook, stirring constantly, just until bubbly. Stir in cream or evaporated milk, mushroom liquid, if used, instant chicken broth and water. Continue cooking and stirring until sauce thickens and bubbles 3 minutes.

5. Add 2 cups of the sauce and half of the mushrooms to drained pasta; toss to mix. Spoon into a 10-cup shallow casserole, pressing pasta up sides of casserole to leave a hollow in center. Add chicken and remaining mushrooms to remaining sauce, blending well. Spoon into hollow in pasta. Sprinkle with Romano cheese.

6. Bake in hot oven (400°) 20 minutes, or until bubbly-hot.

CIPÂTÉ STEW

Inspired by a French-Canadian dish, a trio of meats is simmered in a savory sauce and topped with flaky biscuits.

Bake at 350° for 1 hour,
then at 425° for 15 minutes.
Makes 8 servings.

- 1 broiler-fryer, cut up (about 2½ pounds)
- ⅓ cup all-purpose flour
- 2 teaspoons seasoned salt
- ½ teaspoon lemon-flavored pepper
- 2 tablespoons vegetable oil
- 1 pound boneless chuck, cubed
- ½ pound cooked ham, cubed

- 1 pound small white onions, peeled
- 4 cups water
- 1 can (3 or 4 ounces) sliced mushrooms
- 2 tablespoons bottled steak sauce
- 1 package (9 ounces) frozen cut green beans
  Flaky Biscuits (recipe follows)

1. Shake chicken pieces in a mixture of flour, salt and pepper in a plastic bag.

2. Brown chicken, a few pieces at a time, in oil in a large skillet and place in a 12-cup casserole. Shake beef and ham cubes in seasoned flour. Brown in pan drippings; add to casserole. Brown onions lightly in pan drippings; add to casserole.

3. Stir any remaining seasoned flour into pan drippings; add water; cook, stirring constantly, until mixture thickens and bubbles; add mushrooms with liquid and bottled steak sauce. Pour over meats in casserole; cover. Bake in moderate oven (350°) 1 hour, or until meats are tender.

5. Increase oven temperature to hot (425°); stir cut green beans into meats. Arrange FLAKY BISCUITS in a pretty pattern on top of casserole. Bake 15 minutes, or until biscuits are golden-brown. Serve with glasses of chilled apple cider, if you wish.

FLAKY BISCUITS

Makes 8 biscuits.
- 2 cups sifted all-purpose flour
- 2 teaspoons baking powder
- 1 teaspoon salt
- ¼ cup vegetable shortening
- ¾ cup milk

1. Sift flour, baking powder and salt into a medium-size bowl; cut in shortening with a pastry blender. Stir in milk, just until blended.

2. Turn out onto a lightly floured pastry board and knead several times. Pat out to a ½-inch-thick round. Cut into 8 rounds with a 2½-inch biscuit cutter. Reroll any trims and cut into additional biscuits to be baked on a cooky sheet, along with stew.

FRENCH MARKET FONDUE

The trick to making this casserole puff handsomely is to make ahead and chill before baking. Overnight is best.

Bake at 350° for 45 minutes.
Makes 6 servings.

  1 large Bermuda onion, sliced and separated into rings
  ¼ cup (½ stick) butter or margarine
 12 slices French bread (about ½ loaf)
  3 eggs
  3 cups milk
  1 tablespoon prepared mustard
  1 teaspoon Worcestershire sauce
  ½ teaspoon salt
  2 cups shredded Swiss cheese (8 ounces)
  ¼ cup grated Parmesan cheese
     Paprika

1. Sauté onion rings just until soft in 2 tablespoons of the butter or margarine in a large skillet.
2. While onion cooks, spread bread slices with remaining 2 tablespoons butter or margarine.
3. Beat eggs with milk, mustard, Worcestershire sauce and salt in a medium-size bowl until blended.
4. Place 4 slices of bread in a single layer in buttered 8-cup shallow casserole; top with layers of one third of the onion rings and Swiss cheese; repeat to make 2 more layers; top with Parmesan cheese.
5. Pour egg mixture over; sprinkle with paprika. Cover; chill at least 4 hours, or even overnight; uncover.
6. Bake in moderate oven (350°) 45 minutes, or until puffed and golden. Serve at once with a tossed green salad and a dry white wine.

CHOUCROUTE A L'ALSACIENNE

Sauerkraut and sausages simmer in beef broth and beer—the makings of a memorable meal.

Bake at 350° for 2 hours.
Makes 8 servings.

  2 cans (1 pound, 11 ounces each) sauerkraut
  2 large carrots, pared and chopped
  1 large onion, chopped (1 cup)
  ¼ cup (½ stick) butter or margarine
  1 teaspoon caraway seeds
  1 can condensed beef broth
  1 can (12 ounces) beer
  2 kielbasa sausages (about 1 pound each)
     OR: 2 pounds knackwurst
  6 sprigs parsley
  4 peppercorns
  1 bay leaf

1. Soak sauerkraut 5 minutes in a large pan of cold water; change the water twice; drain well.
2. Sauté carrot and onion until soft in butter or margarine in a 12-cup flame-proof casserole or a large skillet. Stir in drained sauerkraut and caraway seeds; toss to blend well. (If using a skillet, spoon mixture into a 12-cup casserole.)
3. Pour beef broth and beer over sauerkraut. Score sausages and place over sauerkraut.
4. Tie a "bouquet garni" of parsley, peppercorns and bay leaf in cheesecloth. Push under liquid in casserole; cover.
5. Bake in moderate oven (350°) 2 hours, or until liquid is absorbed. Discard "bouquet garni." Serve with cold beer.

SCANDINAVIAN RAGOÛT

Dill and sour cream flavor this festive casserole.

Bake at 350° for 30 minutes.
Makes 6 servings.

  1 pound ground beef
  ½ pound ground veal
     OR: ½ pound ground pork
  1 cup soft white bread crumbs (2 slices)
  1 egg
  1 small can evaporated milk
     OR: ⅔ cup milk
  1 tablespoon grated onion
  1 teaspoon grated lemon rind
 1½ teaspoons salt
  ¼ cup vegetable shortening
  1 medium-size cucumber, halved lengthwise and sliced ¼-inch thick
  1 can (12 or 16 ounces) whole-kernel corn
  1 tablespoon all-purpose flour
  ¼ teaspoon pepper
  1 container (8 ounces) dairy sour cream
  1 tablespoon chopped fresh dill
     OR: 1 teaspoon dried dillweed
  3 cups frozen French fries (from a 2-pound bag)

1. Mix beef, veal or pork, bread crumbs, egg, milk, onion, lemon rind and 1 teaspoon of the salt in a large bowl; shape into 36 small balls. Brown on all sides in shortening in a 12-cup flame-proof casserole or a large skillet; remove and keep warm.
2. Boil cucumber slices in salted water 3 minutes; drain, pouring liquid into a 1-cup measure. Drain corn, adding liquid from can to cucumber water, if needed, to make 1 cup.
3. Blend flour, remaining ½ teaspoon salt and pepper into fat in casserole; slowly stir in the 1 cup of saved vegetable liquid. Cook, stirring constantly, until sauce thickens and bubbles 3 minutes. Stir ½ cup of hot mixture into sour cream and dill in a small bowl; return to casserole and cook slowly 1 minute.
4. Pile browned meat balls in one part of casserole, frozen French fries into a second part; toss cooked cucumber with drained corn and spoon into third section; pour sauce over; cover. (If using a skillet, pile food in a 12-cup casserole and pour sauce over; cover.)
5. Bake in moderate oven (350°) 30 minutes, or until bubbly-hot.

OLD ENGLISH BEEF CASSEROLE

Fill a casserole with all the good ingredients of a stew. Top with pastry and it's a dish fit for a king. Shown on page 71.

Bake at 350° for 2 hours,
then at 425° for 20 minutes.
Makes 8 servings.

 2½ pounds boneless chuck, cubed
  3 tablespoons vegetable oil
  1 pound small white onions, peeled
  1 pound carrots, pared and cut into 2-inch pieces
  ½ pound mushrooms, sliced
     OR: 1 can (6 ounces) sliced mushrooms
  1 envelope (about 1 ounce) brown gravy mix
  1 cup water
  ¼ cup chopped parsley
  1 tablespoon Worcestershire sauce
  2 teaspoons salt
  1 teaspoon leaf basil, crumbled
  ½ teaspoon leaf thyme, crumbled
  ½ teaspoon pepper
  1 package piecrust mix
  1 egg

1. Brown beef in hot oil in a large skillet, a few pieces at a time; remove to a 10-cup deep casserole.
2. Brown onions and carrots in pan drippings; add to casserole with mushrooms and liquid, if canned mushrooms are used.
3. Stir brown gravy mix and water into skillet; cook, stirring up all the cooked-on juices, until mixture bubbles; stir in parsley, Worcestershire sauce, salt, basil, thyme and pepper; pour over meat and vegetables; cover.
4. Bake in moderate oven (350°) 2 hours, or until beef is tender. Increase oven temperature to hot (425°).
5. Prepare piecrust mix, following label directions. Roll out onto a lightly floured pastry cloth or board just to the size of the casserole. (You should make a cardboard pattern before filling the casserole.) Cut diamond shapes with a truffle cutter or sharp-tipped knife in pastry to make a pretty pattern.
6. Roll pastry lightly over rolling pin and transfer to casserole. Beat egg with 1 teaspoon water in a cup; brush over pastry; arrange cut-outs on pastry; brush with egg mixture.
7. Bake in hot oven (425°) for 20 minutes, or until pastry is golden.
Suggested Variation: For BEEF AND KIDNEY CASSEROLE. soak 1 beef kidney overnight in lightly salted water to cover in a glass bowl in the refrigerator. In the morning drain and cut into ½-inch slices. Cut out tubes and white membrane. Dice meat and brown with beef.

Light, tender pastry always adds the crowning touch to favorite dishes, such as this Old English Beef Casserole. Unbaked pastry gets an egg wash and decorative steam vents for a truly professional touch. (Recipe on page 70.)

casseroles for a company meal

You can be the carefree hostess when you make the main course a casserole. From left to right: Pasta Rolls Florentine, Party Paella and Chicken Marengo. All bake unattended while you stay with your guests. Recipes begin on page 76.

Learning the secrets to making superb sauces are part of a chef's training. You, too, will be delighted with how perfectly your sauces come out every time, because, once mastered, the same techniques are used to make white sauce, soufflé bases, gravies and dessert sauces. Follow our simple step-by-step photographs.

MAKE A SAUCE

1. Melt butter or margarine until bubbly in a heavy saucepan over medium-high heat. 2. Then add the flour, salt and other dry seasonings. Stir mixture well with a wire whip until it is smooth and again begins to bubble and cooks 1 minute. 3. Add milk, broth or other liquid and whip briskly until mixture is very smooth. 4. Cook and stir constantly, until the sauce thickens and bubbles 3 minutes. 5. When using leeks, onions, or shallots, add to the saucepan while the butter melts. Sauté, stirring constantly, so that the onions do not brown. If using curry powder or chili powder in a sauce, cook in the hot butter a few minutes before adding flour. 6. Stir shredded cheese or liquid seasonings into the sauce after it has bubbled 3 minutes, just until smooth and well-blended. Cover surface with plastic wrap until ready to serve.

BECHAMEL SAUCE

Makes about 3 cups.

- 3 cups light cream
  OR: 3 cups milk
- 1 bay leaf
- ⅓ cup butter or margarine
- ⅓ cup all-purpose flour
- 2 envelopes or teaspoons instant chicken broth
- 1 teaspoon salt
- ¼ teaspoon white pepper
  Dash nutmeg

1. Scald cream or milk with bay leaf in a small saucepan; let stand 5 minutes; remove bay leaf.
2. Melt butter or margarine in a medium-size saucepan; stir in flour; cook, stirring constantly, until mixture bubbles.
3. Stir in scalded cream or milk, instant chicken broth, salt, pepper and nutmeg. Continue cooking and stirring until sauce thickens and bubbles 3 minutes. This sauce is excellent on lasagna, ravioli, canneloni and other pasta dishes.

WHITE CLAM SAUCE

Makes 3 cups.

- 1 medium-size onion, chopped (½ cup)
- 1 clove garlic, minced
- ¼ cup olive oil or vegetable oil
- 2 cans (8 ounces each) minced clams
- ¼ cup white cooking wine
- ½ cup chopped parsley

1. Sauté onion and garlic in oil until soft in a medium-size saucepan. Add clams with liquid, wine and parsley; cook over low heat, just until hot.
2. For a special sauce; cool mixture slightly and place in electric-blender container; cover. Whirl 30 seconds. Reheat before serving. Serve over spaghetti, maruzzelle or fettuccine.

HOMEMADE TOMATO SAUCE

Makes about 5 cups.

- 1 large onion, chopped (1 cup)
- 1 clove garlic, minced
- ¼ cup olive oil or vegetable oil
- 1 can (2 pounds, 3 ounces) Italian tomatoes
- 1 can (6 ounces) tomato paste
- 2 teaspoons leaf basil, crumbled
- 1 teaspoon salt
- 1 cup water

1. Sauté onion and garlic in oil until soft in a large saucepan; stir in tomatoes, tomato paste, basil, salt and water.
2. Bring to bubbling; reduce heat; simmer, uncovered, stirring frequently, 45 minutes, or until sauce has thickened.
3. Pour into clean jars; cover; cool; refrigerate. Use within 2 weeks.

SPEEDY SAUSAGE SAUCE

Makes 3 cups.

- ½ pound sweet Italian sausages
- 1 jar (24 ounces) meatless spaghetti sauce
- ¼ cup chopped parsley

1. Cut sausages into ½-inch slices. Cook slowly until well done in a medium-size skillet; drain off fat.
2. Add spaghetti sauce and parsley to sausage; bring to bubbling; reduce heat. Simmer 5 minutes to blend flavors.

TOMATO-MEAT SAUCE

Makes about 4 cups.

- 1 pound ground beef
- 2 tablespoons olive oil or vegetable oil
- 1 envelope (1½ ounces) spaghetti sauce mix
- 1 can (2 pounds, 3 ounces) Italian tomatoes
- ¼ cup red cooking wine
- ¼ cup chopped parsley

1. Brown meat in oil in a large skillet; remove with slotted spoon; drain off all but 2 tablespoons fat.
2. Stir spaghetti sauce mix, tomatoes, wine and parsley into drippings in skillet. Heat until bubbly-hot; add meat; reduce heat; simmer 25 minutes.

ZUCCHINI-TOMATO SAUCE

Makes 3 cups.

- 1 large onion, chopped (1 cup)
- 1 clove garlic, minced
- 1 pound zucchini, trimmed and chopped
- ¼ cup olive oil or vegetable oil
- 2 large ripe tomatoes, peeled and chopped
- 2 teaspoons leaf basil, crumbled
- 1½ teaspoons salt
- ¼ teaspoon pepper
  Dash sugar

1. Sauté onion, garlic and zucchini in oil until soft in a medium-size saucepan; stir in tomatoes, basil, salt, pepper, and sugar until well-blended.
2. Heat to bubbling; simmer 30 minutes, or until sauce thickens slightly. Serve with fettuccelle or spaghetti.

QUICK TIPS

- Don't let unused olives or pimientos spoil. Instead, cover with vinegar in a glass jar, screw top on tightly; refrigerate until needed.
- Save those snack food tag-ends. Crush the last of pretzels, potato chips or crackers and use as a casserole topping.
- To give fish a fresh flavor, soak it in salted warm water for 5 minutes; dry on paper towels, then add to your recipe.

Casserole dishes are available in a multitude of sizes, shapes and materials. Here are a few of the basic types, as well as recommendations for their care and use:

- Freezer-to-oven casseroles are those made of glass-ceramic material. The most versatile of containers, these casseroles may be used on a range burner, in the oven, or under the broiler. Don't worry about placing a still-frozen casserole in a hot oven—this space age material can withstand the most drastic changes in temperature. Clean these glass-ceramic casseroles with dish detergent and water, and, if necessary, a scouring pad.
- Besides the freezer-to-oven glass-ceramic dishes, there are a few other ceramic type casseroles. Porcelainware is specially crafted for baking, and should not be used on open flame or under a broiler. Many porcelainware dishes are straight-sided; the soufflé dish is an example, with straight sides that are fluted on the outside. Porcelainware dishes come in sizes ranging from ⅓ cup to several quarts. Pottery and earthenware (including the clay pots described in Chapter 4) are other types of ceramic casseroles. Some may be used top range, but many are made solely for baking, so consult the manufacturer's tag carefully before using.

QUICK TIPS

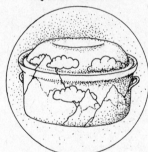

- Aluminum casseroles are flameproof, durable and relatively inexpensive. Most may be used in the oven and under a broiler, depending on the inner cooking surface of the dish. Some aluminum casseroles are treated with a nonstick finish for fat-free browning and easy cleaning. These dishes should never be washed with steel wool or gritty cleansers, as the nonstick surface might be damaged. Also, avoid sharp-edged cooking utensils when using casseroles with nonstick surface.
- Copper casseroles are handsome and durable, though the copper surface requires careful polishing with a cleaner specifically designed for copper. Most are shallow, and can be used on top of the range as well as in the oven.
- Iron and enameled steel casseroles are heavy, durable, and available in a multitude of enameled finishes. Most can be used in the oven and on top of the range, and many are attractive enough to use as serving dishes, right from oven to table.

MOROCCAN LAMB PILAF

Coriander and cumin give this dish its traditional flavor.

Bake at 350° for 1 hour.
Makes 6 servings.

- 1½ pounds lean lamb shoulder, cubed
- 2 tablespoons vegetable oil
- ½ teaspoon coriander seeds, crushed
- ½ teaspoon cumin seeds, crushed
- ⅛ teaspoon pepper
- 1 large onion, chopped (1 cup)
- ¾ cup wheat pilaf (from a 12-ounce package)
- 1 cup chopped celery
- 1½ teaspoons salt
- 2 cups water
- 1 cup chopped parsley

1. Brown lamb cubes, part at a time, in oil in an 8-cup flame-proof casserole or a large skillet; reserve. Stir in coriander, cumin seeds and pepper.
2. Sauté onion until golden in drippings; stir in wheat pilaf, celery, salt and water; bring to boiling. Return meat; toss lightly to mix; cover. (If using a skillet, place lamb in an 8-cup casserole; pour wheat pilaf over and toss to mix; cover.)
3. Bake in moderate oven (350°) 1 hour, or until lamb is tender and liquid is absorbed. Just before serving, stir in chopped parsley.

PARTY PAELLA

The best known Spanish dish in America. Rice, seafood and chicken are baked in a saffron-flavored chicken broth. Pictured on page 72.

Bake at 375° for 1 hour.
Makes 8 to 10 servings.

- 1 broiler-fryer, cut up (about 3 pounds)
- 1 clove garlic, minced
- ¼ cup olive oil or vegetable oil
- 6 strands saffron, crushed
- 1½ cups uncooked long-grain rice
- 1 large onion, chopped (1 cup)
- 1 green pepper, halved, seeded and chopped
- 2 cans condensed chicken broth
- 1 teaspoon salt
- 6 chorizo sausages, cut into 1-inch pieces
  OR: ½ pound pepperoni, sliced
- 1 pound fresh peas, shelled
  OR: 1 cup frozen peas (from a 1½-pound bag)
- 1 can (4 ounces) pimiento, diced
- 12 hard-shelled clams, scrubbed well
  OR: 2 cans (8 ounces each) minced clams
- 1 pound raw shrimp, shelled and deveined

1. Brown chicken with garlic in oil in a large skillet; remove and keep warm. Stir in saffron and rice; sauté until rice is golden; add onion and green pepper; sauté 7 to 10 minutes longer; stir in chicken broth and salt; cover; cook 10 minutes; remove from heat.
2. Layer chicken, rice mixture, chorizo or pepperoni, peas and pimiento in a paella pan or a 12-cup casserole; cover.
3. Bake in moderate oven (375°) 45 minutes. Stir in clams in shell or minced clams and liquid and shrimp; cover. Bake 15 minutes longer, or until rice is tender and liquid is absorbed.
HOSTESS TIP: For an extra festive touch, top PAELLA with cooked lobster claws just before serving. Sangria, a delicious red wine and fruit combination, is the traditional beverage to serve. In the photograph, we pared a lemon and twisted the skin around the handle of the stirrer for a decorative touch.

CHICKEN MARENGO

Marengo is a village in Northern Italy famous for Napoleon's victory over the Austrians in 1800. Shown on page 72.

Bake at 350° for 1 hour, 15 minutes.
Makes 8 servings.

- 2 broiler-fryers, cut up (2½ pounds each)
- ½ cup all-purpose flour
- 2 teaspoons salt
- ½ teaspoon freshly ground pepper
- 3 tablespoons olive oil or vegetable oil
- 3 tablespoons butter or margarine
- 1 large onion, chopped (1 cup)
- 2 cloves garlic, minced
- 1 cup dry white wine
- 3 tablespoons brandy (optional)
- 2 large tomatoes, peeled and chopped
  OR: 1 can (1 pound) tomatoes, chopped
- 6 sprigs parsley
- 1 bay leaf
- 1 teaspoon leaf thyme
- ½ pound mushrooms, sliced
  OR: 1 can (6 ounces) sliced mushrooms

1. Shake chicken pieces in a mixture of flour, salt and pepper in a plastic bag to coat well.
2. Heat oil and butter or margarine in a 12-cup flame-proof casserole or a large skillet. Brown chicken, a few pieces at a time, in hot fat; remove; keep warm.
3. Sauté onion and garlic in drippings until soft; stir in wine and brandy; bring to boiling, stirring constantly. Stir in chopped tomatoes; arrange browned chicken pieces in casserole, spooning part of the sauce over.
4. Tie a "bouquet garni" of parsley, bay leaf and thyme in cheesecloth; push down into sauce; cover. (If using a skillet, place chicken in a 12-cup casserole; pour sauce over and add "bouquet garni"; cover.)
5. Bake in moderate oven (350°) 1 hour. Stir in sliced mushrooms or canned mushrooms and liquid. Bake 15 minutes longer, or until chicken is tender. Remove "bouquet garni" before serving. Garnish with parsley, if desired.
Suggested Variations: For VEAL MARENGO, use 3 pounds of cubed boneless veal instead of the chicken. Omit the brandy and stir in ½ cup brown gravy. Bake in moderate oven (350°) 1 hour, 30 minutes, or until veal is tender. Serve with bread triangles and sprinkle with a mixture of chopped parsley and chives or green onion tops.

PASTA ROLLS FLORENTINE

A dish in the classic tradition of fine Northern Italian cuisine. Pictured on page 72.

Bake at 350° for 35 minutes.
Makes 8 servings.

- Lasagna Noodle Dough (recipe, page 86)
- 2 packages (10 ounces each) frozen chopped spinach, slightly thawed
- 1 container (15 ounces) ricotta cheese
  OR: 1 container (16 ounces) dry cottage cheese
- 1½ cups grated Parmesan cheese
- ¼ cup (½ stick) butter or margarine, softened
- 1 teaspoon salt
- ¼ teaspoon pepper
  Dash grated nutmeg
  Tomato-Meat Sauce (recipe, page 75)
  Béchamel Sauce (recipe, page 75)

1. Prepare LASAGNA NOODLE DOUGH and allow to rest 20 minutes.
2. Cut spinach into cubes and place in a large heavy saucepan; heat slowly, stirring often, until spinach thaws; cover skillet and simmer 3 minutes; drain in strainer, pressing with the back of a wooden spoon, until spinach is dry.
3. Combine spinach with ricotta or cottage cheese, Parmesan cheese, butter or margarine, salt, pepper and nutmeg in a medium-size bowl.
4. Roll out LASAGNA NOODLE DOUGH, one-third at a time, to a 22x10-inch rectangle on a lightly floured pastry cloth or board.
5. Spread dough with one-third of the spinach-cheese mixture; starting at a short end, roll up dough, jelly-roll fashion and place, seam-side down, in the center of a triple-thick piece of cheesecloth; wrap cheesecloth completely around pasta roll and tie ends with kitchen string. Repeat with remaining dough and filling to make 3 rolls.
6. Heat a large kettle of salted water to boiling; cook rolls, one at a time, 20 minutes, or until roll floats to the top of the water. Remove with slotted spoon and cool on wooden board.
7. Remove cheesecloth and cut each roll

into 12 slices. Spread half the TOMATO-MEAT SAUCE in the bottoms of two 10-cup shallow casseroles. Overlap slices in dishes and top with BÉCHAMEL SAUCE. Sprinkle with additional grated Parmesan cheese if you wish.

8. Bake in moderate oven (375°) 30 minutes, or until bubbly-hot.

HOSTESS TIP: Rolls can be made and cooked in boiling water the day ahead, then sealed in plastic bags and refrigerate until ready to cut.

MATAMBRE

The idea for this stuffed flank steak comes from Argentina. Cooking it "en casserole" makes it extra moist and flavorful.

Bake at 350° for 1 hour, 30 minutes.
Makes 6 servings.

1 flank steak, (about 1½ pounds)
 OR: 1 round steak, cut ½-inch thick, (about 1½ pounds)
1 package (10 ounces) frozen mixed vegetables
½ cup finely chopped celery
1 medium-size onion, chopped (½ cup)
2 tablespoons butter or margarine
1 teaspoon garlic salt
½ cup water
 Dry red wine
2 cups soft whole-wheat bread crumbs (4 slices)
2 hard-cooked eggs, shelled and diced
1 can (4 ounces) pimiento, diced
3 tablespoons vegetable oil
½ cup bottled barbecue sauce

1. Ask your meatman to split the steak "butterfly-fashion", or you can do it yourself with a sharp long-bladed knife. Work slowly, cutting with a sawing motion, as evenly as possible, almost through to other edge of steak.
2. Pound steak slightly with a mallet or rolling pin to make an even thinner steak.
3. Combine frozen mixed vegetables with celery, onion, butter or margarine, garlic salt and water in a medium-size saucepan; bring to boiling; cover. Cook 5 minutes. Drain liquid into a 1-cup measure. Add dry red wine or water to vegetable liquid to make ½ cup.
4. Combine bread crumbs, vegetable mixture, eggs and pimiento in a medium-size bowl; moisten with the ½ cup vegetable liquid.
5. Brush prepared steak with part of the bottled barbecue sauce; spread crumb mixture evenly over steak to within 1 inch of edges.
6. Starting at a long side, roll up tightly, tucking in any loose stuffing; tie with kitchen string every 2 inches.
7. Heat oil in a 10-cup oval flame-proof casserole or a large heavy skillet; brown steak roll on all sides in oil; stir in remaining barbecue sauce and ½ cup dry

red wine or water; cover casserole. (If using a skillet, transfer to a 10-cup oval casserole; stir barbecue sauce and wine or water into skillet and cook, stirring constantly, until sauce thickens slightly; pour over meat in casserole; cover.)
8. Bake in moderate oven (350°), basting meat with sauce every 30 minutes, 1 hour, 30 minutes, or until meat is tender when pierced with a two-tined fork. Remove strings and sprinkle with finely chopped parsley, if you wish.

HOSTESS TIP: MATAMBRE can be made the day ahead and baked. Cool, then cover and refrigerate. One hour before serving, remove from refrigerator; skim any fat on the surface of the sauce; cover casserole. Place in oven; turn oven control to moderate (350°) and bake 55 minutes, or until bubbly-hot.

CHICKEN MILIANO

Inspired by a famous Italian dish, our recipe calls for first toasting the rice.

Bake at 350° for 1 hour, 30 minutes.
Makes 6 servings.

1 cup uncooked long-grain rice
2 broiler-fryers, cut up (about 2½ pounds each)
3 tablespoons all-purpose flour
¼ cup olive oil or vegetable oil
1 medium-size onion, chopped (½ cup)
1 clove garlic, minced
1 cup chopped celery
1 teaspoon salt
3 strands saffron, crushed
½ cup dry white wine or water
1 can condensed beef consommé
1 package (10 ounces) frozen cut green beans
¼ cup toasted almonds
 Chopped parsley

1. Spread rice on a 15x10x1-inch jelly-roll pan. Toast in moderate oven (350°), stirring once or twice, 15 minutes, or until golden-brown. Pour at once into a strainer; rinse under cold running water.
2. Shake chicken with flour in a plastic bag until well-coated. Brown, a few pieces at a time, in oil in a 10-cup shallow flame-proof casserole or a large skillet; remove and reserve.
3. Sauté onion and garlic in same pan; stir in rice, celery, salt, saffron and wine or water. Arrange chicken on top; pour consommé over; cover. (If using a skillet, pour rice mixture into a 10-cup shallow casserole; arrange chicken on top; pour consommé over; cover.)
4. Bake in moderate oven (350°) 1 hour and 20 minutes, or until rice is popped and liquid is absorbed. Spoon green beans over chicken in small mounds; cover; bake 10 minutes longer, or until beans are cooked.
5. Sprinkle with toasted almonds and parsley, just before serving. Serve with a dry wine.

SCALLOPED OYSTERS

Oysters were once eaten only in months with the letter "r." Now you can enjoy them year-round.

Bake at 350° for 30 minutes.
Makes 4 servings.

¼ cup (½ stick) butter or margarine
2 cups coarse soda cracker crumbs (about 12 large)
½ cup chopped parsley
1 teaspoon salt
¼ teaspoon pepper
1 pint (about 24) oysters
 OR: 2 cans (8 ounces each) oysters
½ cup light cream
1 teaspoon Worcestershire sauce

1. Melt butter or margarine in a medium-size saucepan; remove from heat; stir in cracker crumbs, parsley, salt and pepper; set aside.
2. Drain juice from oysters into a 2-cup measure; reserve. Sprinkle ⅓ of crumb mixture into a 9-inch pie plate or a 4-cup shallow casserole; layer half the oysters on top, then half of remaining crumbs and rest of oysters.
3. Combine saved oyster juice, cream and Worcestershire sauce and pour over oysters; sprinkle with remaining crumbs.
4. Bake in moderate oven (350°) 30 minutes, or until top is golden.

ROCK CORNISH HENS A L'ORANGE

A recipe to remember when Rock Cornish hens are on special at the market.

Bake at 325° for 1 hour, 15 minutes.
Makes 8 servings.

4 frozen Rock Cornish hens (about 1 pound each), thawed
¼ cup (½ stick) butter or margarine
1 can (6 ounces) frozen concentrate for orange juice
¾ cup water
2 tablespoons bottled steak sauce
2 tablespoons honey
1 teaspoon salt
1 teaspoon leaf rosemary, crumbled

1. Cut hens in half with poultry shears or kitchen scissors.
2. Brown split hens, part at a time, in butter or margarine, in a 12-cup flame-proof casserole or a large skillet; remove hens and keep warm.
3. Stir orange-juice concentrate, water, steak sauce, honey, salt and rosemary into casserole; bring to boiling, scraping to loosen cooked-on juices; return hens to casserole; cover. (If using a skillet, place hens in a 12-cup casserole; pour sauce over; cover.)
4. Bake in slow oven (325°) 1 hour, 15 minutes, basting several times with sauce, or until hens are tender when pierced with a two-tined fork. Serve on OVEN BAKED RICE PILAF (recipe page 84), if you wish, spooning sauce over hens.

PINE TOP PARTY CASSEROLE

The hostesses of this Arizona community developed this dish as the perfect way to use leftover turkey and entertain during the holidays.

Bake at 375° for 45 minutes.
Makes 16 servings.

- **8 cups cooked diced turkey**
- **4 cans cream of chicken soup**
- **2 cups light cream or milk**
- **1 can (4 ounces) green chili peppers, seeded and chopped (optional)**
- **1 bag (about 8 ounces) corn chips, crushed**
- **2 Bermuda onions, chopped**
- **2 cups shredded Monterey Jack cheese (8 ounces)**
- **2 cups shredded Cheddar cheese (8 ounces)**

1. Combine turkey, chicken soup, cream or milk and chili peppers in a large kettle; heat slowly, stirring often, just until bubbly.
2. Divide ⅓ of the corn chips between two 12-cup casseroles; top with half the turkey mixture, chopped onion and shredded cheeses; layer ⅓ of corn chips, remaining turkey mixture, onion and cheeses; top with remaining corn chips.
3. Bake in moderate oven (375°) 45 minutes, or until bubbly-hot.
HOSTESS TIP: This is an especially good dish when guests arrive at various times. Bake one casserole and keep the other on hand for the second flow of company. A heaping platter of chilled marinated vegetables, sour dough bread and a bowl of sliced fruits in wine make a festive, yet easy menu.

COQUILLES ST. JACQUES

Scallop recipes are called Coquilles St. Jacques because scallop shells were used as drinking cups by 14th century pilgrims to the shrine of St. James. Shown on page 79.

Bake at 400° for 12 minutes.
Makes 4 servings.

- **1 pound fresh or frozen sea scallops**
- **1 cup dry white wine**
- **1 teaspoon salt**
- **3 tablespoons butter or margarine**
- **½ pound mushrooms, sliced**
- **¼ cup chopped shallots**
  OR: ¼ cup sliced green onions
- **3 tablespoons all-purpose flour**
- **½ cup heavy cream**
- **2 cups soft white bread crumbs (4 slices)**
- **2 tablespoons melted butter or margarine**
- **2 tablespoons chopped parsley**

1. Wash scallops and quarter. Bring wine and salt to boiling in a large skillet; add scallops; lower heat; simmer very gently, just until tender, about 5 minutes.
2. Remove scallops from liquid with a slotted spoon and divide among 4 scallop shells, au gratin dishes or individual casseroles; reserve liquid (there should be about 1 cup).
3. Melt butter or margarine in a medium-size saucepan; sauté mushrooms until soft; remove with slotted spoon and divide among scallop shells.
4. Sauté shallots or green onions in butter until soft; stir in flour and cook, stirring constantly, until bubbly.
5. Stir in reserved liquid and cream; cook, stirring constantly, until sauce thickens and bubbles 3 minutes. Spoon over scallops and mushrooms, dividing evenly. Toss bread crumbs with melted butter or margarine and parsley until well-blended in a medium-size bowl; sprinkle over shells.
6. Bake in hot oven (400°) 12 minutes, or until crumbs are golden.
HOSTESS TIP: COQUILLES ST. JACQUES can be made up earlier in the day and refrigerated until ready to serve. Do not sprinkle with crumbs until ready to bake. Coquilles will take about 20 minutes to heat through.
Suggested Variation: COQUILLES SARAH BERNHARDT—For a delightful dish from the Victorian era, follow the recipe for COQUILLES ST. JACQUES. substituting shrimp for the scallops and stirring in 2 tablespoons dry Madeira wine into the cream sauce.

BLANQUETTE DE VEAU

A delicate dish, just right for unexpected company.

Bake at 350° for 30 minutes.
Makes 8 servings.

- **5 pounds breast of veal**
- **1 onion studded with 6 whole cloves**
- **1 bay leaf**
- **1 large carrot, pared and diced**
- **1 cup chopped celery with leaves**
- **1 sprig parsley**
- **3 teaspoons salt**
- **½ teaspoon pepper**
- **2 cups water**
- **⅓ cup butter or margarine**
- **½ pound mushrooms, quartered**
- **⅓ cup all-purpose flour**
- **1 cup heavy cream**
- **½ cup milk**
- **½ cup dry white wine**
- **4 large carrots, pared, sliced and cooked**
- **16 small white onions, cooked**
- **2 tablespoons chopped fresh dill**
  OR: 2 teaspoons dillweed

1. Combine breast of veal, onion studded with cloves, bay leaf, carrot, celery, parsley, 2 teaspoons of the salt and ¼ teaspoon of the pepper in a large kettle. Add water.
2. Bring to boiling; lower heat; cover kettle. Simmer 2 hours, or until veal is very tender.
3. Cool veal in broth, then refrigerate until fat rises to top and hardens. Remove meat from bones and cut into cubes. (You should have 4 cups.)
4. Melt butter or margarine in a large saucepan; sauté mushrooms lightly.
5. Stir in flour and cook, stirring constantly, 2 minutes. Combine veal broth, heavy cream, milk and wine in a 4-cup measure; stir into saucepan. Cook, stirring constantly, until mixture thickens and bubbles 3 minutes. Season with the remaining 1 teaspoon salt and ¼ teaspoon pepper.
6. Arrange veal, carrots, onions and dill in a 12-cup casserole; spoon sauce over meat and vegetables to coat.
7. Bake in moderate oven (350°) 30 minutes, or until bubbly-hot. Garnish with parsley, if you wish.

TERIYAKI CASSEROLE

The secret to successful Oriental cooking is to cook the vegetables until crisply tender. Pictured on pages 80 and 81.

Bake at 350° for 15 minutes.
Makes 6 servings.

- **1 boneless sirloin or top round steak (about 1½ pounds)**
- **3 tablespoons peanut oil or vegetable oil**
- **1 clove garlic, halved**
- **1 large onion, sliced and separated into rings**
- **1 large green pepper, halved, seeded and sliced**
- **1 large red pepper, halved, seeded and sliced**
- **1 large zucchini, tipped and sliced**
- **1 large yellow squash, tipped and sliced**
- **½ pound mushrooms, sliced**
- **1 large carrot, pared and cut into thin sticks**
- **½ cup soy sauce**
- **¼ cup saki or dry sherry**
- **1 package (1 pound) Chinese noodles, cooked and drained**
  OR: 1 package (1 pound) fine noodles, cooked and drained

1. Cut very cold steak into very thin slices with a sharp knife.
2. Heat oil with garlic until very hot in a large skillet; remove garlic; brown beef quickly, a few pieces at a time; remove.
3. Add onion rings; sauté 2 minutes; add pepper slices, zucchini, yellow squash, mushrooms and carrots; sauté, stirring constantly, until vegetables glisten and have bright color; add soy sauce and saki or sherry.
4. Cook 5 minutes, or until vegetables are crisply-tender; remove from heat; stir in reserved steak.
5. Arrange cooked noodles in an 8-cup shallow casserole; add meat and vegetables and mix with noodles.
6. Bake in moderate oven (350°) 15 minutes, or until bubbly-hot.

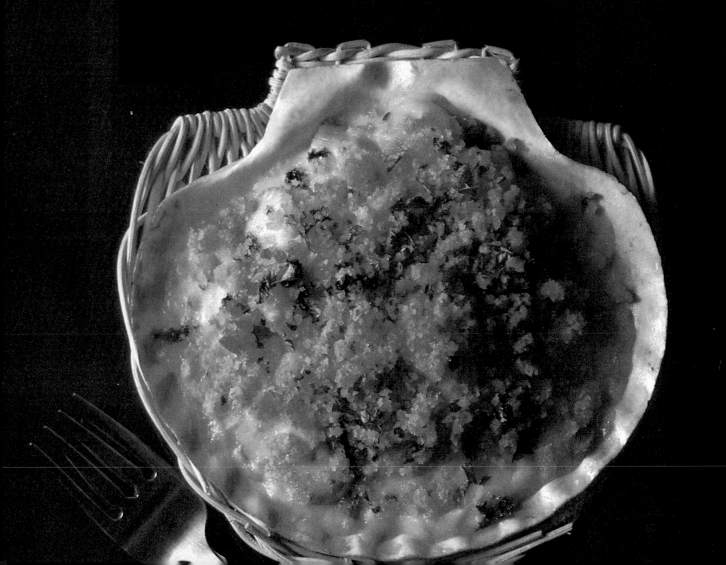

Serve Coquilles St.
Jacques (recipe on page
78) for an elegant,
yet simply company
dish.

**a party
casserole
made
quickly**

East meets West in our colorful Teri-yaki Casserole (recipe on page 78). The Oriental stir-fry method of cooking is teamed with the flavor-blending secret of oven baking. Japanese cooks like to show the beauty of the raw ingredients to their guests. You can have the ingredients ready, then stir-fry and bake. Done in less than 30 minutes.

Spicy Patio Enchiladas make a perfect sunset supper casserole. Recipe appears on page 8

MARYLAND SEAFOOD CASSEROLE

Ella Peigert from the Delmarva Peninsula of Maryland has gained her reputation as a casserole cook with this recipe.

Bake at 375° for 20 minutes.
Makes 8 servings.

- 1 pound fresh or frozen crabmeat
- 1 pound shrimp, cooked, shelled and deveined
- 1 cup mayonnaise or salad dressing
- 1½ cups finely chopped celery
- 1 small green pepper, halved, seeded and chopped
- 1 small onion, finely chopped (¼ cup)
- ½ teaspoon salt
- 1 tablespoon Worcestershire sauce
- 2 cups coarsely crushed potato chips
  Paprika

1. Combine crabmeat, shrimp, mayonnaise or salad dressing, celery, green pepper, onion, salt and Worcestershire sauce in a large bowl. Pour into a greased 10-cup casserole. Top with crushed potato chips; sprinkle with paprika.
2. Bake in moderate oven (375°) 20 minutes, or until mixture is heated.

PATIO ENCHILADAS

Mexican-style crêpes have cornmeal in the batter. Beef and red kidney beans are the filling. An excellent choice for a party dish, shown on page 82.

Bake at 400° for 30 minutes.
Makes 8 servings.

Filling
- 1 large onion, chopped (1 cup)
- 1 clove garlic, minced
- 2 to 4 teaspoons chili powder
- 2 tablespoons olive oil or vegetable oil
- 1 pound ground beef
- 1 can (1 pound, 13 ounces) tomatoes
- 2 cans (1 pound each) red kidney beans, drained
- 2 teaspoons salt
Crêpes
- 1 egg
- 1½ cups water
- 1 cup sifted all-purpose flour
- ½ cup yellow cornmeal
- ¼ teaspoon salt
Topping
- 1 small onion, sliced and separated into rings
- ½ cup pitted olives, sliced
- 1 cup shredded Cheddar cheese (4 ounces)

1. Make filling: Sauté onion and garlic with chili powder in oil just until soft in a large skillet; push to one side. Shape beef into a large patty; brown in same pan, 5 minutes on each side; break up into small pieces. Stir in tomatoes, red kidney beans and salt. Cover; simmer 15 minutes to blend flavors.
2. While filling simmers, make crêpe batter: Beat egg until thick in a medium-size bowl; beat in water, then flour, cornmeal and salt until smooth. (Batter will be thin.)
3. Heat a heavy 8-inch crêpe pan or skillet; test temperature by sprinkling in a few drops of water. When drops bounce about, temperature is right; grease lightly. Pour batter, a scant ¼ cup for each crêpe, into pan; bake 3 minutes, or until top appears dry and underside is golden; turn; bake 2 minutes longer. Repeat to make 16 crêpes.
4. As each is baked, roll up with about ½ cup filling and place in a 12-cup casserole; spoon remaining filling over.
5. Bake in hot oven (400°) 30 minutes, or until bubbly-hot.
6. Arrange topping: Place onion rings and sliced olives in a pretty pattern on top; sprinkle with cheese.

CANNELONI

Some canneloni recipes call for crêpes, but this one uses a noodle dough, true to the style of Italy's Piedmont region.

Bake at 350° for 30 minutes.
Makes 6 servings.

- Lasagna Noodle Dough (recipe, page 86)
- 1 pound ground meatloaf mixture
- 1 large onion, chopped (1 cup)
- 2 cloves garlic, minced
- 1 cup soft white bread crumbs (2 slices)
- 1 egg, beaten
- ½ cup chopped Italian parsley
- 1 teaspoon leaf basil, crumbled
- 1 teaspoon salt
- ¼ teaspoon pepper
- 2 cups Homemade Tomato Sauce (recipe page 75)
  Béchamel Sauce (recipe page 75)

1. Prepare LASAGNA NOODLE DOUGH and allow it to rest 20 minutes.
2. Shape meatloaf mixture into a large patty in a large heavy skillet. Brown 5 minutes on each side, then break up into small pieces; remove with a slotted spoon to a medium-size bowl.
3. Sauté onion and garlic until soft in drippings in skillet; remove from heat. Add cooked meat with bread crumbs, egg, parsley, basil, salt and pepper; mix.
4. Roll out LASAGNA NOODLE DOUGH. one-third at a time, to a 16x16-inch square. Cut into four 4-inch squares. Repeat with remaining dough.
5. Bring 4 quarts of salted water to boiling in a large kettle; add pasta squares, half at a time, to rapidly boiling water; cook 3 minutes; remove with slotted spoon to a large bowl of cold water, then drain on paper towels.
6. Spread 2 tablespoons of filling on each square; roll up, jelly-roll fashion.
7. Spoon TOMATO SAUCE into the bottom of a 12-cup shallow casserole. Arrange CANNELONI. seam side down in dish; cover with BÉCHAMEL SAUCE.
8. Bake in moderate oven (350°) 30 minutes, or until bubbly-hot.
HOSTESS TIP: CANNELONI can be stuffed and placed in TOMATO SAUCE in casserole, covered, and refrigerated. One hour before serving, remove cover; prepare and spoon BÉCHAMEL SAUCE over. Place casserole in oven. Turn oven control to moderate (350°) and bake 45 minutes, or until bubbly-hot.

DELMONICO POTATOES WITH HAM

Our recipe makes enough for a party. You can make two casseroles and freeze the second.

Bake at 325° for 1 hour.
Makes 12 servings.

- 15 medium-size potatoes, washed (about 5 pounds)
- ½ cup (1 stick) butter or margarine
- ½ cup all-purpose flour
- 2 teaspoons salt
- 6 cups milk
- 2 tablespoons prepared mustard
- 2 teaspoons Worcestershire sauce
- 4 cups shredded Cheddar cheese (1 pound)
- 4 cups diced cooked ham
- 3 cups soft white bread crumbs (6 slices)
- 3 tablespoons butter or margarine, melted

1. Cook potatoes in their jackets in boiling salted water in a large kettle, just until tender, about 30 minutes; drain; return to kettle; toss potatoes in kettle over low heat to fluff-dry.
2. While potatoes cook, melt the ½ cup butter or margarine in a large saucepan; blend in flour and salt; cook, stirring constantly, just until bubbly; stir in milk, prepared mustard and Worcestershire sauce. Continue cooking and stirring until sauce thickens and bubbles 3 minutes; stir in cheese until melted.
3. Peel potatoes; cut into ⅛-inch-thick slices. (An egg slicer does a quick job.) Arrange potato slices and ham in a 16-cup casserole or two 8-cup casseroles; pour cheese sauce over.
4. Toss bread crumbs with the 3 tablespoons melted butter or margarine until well-blended in a medium-size bowl; sprinkle over potatoes.
5. Bake in a slow oven (325°) 1 hour for the large casserole, and 45 minutes for the smaller ones, or until bubbly-hot.
HOSTESS TIP: To freeze the second casserole, follow general directions in Chapter 7. To bake: Place uncovered casserole in the oven. Turn oven control to slow (325°) and bake for 1 hour, 45 minutes, or until top is golden.

BALI PARTY CHICKEN

It's the special curry glaze that makes this chicken so special.

Bake at 400° for 1 hour.
Makes 8 servings.

- 2 broiler-fryers, quartered (3 pounds each)
- ⅓ cup all-purpose flour
- 1½ teaspoons salt
- 1 teaspoon ground ginger
- ⅓ cup butter or margarine
  Curry Glaze (recipe follows)
  Oven Baked Rice Pilaf (recipe follows)

1. Shake chicken pieces in mixture of flour, salt and ginger in a plastic bag to coat well.
2. Place butter or margarine in a 16-cup shallow casserole in oven while preheating. Roll chicken in melted butter or margarine to coat well, then arrange, skin side up, in single layer in casserole.
3. Bake in hot oven (400°) 20 minutes, or until chicken begins to turn golden.
4. While chicken bakes, make CURRY GLAZE. Spoon half of the mixture over chicken; bake 20 minutes; spoon remaining glaze over and bake 20 minutes longer, or until chicken is richly browned. Serve with OVEN BAKED RICE PILAF that bakes alongside at the same temperature setting.

CURRY GLAZE

Makes about 2 cups.

- 1 medium-size onion, chopped (½ cup)
- 6 slices bacon, finely diced
- 2 tablespoons all-purpose flour
- 1 tablespoon curry powder
- 1 tablespoon sugar
- 1 can condensed beef broth
- 2 tablespoons flaked coconut
- 2 tablespoons applesauce
- 2 tablespoons catsup
- 2 tablespoons lemon juice

Combine all ingredients in a medium-size saucepan. Bring to boiling, stirring constantly; lower heat, simmer 15 minutes, or until thickened.

OVEN BAKED RICE PILAF

Makes 8 servings.

- 1½ cups uncooked long-grain rice
- 3 tablespoons vegetable oil
- ¼ cup sliced green onions
- 4 envelopes or teaspoons instant chicken broth
- 4 cups water
- ½ cup raisins (optional)
- ¼ cup toasted almonds or chopped dry-roasted peanuts (optional)

1. Sauté rice in oil in a skillet until golden; stir in green onions; sauté 2 minutes. Add instant chicken broth and water; bring to boiling; cover. Pour rice mixture into an 8-cup casserole.
2. Bake in hot oven (400°), 1 hour, or until liquid is absorbed and rice is tender. Stir in raisins and nuts. (Rice can be baked at 350° to 375°, too.)

SHOULDER LAMB CHOPS INDIENNE

Casserole cooking makes meaty shoulder chops extra moist and tender.

Bake at 375° for 1 hour, 30 minutes.
Makes 6 servings.

- 6 shoulder lamb chops (about 2 pounds)
- 2 tablespoons vegetable oil
- 1 large onion, chopped (1 cup)
- 2 tablespoons curry powder
- 1 teaspoon salt
- ½ teaspoon ground ginger
- ½ teaspoon ground cardamom
- 2 envelopes instant chicken broth
- 1½ cups water
- 1 small eggplant, diced
- ½ cup raisins
- 1 jar (8 ounces) applesauce
- 2 tablespoons lemon juice

1. Brown chops, a few at a time, in oil in a large skillet; place meat in a 10-cup casserole.
2. Sauté onion in pan drippings until soft; stir in curry powder and cook 2 minutes; add salt, ginger, cardamom, chicken broth and water. Bring to boiling, stirring constantly. Stir in eggplant, raisins, applesauce and lemon juice; pour over lamb.
3. Bake in moderate oven (375°) 1 hour, 30 minutes, or until lamb chops are tender, when pierced with a two-tined fork. Serve with spicy chutney and fluffy rice, if you wish.

QUICK TIPS

The nose knows. Train your nose to tell you about food:
● Check a casserole that smells done, even if the cooking time isn't up. The oven thermometer could be inaccurate.
● Smell vegetables and fruits before you buy them. Fragrant produce will be the most flavorful when cooked.
● Sniff raw fish, meat and poultry. If it has an "off", slightly rancid smell, throw it out. Food is costly, but your health is priceless.

COQ AU VIN

Chicken in wine is a classic French dish. Serve with crusty bread and red wine.

Bake at 325° for 1 hour, 30 minutes.
Makes 8 servings.

- ½ pound thickly sliced bacon
- 2 broiler-fryers, cut up (about 2½ pounds each)
- ⅓ cup all-purpose flour
- 2 teaspoons salt
- ½ teaspoon freshly ground pepper
- 1 pound small white onions, peeled
- 2 cloves garlic, minced
- 3 cups dry red wine
- 2 sprigs parsley
- 2 sprigs celery leaves
- 1 bay leaf
- 1 teaspoon leaf thyme
- ½ teaspoon leaf rosemary
- ½ pound fresh mushrooms
- 3 tablespoons butter or margarine

1. Cut bacon into 1-inch pieces; place in a small saucepan; cover with water. Bring to boiling; lower heat and simmer 10 minutes. Dry bacon on paper towels. Fry bacon until crisp in a 12-cup flame-proof casserole or a large kettle. Remove bacon with a slotted spoon and reserve.
2. Shake chicken pieces with flour, salt and pepper in a plastic bag to coat well. Brown chicken, a few pieces at a time, in casserole; remove and reserve.
3. Brown onions in pan drippings until golden; stir in garlic and cook 2 minutes; stir in red wine and bring to boiling, scraping brown bits from bottom of casserole.
4. Return chicken and bacon to casserole; tie a "bouquet garni" of parsley, celery leaves, bay leaf, thyme and rosemary in cheesecloth; push down into liquid in casserole; cover. (If using a kettle, place chicken and bacon in a 12-cup casserole; ladle sauce and onions over; tuck in "bouquet garni"; cover casserole.)
5. Bake in slow oven (325°) 1 hour, 30 minutes, or until chicken is tender. Remove "bouquet garni".
6. While casserole cooks, wipe mushrooms with a damp paper towel. Sauté in melted butter or margarine until soft in a small skillet; add to casserole with pan juices for last 15 minutes of baking. Sprinkle with chopped parsley just before serving, if you wish.
HOSTESS TIP: The finished dish can be held in a very slow oven for 1 hour before serving. COQ AU VIN can be made the day before. Cool, then cover and refrigerate. One hour before serving, remove casserole from refrigerator; place in oven. Turn oven control to moderate (350°) and bake 1 hour, or until bubbly-hot.
Suggested Variation: COQ AU VIN BLANC —For those who prefer the flavor of white wine, follow the recipe for COQ AU VIN, except use 3 cups dry white wine in place of the dry red wine.

NORWEGIAN FISH BAKE

A trio of Scandinavian favorites; fish, dill and sour cream are topped with buttered crumbs.

Bake at 350° for 40 minutes.
Makes 6 servings.

- 2 pounds fresh cod, haddock or flounder fillets
  OR: 2 packages (1 pound each) frozen cod, haddock or flounder fillets
- ¼ cup all-purpose flour
- 2 teaspoons salt
- ¼ teaspoon pepper
- 1 cup milk
- 2 cups soft white bread crumbs (4 slices)
- ¼ cup (½ stick) butter or margarine, melted
- 1 tablespoon chopped fresh dill
  OR: 1 teaspoon dillweed
- 1 container (8 ounces) dairy sour cream

1. Cut fresh or frozen fish into serving-size pieces; coat with mixture of flour, salt and pepper. Arrange in a single layer in a 13x9x2-inch casserole; pour milk over coated fillets.
2. Bake in moderate oven (350°) 30 minutes, or until fish flakes easily.
3. While fish bakes, mix crumbs and melted butter or margarine in a small bowl. Stir dill into sour cream container.
4. Remove fish from oven; spoon sour-cream mixture over, then top with buttered crumbs.
5. Bake 10 minutes longer, or just until the sour cream mixture is set.

CARBONADE FLAMANDE

A delicious way to prepare the less tender cuts of beef.

Bake at 325° for 1 hour, 45 minutes.
Makes 6 servings.

- 1 boneless chuck or round steak (about 2 pounds)
- 3 large onions, sliced
- 1 can (12 ounces) beer
- 1 teaspoon salt
- 1 teaspoon leaf tarragon, crumbled
- 1 bay leaf
- ¼ teaspoon freshly ground pepper
  Oven Braised Vegetables (recipe follows)

1. Trim a 2-inch piece of fat from steak. Render fat in an 8-cup flame-proof casserole or a large skillet. Cut steak into 1-inch cubes; brown well on all sides in fat; remove and reserve.
2. Sauté onions until soft in drippings in casserole; stir in beer, salt, tarragon, bay leaf and pepper; return beef to casserole; cover. (If using a skillet place browned beef in an 8 cup casserole; pour sauce over; cover.)
3. Bake in slow oven (325°) 1 hour, 45

minutes, or until meat is very tender.
4. To serve, surround with OVEN BRAISED VEGETABLES.

OVEN BRAISED VEGETABLES

Bake at 325° for 45 minutes.
Makes 6 servings.

- 3 tablespoons butter or margarine
- 6 medium-size boiling potatoes, pared and quartered
- 6 large carrots, pared and cut into 1-inch pieces
- 2 envelopes or teaspoons instant beef broth
- 1 cup boiling water

1. Melt butter or margarine in a 6-cup flame-proof casserole or a large saucepan. Toss potatoes and carrots in butter to coat evenly. Add instant beef broth and water; bring to boiling; cover. (If using a saucepan, place in a 6-cup casserole; cover.)
2. Bake in slow oven (325°) 45 minutes, basting occasionally, or until vegetables are tender and cooked through.

PORK SATÉ

This spicy Indonesian casserole comes from the recipe files of Agnes Bos, a Family Circle copy editor.

Bake at 325° for 1 hour, 30 minutes.
Makes 6 servings.

- 2 pounds lean boneless pork
- ¼ cup soy sauce
- 3 tablespoons lemon juice
- 3 medium-size onions, chopped (1½ cups)
- 2 cloves garlic, minced
- 1 cup salted peanuts
- 2 tablespoons brown sugar
- 1 tablespoon coriander seeds
- ½ to 1 teaspoon red pepper flakes
- ½ cup (1 stick) butter or margarine
- ½ cup chicken broth or water

1. Cut pork into 1-inch cubes. (You can buy a 3½ pound loin of pork. First, cut meat from bones; trim, then cube. Bake the bones along with the casserole and serve as a nibble with bottled barbecue sauce, if you wish.) Place pork cubes in an 8-cup shallow casserole.
2. Combine soy sauce, lemon juice, onion, garlic, peanuts, brown sugar, coriander and red pepper flakes in an electric blender container; cover; process on low 30 seconds; remove cover and push mixture down into blades with a thin rubber spatula. (If mixture is too stiff, add a few tablespoons of the chicken broth.) Continue to process, turning blender on and off, until smooth; pour into a small heavy saucepan.
3. Heat slowly, stirring constantly, until mixture boils; remove from heat; stir in butter or margarine and remaining chicken broth until butter melts.

4. Spoon sauce over pork in casserole; cover.
5. Bake in slow oven (325°) 1 hour, 30 minutes, stirring several times, or until pork is tender. Serve with hot fluffy rice and cold marinated vegetables, such as pickled beets, cauliflower, carrot sticks and cucumber slices, if you wish. Agnes Bos's family prefers French bread to get up every last bit of sauce. *Suggested Variations:* When fresh pork shoulder is on special, you can trim, bone and cube it for a more economical version of this recipe.

SEAFOOD SUPREME

Try this casserole when you want to serve something special that doesn't take a lot of time.

Bake at 350° for 30 minutes.
Makes 6 servings.

- 1 package (8 ounces) medium-size shells or elbow macaroni
- 2 cans (about 6 ounces each) lobster meat
  OR: 1 can (about 6 ounces) lobster or crab meat and 1 can (about 7 ounces) tuna
- 1 tablespoon lemon juice
- 3 tablespoons butter or margarine
- 3 tablespoons all-purpose flour
- 1 teaspoon salt
- ⅛ teaspoon pepper
- 1½ cups milk
- 1 cup shredded Cheddar cheese (4 ounces)
- 1 teaspoon dry mustard
- 1 package (10 ounces) frozen peas with sliced mushrooms

1. Cook pasta in boiling salted water in a large kettle following label directions; drain; return to kettle.
2. Drain lobster or crab; remove any bony tissue; cut into bite-size pieces and place in a medium-size bowl; sprinkle lemon juice over. Or, flake tuna and place in medium-size bowl with lobster or crabmeat; stir in lemon juice.
3. Melt butter or margarine in a medium-size saucepan; stir in flour, salt and pepper. Cook, stirring constantly, until mixture bubbles; stir in milk. Continue cooking and stirring until sauce thickens and bubbles 3 minutes.
4. Spoon ½ cup of sauce over seafood and stir gently. Stir cheese and mustard into remaining sauce until cheese melts. Fold into pasta in kettle.
5. Line an 8-cup casserole with pasta, making a hollow in the center; spoon seafood mixture into hollow; cover.
6. Bake in moderate oven (350°) 30 minutes, or until bubbly-hot.
7. While casserole bakes, cook peas with mushrooms, following label directions; drain and season with butter or margarine and herb-seasoned salt, if you wish. Uncover casserole; spoon peas and mushrooms around edge; serve.

BEEF A LA MODE

Red wine helps to tenderize a less-tender cut of beef and make a superb gravy, too. Shown on page 87.

Bake at 325° for 3 hours.
Makes 10 to 12 servings.

- 1 round or boneless chuck roast (about 4 pounds)
- 2 cups red Burgundy wine
- 1 large onion, sliced
- 2 cloves garlic, minced
- 2 bay leaves
- 1 teaspoon leaf thyme, crumbled
- 2 teaspoons salt
- ½ teaspoon freshly ground pepper
- 2 tablespoons olive oil or vegetable oil
- 1 can condensed beef broth
- ⅓ cup all-purpose flour
  Butter Braised Vegetables (recipe follows)

1. Place meat in a large glass or ceramic bowl; pour mixture of Burgundy, sliced onion, garlic, bay leaves, thyme, salt and pepper over. Cover; store in refrigerator overnight, turning meat several times to marinate on all sides.
2. When ready to cook, remove meat from marinade and pat dry with paper towels; brown in hot oil in a 12-cup flame-proof casserole or a large heavy kettle; add marinade with broth and vegetables; cover. (If using a kettle, place browned meat in a 12-cup casserole along with marinade; cover.)
3. Bake in slow oven (325°) 3 hours, or until meat is very tender when pierced with a two-tined fork; remove from casserole and keep warm; remove bay leaves from cooking liquid.
4. Pour liquid, half at a time, into an electric blender container; add flour, half at a time; cover container; whirl at high speed 1 minute. (Or press liquid through a sieve with a wooden spoon into a bowl; cool slightly; stir in flour until well-blended.) Pour liquid into a large saucepan; bring to boiling. Cook, stirring constantly, until sauce thickens and bubbles 3 minutes.
5. Return beef and part of the sauce to casserole; surround with BUTTER BRAISED VEGETABLES; spoon remaining sauce over meat, just before serving.

BUTTER BRAISED VEGETABLES

Makes 10-12 servings.

- 1 pound green beans, tipped
- 1 pound small white onions, peeled
- 1 pound carrots, pared and cut into 5-inch pieces
- ¼ cup (½ stick) butter or margarine
- 1 envelope or teaspoon instant chicken broth
- ½ cup water

1. Sauté whole green beans in butter or margarine in a large skillet until a bright green; remove; brown white onions and carrots in the same skillet. Combine instant chicken broth and hot water in a cup; pour into skillet; cover.
2. Simmer 25 minutes; return green beans to skillet; simmer 10 minutes longer, or until vegetables are tender.

LASAGNA

There are almost as many recipes for Lasagna as there are cooks who make it. This is our favorite.

Bake at 350° for 30 minutes.
Makes 8 servings.

  Lasagna Noodle Dough (recipe follows)
  OR: 9 lasagna noodles (from a 1-pound package)
- 1 container (15 ounces) ricotta cheese
  OR: 1 container (16 ounces) cottage cheese
- 2 eggs
- 1 package (10 ounces) frozen chopped spinach, thawed and drained well
- 1 teaspoon salt
  Tomato-Meat Sauce (recipe, page 75)
- ½ cup grated Parmesan cheese
- 1 package (6 ounces) sliced mozzarella cheese

1. Prepare LASAGNA NOODLE DOUGH.
2. Bring 4 quarts of salted water to boiling in a large kettle; add 9 lasagna noodles. (Save remaining noodles for another recipe.) Return to boiling and cook 5 minutes; remove with slotted spoon to a large bowl of cold water, then drain on paper towels. OR: Cook packaged lasagna noodles, following label directions and drain on paper towels.
3. Combine ricotta or cottage cheese and eggs in a large bowl; stir in drained spinach and salt.
4. To assemble: Spoon 1 cup TOMATO-MEAT SAUCE in bottom of a 12-cup shallow casserole; lay 3 lasagna noodles on top; spoon part of the cheese-spinach mixture over; add part of the Parmesan cheese. Continue layering twice, ending with sauce and Parmesan cheese.
5. Bake in moderate oven (350°) 30 minutes. Arrange slices of mozzarella cheese on top. Bake 5 minutes longer, or until cheese melts. Cool 10 minutes before serving.

LASAGNA NOODLE DOUGH

Makes about 1½ pounds.

- 3 cups sifted all-purpose flour
- 2 teaspoons salt
- 3 eggs
- 2 tablespoons olive oil or vegetable oil
- ¼ cup lukewarm water

1. Sift flour and salt onto a large wooden board; make a well in center; add eggs, oil and water. Work liquids into flour with fingers to make a stiff dough. (Or make dough in a large bowl, but it's not as much fun.)
2. Knead dough on board (do not add additional flour) 10 minutes, or until dough is smooth and soft.
3. Wrap dough in plastic wrap. Let stand 20 minutes. Cut into quarters; keep dough you are not working with wrapped, or it will dry out.
4. Roll out dough quarter on wooden board to a 10x8-inch rectangle. (Do not use additional flour, but if dough really sticks, sprinkle board lightly with cornstarch.) This takes a lot of pressure. Repeat with remaining dough.
5. Cut dough into four 10x2-inch strips and lay in a single layer on clean towels to dry for 1 hour.

ARROZ CON CERDO

Toast the rice first in a skillet, so it will puff later while baking in its sauce.

Bake at 350° for 1 hour.
Makes 8 servings.

- 8 slices bacon
- 2 pounds boneless lean pork shoulder, cubed
- 1 large onion, chopped (1 cup)
- 1 clove garlic, minced
- 2 cups uncooked rice
- 5 envelopes instant chicken broth
  OR: 5 chicken bouillon cubes
- ¼ teaspoon saffron, crushed
- 6 cups water
- 1 pound fresh peas, shelled and cooked
  OR: 1 package (10 ounces) frozen peas, cooked
- ¼ cup chopped dry-roasted peanuts
- 1 pimiento, diced

1. Sauté bacon until almost crisp in a large skillet; roll each slice while still warm around tines of a fork to make bacon curls; drain on paper towels.
2. Pour all but 2 tablespoons drippings into a cup. Brown pork, a few pieces at a time, in same skillet; remove.
3. Return 2 tablespoons bacon drippings to pan; add onion and garlic; sauté until soft; push to one side. Add rice and sauté, stirring constantly, until golden. Stir in instant chicken broth or bouillon cubes, saffron and water; bring to boiling. (If using bouillon cubes, crush with spoon until dissolved.)
4. Pour into a 12-cup casserole; top with browned pork; cover.
5. Bake in moderate oven (350°) 1 hour, or until liquid is absorbed and rice is tender; fluff up with a fork. Stand bacon curls in a ring in center; spoon cooked peas around edge. Sprinkle chopped peanuts and diced pimiento over top.
COOK'S TIP: Saffron, a Spanish seasoning, is expensive, but a very little goes a long way to give rice a rich golden color and unusual flavor.

Beef a la Mode, a classic French pot roast, is surrounded with Butter Braised Vegetables. (See recipe page 86.)

seasonings are the magic flavor touch

From left to right:
Bay leaves for poultry;
curry powder for curries;
fresh dill for fish dishes;
freeze-dried chives
to use as a topping;
chicken-flavored rice mix
for a casserole base;
tomato paste for a
richly-flavored sauce;
red pepper flakes used in
many Mexican foods;
leaf thyme, the favorite
French herb;
saffron for exotic entrees.

Stir in a spoon-
ful of aromatic, subtle or
pungent seasonings and add
lively flavor and interest
to everyday dishes. Use
them to acquaint your
family with the varied
cuisines of the world:
Read suggestions on seasoning labels and start
with just a little. Next
time, increase the amount
to suit the family's taste.

in your casserole cookery

Dieters need not feel deprived when they can enjoy a casserole as rich as Zucchini Bolognese (recipe, page 92) without worrying about extra inches on the waistline. Zucchini slices take the place of calorie-rich lasagna noodles. A little meat and low-calorie cheese are included, too.

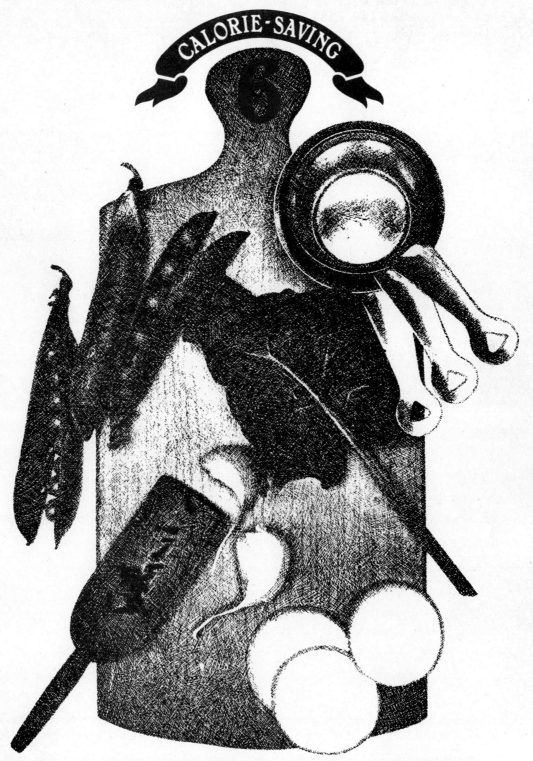

A DIETER'S DELIGHT

Pare the calories, but not the flavor. That's the secret behind many successful diets,
as well as the basis for our diet-watching casseroles. They start with
lean meats, seafood and vegetables — a dieter's basics. We've given these foods extra
flavor — but few extra calories — with a variety of herbs and seasonings.

MONTEREY PORK

Cubed pork simmers in a pepper and tomato sauce. Rice is even included in this calorie counter's special.

Bake at 350° for 1 hour.
Makes 6 servings at 307 calories each.

- 1½ pounds lean boneless pork shoulder, cubed
- 1 large onion, chopped (1 cup)
- 1 large green pepper, halved, seeded and chopped
- 1½ teaspoons chili powder
- 1 can (1 pound) tomatoes
- ½ cup chopped celery
- 1 teaspoon salt
- ⅛ teaspoon pepper
- 3 cups hot cooked rice

1. Brown pork, a few pieces at a time, in a large nonstick skillet; remove with a slotted spoon and reserve.
2. Sauté onion and green pepper until soft, then stir in chili powder; cook 2 minutes; return meat with tomatoes, celery, salt and pepper to skillet and mix well. Spoon into a 6-cup casserole.
3. Bake in moderate oven (350°) 1 hour, or until pork is tender. Spoon over ½ cup cooked rice per serving.

ZUCCHINI BOLOGNESE

Long slender slices of zucchini take the place of lasagna noodles in this calorie-saving version of an Italian classic. Pictured on page 90.

Bake at 350° for 1 hour.
Makes 6 servings at 273 calories each.

- 4 large zucchini (about 2 pounds)
- 2 medium-size onions, sliced
- 2 sweet or hot Italian sausages
- ¾ cup water
- 1 package (8 ounces) low-fat mozzarella cheese, diced
- ¼ pound mushrooms, sliced (optional)
- 1½ teaspoons salt
- 1 teaspoon leaf oregano, crumbled
- ½ teaspoon garlic powder
- ½ teaspoon sugar
- ¼ teaspoon pepper
- 1 can (1 pound, 4 ounces) tomatoes in tomato purée
- ½ cup low-fat ricotta cheese (from a 15-ounce container)

1. Trim zucchini; cut into very thin lengthwise slices with a very sharp knife.
2. Place onion slices and Italian sausages in a large skillet with water; cook over medium heat, stirring often, until water evaporates; then stir constantly until onion slices are golden; remove from heat; chop up sausages.
3. Layer one-third of the zucchini slices in a 8-cup shallow casserole; top with part of the cheese and mushroom slices. Combine salt, oregano, garlic powder, sugar and pepper in a cup; sprinkle part over; layer with one-third of the onion-meat mixture and tomatoes in purée. Repeat to make 3 layers; cover casserole with aluminum foil.
4. Bake in moderate oven (350°) 40 minutes; remove foil; bake 20 minutes longer, or until zucchini is tender and casserole is bubbly. Spoon ricotta on top. Let stand 10 minutes before serving.
Suggested Variations: A cup of diced cooked chicken, ½ pound ground lean beef or ½ pound chicken livers can be substituted for the Italian sausages in this recipe. To save a few more calories, use low-fat cottage cheese rather than the ricotta on top.

KEY WEST PORK

From Florida comes the inspiration for this sweet-sour combination of tropical fruits that go so well with pork.

Bake at 350° for 1 hour, 30 minutes.
Makes 8 servings at 263 calories each.

- 2 pounds lean boneless pork shoulder, cubed
- 2 tablespoons vegetable oil
- 1 large onion, chopped (1 cup)
- 2 envelopes or teaspoons instant chicken broth
- 1¼ cups water
- 2 teaspoons salt
- 1 acorn squash, cut into ½-inch slices, pared and seeded
- 1 package (9 ounces) frozen artichoke hearts
- 1 teaspoon grated lime rind
- 1 tablespoon lime juice
- 1 can (8 ounces) pineapple chunks in pineapple juice
- 3 tablespoons cornstarch

1. Brown pork cubes, a few at a time, in oil in a 10-cup flame-proof casserole or a large kettle; remove; reserve. Drain on paper towels. Pour off all but 1 tablespoon pan drippings. Sauté onion in pan drippings until soft; return browned pork to casserole; add chicken broth, water and salt; bring slowly to boiling; cover. (If using a skillet, spoon pork mixture into a 10-cup casserole; cover.)
2. Bake in moderate oven (350°) 1 hour, or until pork is almost tender; add acorn squash slices and bake 15 minutes; add artichoke hearts and bake 15 minutes longer, or until meat and vegetables are tender; stir in lime rind and juice.
3. Drain liquid from pineapple into a small saucepan; blend in cornstarch; add pineapple chunks to kettle.
4. Stir 1½ cups hot cooking liquid from casserole into saucepan. (A bulb baster does a quick job.) Cook, stirring constantly, until sauce thickens and bubbles 1 minute. Taste and sweeten with liquid or granulated sweetener, if you wish. Spoon over pork and vegetables. Garnish with lime slices, if you wish. Serve a low-calorie fruit gelatin as dessert.

PACIFIC TUNA SOUFFLÉ

Here's one way to beat the high cost of eating while on a diet.

Bake at 325° for 45 minutes.
Makes 4 servings at 259 calories each.

- 3 tablespoons butter or margarine
- 3 tablespoons all-purpose flour
- ½ teaspoon salt
- Dash pepper
- 1 cup skim milk
- 2 teaspoons finely minced onion
- ⅛ teaspoon leaf marjoram, crumbled
- 1 teaspoon Worcestershire sauce
- 1 teaspoon lemon juice
- 4 eggs, separated
- 1 can (about 7 ounces) water-pack tuna, drained and flaked

1. Melt butter or margarine in a small saucepan; blend in flour, salt and pepper; cook, stirring constantly, until bubbly; stir in milk.
2. Cook, stirring constantly, until sauce thickens and bubbles 3 minutes; stir in onion, marjoram, Worcestershire sauce and lemon juice; cool sauce slightly.
3. Beat egg whites in a medium-size bowl until stiff but not dry.
4. Beat egg yolks in a large bowl until thick and lemon-colored; blend in cooled sauce; gently fold in flaked tuna and beaten egg whites.
6. Pour mixture into a 6-cup soufflé dish or straight-sided casserole.
7. Bake in slow oven (325°) 45 to 50 minutes, or until center is firm when lightly pressed with fingertip. Serve soufflé immediately.

QUICK TIPS

Calories do count, so here are a few ways to cut casserole calories:
- Trim all visible fat from meat before browning or braising.
- Brown meats in a nonstick skillet.
- Substitute cooked shredded cabbage, lettuce or spinach for the bed of pasta or rice in your favorite recipe.
- Use skim milk, skim evaporated milk or chicken or beef broth for cream and whole milk in sauces.
- Substitute low-fat cheese, such as low-fat cottage cheese and low-fat mozzarella, for whole-milk cheese.
- Remove every speck of fat from stews or pot roasts before thickening gravy by refrigerating food or adding a few ice cubes to liquid. Wait for fat to harden, then skim off.

CHICKEN BREASTS CACCIATORE

Spaghetti sauce mix in an envelope gives a zesty flavor to baked chicken breasts.

Bake at 350° for 1 hour.
Makes 6 servings at 177 calories each.

- 3 **chicken breasts, split (about 12 ounces each)**
- 1 **Bermuda onion, cut in 6 slices**
- 1 **envelope (1½ ounces) spaghetti sauce mix**
- 1 **can (1 pound) tomatoes**

1. Brown chicken breasts in a large nonstick skillet; arrange in single layer in an 8-cup shallow casserole. Top each chicken breast with an onion slice.
2. Blend spaghetti sauce mix into drippings in skillet; stir in tomatoes; bring to boiling, stirring constantly. Spoon around chicken breasts and onions; cover casserole.
3. Bake in moderate oven (350°) 1 hour, or until chicken breasts are tender. Serve with Italian green beans, if you wish.
Suggested Variation: PORK CHOP CACCIATIORE. making 6 servings at 287 calories each, is another version of this recipe. Follow the recipe for CHICKEN BREASTS CACCIATORE. using 6 well-trimmed loin pork chops, cut ¾-inch thick. Add 1 large green pepper seeded and cut into 6 slices to Bermuda onions slices and bake in moderate oven (350°) for 1 hour, 15 minutes, or until chops are tender when pierced with a fork.

RUTH MUMBAUER'S DIET STEW

Try her method for browning onions and beef, without using a drop of fat.

Bake at 325° for 2 hours.
Makes 6 servings at 304 calories each.

- 1 **small onion, chopped (¼ cup)**
- ½ **cup water**
- 1½ **pounds lean boneless beef round, cubed**
- 1 **can condensed beef broth**
- 1 **cup dry red wine or water**
- 1 **bay leaf**
- 1 **teaspoon seasoned salt**
- ¼ **teaspoon seasoned pepper**
- 6 **small potatoes, pared**
- 3 **cups sliced celery**
- 3 **small zucchini, tipped and cut into sticks**
- 3 **cups shredded lettuce**
- 12 **cherry tomatoes**

1. Simmer onion in the ½ cup water in a nonstick large skillet for 10 minutes or just until water evaporates. Continue cooking and stirring constantly over low heat until onion browns lightly; spoon into a 12-cup casserole.
2. Brown beef, a few pieces at a time, in same skillet; place in casserole; stir beef broth, wine or water, bay leaf, seasoned salt and pepper into skillet;

bring to boiling, stirring up the cooked-on juices; pour over beef in casserole; cover casserole.
3. Bake in slow oven (325°) 1 hour; stir in potatoes; cover; bake 30 minutes; stir in celery and zucchini; cover; bake 15 minutes; stir in lettuce and cherry tomatoes; cover; bake 15 minutes longer, or until meat and vegetables are tender. Remove bay leaf. Serve in heated soup bowls.
Suggested Variations: Lean lamb or pork can be substituted for the beef in this recipe. Chicken broth, green beans, carrots, broccoli or cauliflower can also be used in place of the beef broth and listed vegetables.

DIETER'S CURRIED LAMB

Lean lamb, green beans and yellow squash make good eating that's low in calories, too.

Bake at 350° for 1 hour, 30 minutes.
Makes 8 servings at 253 calories each.

- 2 **pounds lean boneless lamb shoulder, cubed**
- 2 **tablespoons vegetable oil**
- 1 **large onion, chopped (1 cup)**
- 2 **cloves garlic, minced**
- 1 **tablespoon curry powder**
- 1 **teaspoon salt**
- ¼ **teaspoon pepper**
- 1 **can condensed chicken broth**
- 1¼ **cups water**
- 3 **large yellow squash, tipped and sliced**
- 1 **pound green beans, tipped and cut into 1-inch pieces**
- 2 **tablespoons all-purpose flour**
- ¼ **cup water**

1. Brown lamb, a few pieces at a time, in oil in a 10-cup flame-proof casserole or a large kettle; remove and reserve; drain on paper towels. Pour off all but 1 tablespoon pan drippings. Sauté onion and garlic in pan drippings. Stir in curry powder and cook 2 minutes; return lamb to casserole; stir in salt, pepper, chicken broth and the 1¼ cups water.
2. Bring slowly to boiling; lower heat; cover. (If using a kettle, spoon lamb mixture into a 10-cup casserole; cover.)
3. Bake in moderate oven (350°) 1 hour, or until meat is almost tender; add yellow squash and green beans; cover; bake 30 minutes, or until meat and vegetables are tender when pierced with a fork.
4. Combine flour and ¼ cup water in a small saucepan; stir in 1½ cups hot cooking liquid from casserole. (A bulb baster does a quick job.) Cook, stirring constantly, until sauce thickens and bubbles 3 minutes. Spoon over lamb and vegetables. Top with chopped fresh mint, if you wish.
Suggested Variation: Chicken breasts, green onions, broccoli flowerets and sliced mushrooms can be substituted for the lamb and vegetables in this recipe.

KOREAN CHICKEN

Quarters of chicken are baked in a soy-green onion sauce and served with pineapple chunks.

Bake at 350° for 1 hour.
Makes 4 servings at 323 calories each.

- 1 **broiler-fryer, quartered (about 3 pounds)**
- 1 **can (8 ounces) pineapple chunks in pineapple juice**
  Water
- ¼ **cup sliced green onions**
  OR: 1 small onion, chopped (¼ cup)
- ¼ **cup soy sauce**
  Water chestnuts (optional)

1. Arrange chicken quarters, skin-side down, in a 12-cup shallow casserole.
2. Drain juice from pineapple chunks into a 2-cup measure; add enough water to make 1 cup; reserve chunks.
3. Add green onions and soy sauce to pineapple liquid; spoon over chicken.
4. Bake in moderate oven (350°) 30 minutes; turn chicken, skin-side up; bake 15 minutes longer; add pineapple chunks and baste with sauce. Bake 15 minutes longer, or until chicken is golden and tender. Top with sliced water chestnuts, if you wish.

LOW-CALORIE VEAL MARENGO

Even classic dishes are possible on a diet, when you know how to trim the calories.

Bake at 350° for 1 hour, 30 minutes.
Makes 6 servings at 271 calories each.

- 1 **tablespoon vegetable oil**
- 1½ **pounds boneless lean veal, cubed**
- 1 **large onion, chopped (1 cup)**
- 1 **clove garlic, minced**
- 2 **tablespoons all-purpose flour**
- 4 **medium-size tomatoes, peeled and chopped**
- 1 **can condensed beef broth**
- ½ **cup dry white wine**
- 1 **teaspoon salt**
- ¼ **teaspoon freshly ground pepper**
- 1 **teaspoon leaf thyme, crumbled**
- 1 **bay leaf**
- 1 **pound mushrooms, sliced**

1. Heat oil in a large nonstick skillet; brown veal, a few pieces at a time in oil; remove and reserve.
2. Sauté onion and garlic in pan drippings until soft; sprinkle flour over and toss to blend well.
3. Add tomatoes, beef broth, wine, salt, pepper, thyme and bay leaf; bring to boiling. Place veal in an 8-cup casserole; spoon sauce over; cover.
4. Bake in moderate oven (350°) 1 hour, or until veal is nearly tender. Add mushrooms; bake 30 minutes longer. Remove bay leaf; sprinkle with chopped parsley, if you wish.

FISH FILLETS, FLORIDA-STYLE

Orange juice and rind give fish a fresh flavor yet keep the calories low.

Bake at 350° for 15 minutes for fresh fish or 30 minutes for frozen.
Makes 4 servings at 140 calories each.

- 4 small fresh fillets of sole, cod or flounder (about 1 pound)
  OR: 1 package (1 pound) frozen fillets of sole, cod or flounder
- 1 teaspoon grated orange rind
- 1 teaspoon salt
- ⅓ cup orange juice
  Steamed zucchini and yellow squash

1. Place fresh fillets in a single layer or block of frozen fish in a 6-cup shallow casserole. Sprinkle with orange rind and salt; pour orange juice over.
2. Bake in moderate oven (350°), basting once or twice with juices in pan, 15 minutes for fresh fish or 30 minutes for frozen, or until fish flakes easily with a fork. Serve with steamed zucchini and yellow squash, if you wish.

CALORIE SAVER'S PAELLA

Even dieters can enjoy this favorite from sunny Valencia when it's made this calorie-saving way.

Bake at 350° for 1 hour.
Makes 6 servings at 363 calories each.

- 1 broiler-fryer, cut up (about 2 pounds)
- 1 large onion, chopped (1 cup)
- 1 clove garlic, minced
- 1 cup uncooked long-grain rice
- 6 small slices salami, diced
- 2 teaspoons salt
- ¼ teaspoon pepper
- ⅛ teaspoon saffron, crushed
- 1 can (1 pound) tomatoes
- 1½ cups water
- 1 envelope instant chicken broth
  OR: 1 chicken bouillon cube
- 1 pound fresh shrimp, shelled and deveined
  OR: 1 package (12 ounces) frozen deveined shelled raw shrimp
- 1 can (4 ounces) pimiento, drained and cut in large pieces

1. Place chicken, skin-side down, in a single layer on rack of broiler pan.
2. Broil, 4 inches from heat, 10 minutes; turn; broil 10 minutes longer, or until lightly browned; reserve.
3. Pour 2 tablespoons drippings from broiler pan into a large skillet. Stir in onion and garlic; sauté until soft; spoon into a 12-cup casserole with rice, salami, salt, pepper and saffron.
4. Combine tomatoes with water and instant chicken broth or bouillon cube in skillet; bring to boiling, crushing bouillon cube, if using, with a spoon. Stir

into rice mixture with shrimp. Arrange chicken and pimiento on top; cover.
5. Bake in moderate oven (350°) 1 hour, or until liquid is absorbed and chicken is tender. Garnish with parsley.

CLAM SOUFFLÉ WITH LEEK SAUCE

Clam fans will like the flavor. The calories even include the Leek Sauce.

Bake at 350° for 50 minutes.
Makes 4 servings at 217 calories each.

- 1 can (about 8 ounces) minced clams
  Skim milk
- ¼ cup all-purpose flour
- 1 teaspoon salt
- ¼ teaspoon bottled red-pepper seasoning
- 4 eggs, separated
  Leek Sauce (recipe follows)

1. Drain liquid from clams into a 1-cup measure; add skim milk to make 1 cup; reserve clams.
2. Combine liquid with flour, salt and red-pepper seasoning in a small saucepan; cook, stirring constantly, until mixture thickens and bubbles 3 minutes; remove from heat. Let cool.
3. Beat egg whites just until they form soft peaks in a medium-size bowl.
4. Beat egg yolks well in a large bowl; beat in cooled sauce very slowly; stir in minced clams, then fold in beaten egg whites until no streaks of white or yellow remain. Pour into a 4-cup soufflé dish or straight-sided casserole.
5. Set dish in a baking pan; place on oven shelf; pour boiling water into pan to a depth of about an inch.
6. Bake in moderate oven (350°) 50 minutes, or until puffy-firm and golden. Remove from pan of water. Serve at once with LEEK SAUCE.

LEEK SAUCE

Makes about 1½ cups at 15 calories per tablespoon.

- 1 large leek, washed and sliced
  OR: 1 large onion, chopped (1 cup)
- 2 tablespoons butter or margarine
- 2 tablespoons all-purpose flour
- ½ teaspoon salt
- ¼ teaspoon white pepper
- 1 cup skim milk

1. Sauté leek or onion in butter or margarine in a medium-size saucepan until soft; remove with a slotted spoon and reserve.
2. Stir flour, salt and pepper into saucepan; cook, stirring constantly, until mixture bubbles; stir in milk. Continue cooking and stirring until sauce thickens and bubbles 3 minutes. Return leeks to saucepan and simmer 5 minutes to blend flavors. LEEK SAUCE is also a great low-calorie topping for fish and chicken dishes.

DIETER'S CHICKEN IN WINE

Try Family Circle's method of frying chicken without extra fat. Use the natural fat from the chicken (calories already counted) to sauté the vegetables.

Bake at 350° for 30 minutes.
Makes 4 servings at 301 calories each.

- 1 broiler-fryer, cut up (2½ pounds)
- 1 large onion, chopped (1 cup)
- 1 clove garlic, minced
- 1¾ cups water
- ½ cup dry red wine
- 1 teaspoon salt
- 1 teaspoon leaf tarragon, crumbled
- 1 bay leaf
- ½ pound small white onions, peeled
- 1 pound mushrooms, halved
- 2 envelopes or teaspoons instant beef broth
- 2 tablespoons all-purpose flour

1. Place chicken pieces, skin side down, in a large heavy skillet over very low heat. (Do not add fat.) Cook slowly until skin side is a rich brown, about 10 minutes; turn and brown other side.
2. Remove chicken from skillet and place in an 8-cup casserole. Remove 2 tablespoons of the chicken drippings from skillet.
3. Sauté chopped onion and garlic slowly, until soft, in remaining drippings in skillet; stir in 1 cup of the water, red wine, salt, tarragon and bay leaf. Bring to boiling. Pour over chicken in casserole; cover
4. Bake in a moderate oven (350°) 30 minutes, or until the chicken is tender.
5. While chicken bakes, return reserved chicken drippings to skillet; brown peeled onions slowly; add mushrooms to skillet. Toss to coat with pan drippings.
6. Add instant beef broth and ½ cup water to skillet; cover. Simmer 5 minutes. Remove mushrooms with a slotted spoon and reserve. Continue cooking onions, 15 minutes, or until tender and broth has evaporated, leaving a rich brown residue. (Watch carefully as onions could scorch.)
7. Stir liquid from casserole into skillet (a bulb baster does a quick job). Bring to boiling. Blend flour with remaining ¼ cup cold water to make a smooth paste. Stir flour mixture into boiling liquid in skillet. Continue cooking and stirring until mixture thickens and bubbles 3 minutes. Pour over chicken and vegetables. Garnish with chopped parsley, if you wish.
Suggested Variations: This is an excellent basic recipe for the dieter. You can use dry white wine instead of the red wine or 1 can condensed chicken broth can be substituted for the 1 cup water and ½ cup red wine in Step 3. You can use a 6-ounce can of mushrooms for the fresh ones. You need the small white onions to make the rich brown residue in the skillet, which makes the marvelous sauce that has flavor but few calories.

Party-time or family suppertime, it's great to know that dinner is a make-ahead, such as Beef a la Lindstrom (recipe, page 105). Our Scandinavian dish combines economical meat balls and spring vegetables with a dill-flavored sauce and rice.

Surprise everyone with a puffy Freezer Cheese Soufflé (recipe, page 98). Make and freeze for that inevitable night when you haven't had a minute to think about dinner but want to serve something special.

PUT DINNER ON ICE

From freezer to oven to table. With three easy steps, dinner's ready. Of course,
freezer casseroles involve a little work ahead of time, but you can do this when you
want. Here are the recipes to start you off, along with tips on freezing,
freezer-to-oven casserole baking, and more.

RITA FIORILLO'S BEEF STEW

So simple to fix, so delicious to eat. Make a batch when chuck is on special.

Bake at 350° for 1 hour, 30 minutes.
Makes 12 individual casseroles.

 4 pounds boneless beef chuck
       or round
 1 can (1 pound, 1 ounce) Italian
       tomatoes, drained
 ⅓ cup red wine vinegar
 2 tablespoons olive oil or
       vegetable oil
 2 tablespoons chopped parsley
 1 tablespoon salt
 2 teaspoons leaf oregano, crumbled
 1½ teaspoons garlic powder
 1 teaspoon leaf basil, crumbled
 ¼ teaspoon pepper
       Buttered noodles
       Seasoned Italian green beans

1. Trim all fat from beef; cut into 1½-inch cubes.
2. Place beef, tomatoes, vinegar, oil, parsley, salt, oregano, garlic powder, basil, and pepper in a 12-cup flame-proof casserole; cover.
3. Bake in moderate oven (350°) 1 hour, 30 minutes, or just until beef is tender; cool casserole.
4. Divide mixture among 12 freezing-cooking bags (10x8-inches). Close and freeze, following label directions.
5. To serve: Place frozen bag in a large saucepan of boiling water. Allow water to return to boil; boil 20 minutes. Open bag and turn into individual casseroles lined with buttered noodles; spoon Italian green beans around edge. Serve with a tossed greens salad.

KASHMIR TURKEY CURRY

Freeze this leftover turkey dish, then serve when the family least expects it.

Bake at 350° for 1 hour, 45 minutes.
Makes two 4-serving casseroles.

 1 large onion, chopped (1 cup)
 2 cups thinly sliced celery
 ¼ cup (½ stick) butter or margarine
 2 to 4 teaspoons curry powder
 ¼ cup all-purpose flour
 4 cups turkey broth
       OR: 2 cans (about 14 ounces)
       chicken broth
 1½ teaspoons salt
 5 cups diced cooked turkey
 8 cups hot cooked rice (2 cups
       uncooked rice)

1. Sauté onion and celery in butter or margarine until soft in a large saucepan; stir in curry powder and cook 2 minutes; stir in flour. Cook, stirring constantly, until bubbly. Add broth and salt; continue cooking and stirring until mixture thickens and bubbles 3 minutes; remove from heat; add diced cooked turkey.
2. Place hot cooked rice in a large bowl;

stir in curry mixture until well-blended.
3. Line two 6-cup shallow freezer-to-oven casseroles with heavy-duty aluminum foil, allowing enough overlap to cover food and make a tight seal.
4. Spoon rice and curry mixture into prepared casseroles; cool; cover with foil overlap; seal tightly. Label, date and freeze. When frozen solid, remove foil-wrapped food from casserole; return food to freezer.
5. To bake: Remove foil from frozen food; return to same casserole; cover.
6. Bake in moderate oven (350°) 1 hour, 45 minutes, or until bubbly-hot.

FREEZER CHEESE SOUFFLÉ

Whip up a soufflé or two on a quiet day —then you'll always be ready for guests with a spectacular dish in an hour. Shown on page 96.

Bake at 350° for 1 hour.
Makes 6 servings.

 2 tablespoons finely chopped
       shallots
       OR: 1 small onion, chopped
 ⅓ cup butter or margarine
 ⅓ cup all-purpose flour
 1 teaspoon salt
 1½ cups milk
 1 tablespoon prepared mustard
       Few drops bottled red-pepper
       seasoning
 1½ cups shredded Cheddar cheese
       (6 ounces)
 6 eggs, separated

1. Butter a 6-cup soufflé dish or straight-sided casserole.
2. Sauté shallots or onion in butter or margarine until soft in medium-size saucepan about 5 minutes. Stir in flour and salt; cook, stirring constantly, until mixture bubbles. Gradually stir in milk. Continue cooking and stirring until mixture thickens and bubbles 1 minute. Stir in mustard, red-pepper seasoning and cheese. Remove from heat.
3. Beat egg whites until stiff in a large bowl. Beat yolks well in a metal medium-size bowl; beat hot cheese sauce into yolks. Fold yolk mixture into egg whites until no streaks of yellow or white remain. Pour into prepared dish. Cover with plastic wrap or aluminum foil; label, date and freeze.
4. To bake: Place unwrapped frozen soufflé in cold oven; set oven temperature to moderate (350°); bake for 1 hour, or until puffed and golden.
HOSTESS TIP: For individual soufflés, divide mixture among six 1-cup soufflé dishes or straight-sided casseroles. Bake for 45 minutes.
Suggested Variations: One cup finely diced ham may be substituted for 1 cup of the cheese in this recipe. Swiss cheese can be substituted fo. the Cheddar cheese and 1 teaspoon leaf basil, crumbled, can be added as well.

LASAGNA ROLLUPS

Chicken and spinach are blended into an unforgettable pasta dish.

Bake at 400° for 40 minutes.
Makes 8 individual casseroles.

 1 broiler-fryer (about 2½ pounds)
 1½ cups water
 1 small onion, peeled and sliced
 1 teaspoon salt
 ¼ teaspoon pepper
 1 envelope (1½ ounces) spaghetti
       sauce mix
 1 can (1 pound, 12 ounces) tomato
       purée
 2 tablespoons butter or margarine
 1 package (10 ounces) frozen
       chopped spinach, thawed
 ¼ teaspoon ground nutmeg
 1 package (1 pound) fluted-edge
       lasagna noodles
 1 package (6 ounces) sliced
       mozzarella cheese

1. Cook chicken with water, onion, salt and pepper about 45 minutes, or until tender, in a large saucepan.
2. While chicken cooks, combine spaghetti sauce mix, tomato purée, and butter or margarine in a medium-size saucepan. Bring to boiling; reduce heat; cover. Simmer 30 minutes.
3. Remove chicken from broth; cool; reserve broth. Skin chicken; remove from bones, cut meat into small pieces.
4. For filling: Combine ½ cup of the reserved broth with half of the chicken and half of the spinach in an electric blender container; cover. Whirl until smooth, about 1 minute. Place mixture in medium-size bowl, scraping sides of blender container with rubber spatula. Repeat with remaining chicken, spinach and ½ cup broth; add to mixture in bowl; add nutmeg, blending well. (If you do not have a blender, chop chicken and spinach as fine as possible, then stir in enough chicken broth to make a smooth paste.)
5. Cook lasagna noodles in a kettle, until firm-tender; cool noodles in a large bowl of cold water.
6. To make rollups: Remove lasagna noodles, one at a time, from cold water and drain on paper towels. Spread with scant ¼ cup chicken mixture; roll up, jelly-roll fashion. Repeat with remaining lasagna noodles.
7. Place 2 lasagna rolls in each of 8 individual freezer-to-oven casseroles or 1-cup disposable aluminum pans.
8. Divide tomato sauce among casseroles; cut mozzarella cheese in lengthwise strips and arrange on rollups. Cover each dish with heavy-duty aluminum foil; label, date and freeze.
9. To bake: Remove casserole from freezer and loosen foil around casserole.
10. Bake in hot oven (400°) 30 minutes, then remove foil and bake 10 minutes longer, or until bubbly-hot and mozzarella cheese is melted.

CHICKEN STUFFED CRÊPES

You don't have to wait for a special occasion to serve crêpes.

Bake at 400° for 40 minutes.
Makes 8 individual casseroles.

- 2 broiler-fryers (about 2½ pounds each)
- 3 cups water
- 1 medium-size onion, sliced
  Handful celery leaves
- 3 teaspoons salt
- 6 peppercorns
- ⅓ cup liquid margarine
- ⅓ cup all-purpose flour
- 1 tall can evaporated milk
- ¼ teaspoon white pepper
- ⅔ cup grated Parmesan cheese
  Crêpes (recipe follows)

1. Combine chickens, water, onion, celery leaves, 2 teaspoons of the salt and peppercorns in a large kettle. Bring to boiling; lower heat; cover kettle. Simmer 45 minutes, or until chickens are tender.
2. Remove chickens from broth; strain and reserve broth. Slip skin from chicken; remove meat from bones; cut into tiny pieces; place in a medium-size bowl; reserve.
3. Combine liquid margarine and flour in a large saucepan. Cook, stirring constantly, 3 minutes, over medium heat. Stir in reserved broth, evaporated milk, remaining 1 teaspoon salt and pepper.
4. Cook, stirring constantly, until mixture thickens and bubbles 3 minutes. Add 1½ cups of sauce to chicken. Stir ⅓ cup of the cheese into remaining sauce and reserve.
5. Unroll one crêpe at a time and spread with ¼ cup of chicken mixture. Place 2 filled crêpes in each of 8 individual freezer-to-oven casseroles or 1-cup disposable aluminum pans. Pour ¼ cup of reserved sauce over each set of crêpes and sprinkle with part of remaining Parmesan cheese.
6. Cover each dish with heavy-duty aluminum foil; label, date and freeze.
7. To bake: Remove crêpes from freezer and loosen foil around container.
8. Bake in hot oven (400°) 30 minutes, then remove foil and bake 10 minutes longer, or until sauce is bubbly-hot and browned.
HOSTESS TIP: Crêpes can be layered in a 12-cup shallow freezer-to-oven casserole. Bake, covered, 45 minutes; uncover and bake 15 minutes longer.

CRÊPES

Makes sixteen 8-inch crêpes.
- 4 eggs
- 2 cups milk
- 2 teaspoons liquid margarine
- 1½ cups sifted all-purpose flour
- 1 teaspoon salt
  Liquid margarine

1. Beat eggs until foamy in a medium-size bowl; stir in milk and the 2 teaspoons liquid margarine. Beat in flour and salt until smooth.
2. Heat an 8-inch skillet or crêpe pan until very hot. Brush lightly with liquid margarine. Pour in batter, a scant ¼ cup at a time; quickly tilt pan so batter spreads and covers bottom.
3. Cook over medium to medium-high heat until edges of crêpe brown; turn and cook about 1 minute longer, or until bottom browns.
4. Turn crêpe out onto cooky sheet by flipping pan upside down; roll up crêpe, jelly-roll fashion. Repeat with remaining batter to make 16 crêpes.

MONTEREY SHRIMP SCALLOP

Freezing improves its flavor.

Bake at 350° for 1 hour, 45 minutes.
Makes two 6-serving casseroles.

- 1 cup uncooked rice
- 1 envelope or teaspoon instant vegetable or chicken broth
- 1¼ cups water
- 1 tablespoon cut chives
- 2 cans condensed cream of shrimp soup
- 1 cup milk
- 1 tablespoon Worcestershire sauce
- 1 tablespoon dry sherry
- 1 package (2 pounds) frozen shelled deveined raw shrimp
- 2 packages (9 ounces each) frozen artichoke hearts
- 1 can (6 ounces) sliced mushrooms

1. Cook rice according to label directions in a kettle 20 minutes, or until almost tender. (It will finish cooking in the oven.) Drain; return to kettle.
2. Dissolve the instant vegetable or chicken broth in the 1¼ cups water in a 2-cup measure; stir in chives; pour over drained rice.
3. Heat soup slowly with milk, Worcestershire sauce and sherry in a medium-size saucepan; stir until smooth.
4. Cook shrimp and artichoke hearts in separate saucepans, following label directions; drain. Fold the shrimp, artichokes and mushrooms with liquid into sauce.
5. Line two 8-cup shallow freezer-to-oven casseroles with heavy-duty aluminum foil, allowing enough overlap to cover food and make a tight seal.
6. Make alternate layers of shrimp mixture and rice, dividing evenly and ending with shrimp, in the two prepared dishes. Cool; cover with foil overlap; seal tightly. Label, date and freeze. When frozen solid, remove casseroles; return wrapped food to freezer.
7. To bake: Remove foil from frozen food; return to same casserole; cover.
8. Bake in a moderate oven (350°) 1 hour. Uncover; top with 1 cup of bread cubes, if you wish. Bake 45 minutes longer, or until bubbly-hot.

STEAK PIZZAIOLA

Put up a batch when beef is on special.

Makes 12 individual casseroles.

- 2 large onions, chopped (2 cups)
- 2 cloves garlic, minced
- ⅓ cup olive oil or vegetable oil
- 1 can (2 pounds, 3 ounces) Italian tomatoes
- 2 teaspoons salt
- ½ teaspoon seasoned pepper
- 3 pounds boneless chuck
  Unseasoned instant meat tenderizer

1. Sauté onion and garlic in oil until soft in large saucepan. Stir in tomatoes, salt and pepper. Simmer sauce, uncovered, 10 minutes; reserve.
2. While sauce simmers, trim any excess fat from steak and score remaining fat edge every inch. Sprinkle meat with tenderizer, following label directions.
3. Heat a large skillet. Pan-broil steak in skillet, turning once, 5 minutes on each side, or until steak is done as you like it.
4. Place steak on a cutting board; carve into thin slices. Return to skillet. Stir in tomato sauce; simmer 3 minutes to blend flavors.
5. Divide mixture among 12 freezing-cooking bags (10x8-inches). Close and label bags and freeze, following manufacturer's directions.
6. To serve: Place frozen bag in a large saucepan of boiling water. Allow water to return to boil, then boil 20 minutes. Open bag and spoon over cooked thin spaghetti in individual casseroles. Serve with hot garlic bread and a tossed salad, if you wish.

QUICK TIPS

WHAT TO DO WHEN THE POWER GOES OFF OR THE FREEZER BREAKS DOWN:
- Keep freezer door closed tightly—if freezer is fully stocked, the contents will stay frozen for at least two days; if it is half-full, the food will stay frozen for about one day.
- For periods longer than a day or two, buy dry ice—25 pounds for each cubic foot of freezer space—and place large chunks (with gloved hands) on top of the food. If the freezer is fully stocked, the dry ice will keep the food frozen three to four days; in a half-filled freezer, the dry ice will keep the food frozen up to two to three days.
- If foods have partially thawed, but still have ice crystals in their packages, they can be safely refrozen. To make sure food is only partially thawed (when ice crystals are not discernible), slip a thermometer between the food and its wrapping. If the temperature is 40°F. or lower, the food can be safely refrozen.
- If uncooked foods have thawed, cook, then safely refreeze. Any cooked foods should be heated and eaten.

CHICKEN BREASTS MANDALAY

Check supermarket ads for a special on chicken breasts, then freeze a batch in this spicy sauce.

Bake at 350° for 1 hour, 30 minutes.
Makes four 4-serving casseroles.

- 8 chicken breasts (about 12 ounces each)
- ⅓ cup all-purpose flour
- 1 to 2 tablespoons curry powder
- 1 tablespoon salt
- ½ cup vegetable oil
- 4 envelopes or teaspoons instant beef broth
  OR: 4 beef bouillon cubes
- 2 large onions chopped (2 cups)
- 2 cups water
- 1 jar (8 ounces) junior apricots (baby-pack)
- ¼ cup lemon juice
- 2 tablespoons soy sauce

1. Halve chicken breasts. Shake with mixture of flour, curry powder and salt in a plastic bag to coat lightly.
2. Line four 4-cup shallow freezer-to-oven casseroles with heavy-duty aluminum foil; allow enough overlap to cover food and seal tightly. Brown chicken in oil in a large skillet; divide chicken pieces among casseroles.
3. Stir instant broth or bouillon cubes, onion, water, apricots, lemon juice and soy sauce into drippings in skillet; bring to boiling, crushing bouillon cubes, if used, with a spoon. Pour over chicken in casseroles. Cool; cover with foil overlap; seal tightly. Label, date and freeze. When frozen solid, remove casseroles; return food to freezer.
4. To bake: Remove foil from the frozen food; return to same casserole; cover.
5. Bake in moderate oven (350°) 1 hour, 30 minutes, or until chicken is tender and sauce is bubbly-hot. Serve over prepared chicken-flavored rice mix, if you wish; pass any extra sauce separately.

CASSOULET FOR A CROWD

Turkey is often an excellent buy and this is a great way to serve it.

Bake at 350° for 1 hour, 30 minutes.
Makes two 8-serving casseroles.

- 1 frozen turkey (about 6 pounds), thawed
- 2 ham hocks (about 1 pound each)
- 8 cups water
- 1 cup grated carrot
- 2 large onions, chopped (2 cups)
- 3 teaspoons salt
- 2 cloves garlic, sliced
- 2 bay leaves
- 1 teaspoon leaf thyme, crumbled
- 3 sprigs parsley
- 1 package (2 pounds) dried large lima beans

1. Place turkey with giblets and ham hocks in a kettle. Add water, carrot, onion and salt.
2. Tie garlic, bay leaves, thyme and parsley sprigs in cheesecloth. Push under liquid in kettle.
3. Bring slowly to boiling; reduce heat; cover. Simmer 2 hours, or until turkey is tender. Discard herb bag. Place meats, giblets and liquid in a large bowl.
4. Remove meats and giblets from liquid; allow broth to stand 15 minutes; skim all fat from surface; reserve. Take skin, fat and bones from turkey and ham; cut meats and giblets into small pieces.
5. Pick over beans and rinse under running water; combine with reserved broth in a kettle; heat to boiling and boil 2 minutes; cover. Remove from heat; let stand 1 hour. Bring beans to boiling; reduce heat; simmer 2 hours, or until beans are tender. Stir in meats and giblets.
6. Line two 8-cup shallow freezer-to-oven casseroles with heavy-duty aluminum foil, allowing enough overlap to cover food and make a tight seal.
7. Divide bean mixture between prepared casseroles; cool; cover with overlap of foil; seal tightly. Label, date and freeze. When frozen solid, remove casseroles and return food to freezer.
8. To bake: Remove foil from frozen food; return to same casserole; cover.
9. Bake in moderate oven (350°) 1 hour, 30 minutes, or until bubbly-hot. Sprinkle with chopped parsley, if you wish.

LAMB PASTICHIO

Adding cinnamon to a lamb dish is characteristic of Greek cooking.

Bake at 350° for 1 hour, 45 minutes.
Makes two 6-serving casseroles.

- 1 clove garlic, minced
- 1 tablespoon vegetable oil
- 1½ pounds ground lamb
- ½ teaspoon ground cinnamon
- 1½ teaspoons salt
- ¼ teaspoon pepper
- 1 can (2 pounds, 2 ounces) tomatoes in purée
- 1 package (1 pound) elbow macaroni
- ½ cup (1 stick) butter or margarine
- ½ cup all-purpose flour
- 1 teaspoon salt
- 4 cups milk
- 3 eggs

1. Sauté garlic in oil until brown in a large skillet; remove garlic. Shape lamb into a large patty; brown 5 minutes on each side in skillet, then break up into chunks. Add cinnamon, 1½ teaspoons of the salt and pepper; mix thoroughly. Stir in tomatoes in purée; cook 2 minutes longer. Remove from heat.
2. Cook macaroni in salted boiling water in a large kettle until not quite tender, about 8 minutes. Drain well; return to kettle; reserve.
3. Melt butter or margarine in a large saucepan; add flour and remaining 1 teaspoon salt. Cook, stirring constantly until bubbly. Add milk; cook, stirring constantly, until sauce is thickened and bubbles 3 minutes. Beat eggs in a small bowl; beat in 1 cup of the hot sauce; return to saucepan. Cook 2 minutes.
4. Line two 13x9x2-inch freezer-to-oven casseroles with heavy-duty aluminum foil, allowing enough overlap to cover food and make a tight seal.
5. Layer macaroni and lamb mixture in prepared casseroles; spoon sauce over. Cool. Cover with overlap of foil; seal tightly. Label, date and freeze. When frozen solid, remove foil-wrapped food from casseroles; return food to freezer.
6. To bake: Remove foil from frozen food; return to same casserole; cover.
7. Bake in moderate oven (350°) 1 hour, 45 minutes, or until bubbly-hot.

BEER AND BEEF RAGOÛT

Freezing stews improves their flavor.

Bake at 350° for 1 hour, 30 minutes.
Makes two 6-serving casseroles.

- 3 pounds lean boneless beef chuck, cubed
- 2 tablespoons vegetable oil
- 2 large onions, sliced and separated into rings
- 1 clove garlic, minced
- 2 teaspoons salt
- ½ teaspoon leaf thyme, crumbled
- ¼ teaspoon seasoned pepper
- 1 bay leaf
- 1 can condensed beef broth
- 1 can (12 ounces) beer
- 1 package (1 pound) wide noodles, cooked firm-tender and drained
- ¼ cup all-purpose flour
- ½ cup water

1. Brown beef, part at a time, in oil in a kettle; remove and reserve.
2. Sauté onion rings and garlic until soft in same kettle; stir in salt, thyme, seasoned pepper, bay leaf, beef broth and beer; return meat to kettle; cover.
3. Simmer 1½ hours, or until beef is tender when pierced with a fork.
4. Line two 8-cup casseroles with heavy-duty aluminum foil, allowing enough overlap to cover and seal food.
5. Divide drained noodles between casseroles; spoon meat and onions over.
6. Bring liquid in kettle to boiling; blend flour and water until smooth in a cup; stir into boiling liquid. Cook, stirring constantly, until gravy thickens and bubbles 3 minutes; pour over meat mixture in casseroles. Cool; cover with foil overlap; seal tightly. Label, date and freeze. When frozen solid, remove casseroles; return food to freezer.
7. To bake: Remove foil from the frozen food; return to same casserole; cover.
8. Bake in moderate oven (350°) 1 hour, 30 minutes, or until bubbly-hot.

PORK AND BEANS VALENCIA

Orange marmalade teams with chunks of pork and husky lima beans.

Bake at 350° for 1 hour, 30 minutes.
Makes two 6-serving casseroles.

- 1 **package (1 pound) dried lima beans**
- 6 **cups water**
- 2 **pounds lean boneless pork, cubed**
- 3 **tablespoons vegetable oil**
- 2 **teaspoons salt**
- 2 **bay leaves**
- 1 **teaspoon leaf rosemary, crumbled**
- 2 **cans (8 ounces each) tomato sauce with mushrooms**
- 1 **large onion, chopped (1 cup)**
- ⅓ **cup orange marmalade**
- 2 **tablespoons cider vinegar**
- 1 **tablespoon Worcestershire sauce**
- 2 **teaspoons dry mustard**

1. Pick over beans and rinse; combine with water in a large kettle; bring to boiling; boil for 2 minutes; remove from heat; cover; let stand 1 hour.
2. Brown pork cubes in oil in a large skillet. Stir into beans with salt, bay leaves and rosemary; cover. Bring to boiling; then simmer 2 hours; remove bay leaves from cooking liquid.
3. Stir in tomato sauce with mushrooms, onion, marmalade, vinegar, Worcestershire sauce and dry mustard.
4. Line two 6-cup freezer-to-oven casseroles with heavy-duty aluminum foil, allowing enough overlap to cover food and make a tight seal. Divide mixture between two casseroles. Cool; cover with foil overlap; seal tightly. Label, date and freeze. When food is frozen solid, remove casseroles; return foil-wrapped food to freezer.
5. To bake: Remove foil from the frozen food; return to same casserole; cover.
6. Bake in moderate oven (350°) 1 hour. Uncover and stir well. Cover again and bake 30 minutes longer, or until beans are very tender.

MARVELOUS MEAT BALLS

Chinese food fans, this is for you.

Bake at 350° for 1 hour.
Makes four 4-serving casseroles.

- 2 **pounds ground round or chuck**
- 2 **pounds ground pork**
- ½ **cup all-purpose flour**
- ½ **teaspoon ground ginger**
- 1 **cup light cream or milk**
- ¼ **cup soy sauce**
- ¼ **cup (½ stick) butter or margarine**
  Ginger Sauce (recipe follows)
- 2 **medium-size green peppers**
- 1 **can (5 ounces) water chestnuts**

1. Combine ground beef and pork, flour and ginger in a large bowl of an electric mixer; beat until blended, then beat in cream and soy sauce, 1 tablespoon at a time, until mixture is smooth.

2. Shape into 64 meat balls. (Shaping can be done ahead and meat balls chilled until ready to cook.)
3. Brown meat balls, part at a time, in butter or margarine in a large skillet. Reserve pan drippings for GINGER SAUCE.
4. Halve green peppers, remove seeds; cut peppers in small squares. Drain water chestnuts; cut into thin slices.
5. Line four 4-cup shallow freezer-to-oven casseroles with heavy-duty aluminum foil, allowing enough overlap to cover food and make a tight seal.
6. Divide meat balls, green peppers and water chestnuts among casseroles; pour GINGER SAUCE over; cool; cover with overlap of foil; seal tightly. Label, date and freeze. When frozen solid, remove from casseroles; return food to freezer.
7. To bake: Remove foil from frozen food; return to same casserole; cover.
8. Bake in moderate oven (350°) 1 hour, or until bubbly-hot. Serve over stir-fried vegetables, if you wish.
GINGER SAUCE—Makes about 4 cups. After all meat balls are cooked, tip skillet so fat will rise to top; pour off all fat, leaving brown drippings in pan. Measure ½ cup fat; return to pan; blend in ½ cup all-purpose flour and 2 teaspoons ground ginger. Cook, stirring constantly, just until bubbly. Stir in 4 cups water and ⅓ cup soy sauce; continue cooking and stirring, until sauce thickens and bubbles 3 minutes; pour over casseroles.

LINGUINE ALLA MARIA TERESA

Make up a batch of these pasta and ham casseroles when you have ham on hand.

Bake at 375° for 1 hour, 30 minutes.
Makes three 6-serving casseroles.

- 2 **packages (1 pound each) linguine or spaghetti**
- 8 **cups diced cooked ham OR: 1 can (2 pounds) ham, diced**
- ¾ **cup (1½ sticks) butter or margarine**
- 1 **can (6 ounces) sliced or chopped mushrooms**
- ½ **cup all-purpose flour**
- 2 **teaspoons salt**
- 2 **tall cans evaporated milk**
- 2 **envelopes or teaspoons instant chicken broth**
- 2⅔ **cups water**
- 1 **cup grated Romano cheese**

1. Cook pasta in a kettle, for 5 minutes; drain; return to kettle.
2. While pasta cooks, brown ham slightly in butter or margarine in a large kettle; remove with slotted spoon to a large bowl; reserve.
3. Drain mushroom liquid into a cup; reserve mushrooms. Blend flour and salt into drippings in kettle; cook, stirring constantly, just until bubbly. Stir in mushroom liquid, milk, instant chicken broth and water. Continue cooking and stirring until sauce thickens and bubbles

for about 3 minutes.
4. Add 4 cups of the sauce and reserved mushrooms to the drained pasta; toss with a fork to mix.
5. Line three 6-cup shallow freezer-to-oven casseroles with heavy-duty aluminum foil, allowing enough overlap to cover food and make a tight seal.
6. Divide pasta mixture among prepared casseroles, pressing pasta up sides of casseroles to leave a hollow in each center. Add reserved ham to remaining sauce, blending well. Spoon into hollows in pasta. Sprinkle with Romano cheese. Cool; cover with overlap of foil; seal tightly. Label, date and freeze. When frozen solid, remove casseroles; return food to freezer.
7. To bake: Remove foil from frozen food; return to same casserole; cover.
8. Bake in moderate oven (375°) 1 hour; remove cover; bake 30 minutes longer, or until bubbly-hot.

COMPANY HAM BAKE

Keep a couple of these casseroles in the freezer for unexpected company.

Bake at 400° for 1 hour.
Makes three 6-serving casseroles.

- 1 **bag (1½ pounds) frozen corn**
- 1 **bag (1½ pounds) frozen lima beans**
- 2 **cups water**
- 1 **teaspoon salt**
- 1 **can (2 pounds) ham**
- 1 **can (4 ounces) green chili peppers, seeded and chopped**
- 1 **large onion, chopped (1 cup)**
- ½ **cup (1 stick) butter or margarine**
- ½ **cup all-purpose flour**
- 2 **envelopes or teaspoons instant chicken broth**
- 2 **tall cans evaporated milk**

1. Cook corn and lima beans in salted water in a large kettle 5 minutes; drain, reserving cooking liquid. Return vegetables to kettle; reserve.
2. Open can of ham and cut into 1-inch cubes; add to kettle with chili peppers.
3. Sauté onion in butter or margarine until soft in a large saucepan; stir in flour and instant chicken broth; cook, stirring constantly, just until bubbly; stir in reserved cooking liquid and evaporated milk. Cook, stirring constantly, until mixture thickens and bubbles 3 minutes. Combine with ham and vegetables.
4. Line three 6-cup shallow freezer-to-oven casseroles with heavy-duty aluminum foil, allowing enough overlap to cover food and make a tight seal.
5. Divide ham mixture among prepared casseroles; cool; cover with overlap of foil; seal tightly. Label, date and freeze. When frozen solid, remove casseroles; return food to freezer.
6. To bake: Remove foil from frozen food; return to same casserole; cover.
7. Bake in hot oven (400°) 45 minutes; remove cover. Bake 15 minutes longer.

DOUBLE PEPPER BEEF

Have on hand for the nights when everyone is on a different timetable.

Makes 12 individual casseroles.

- 4 **medium-size green peppers, halved, seeded and thinly sliced**
- 4 **medium-size sweet red peppers, halved, seeded and thinly sliced**
- 2 **tablespoons olive oil or vegetable oil**
- 3 **pounds boneless chuck**
- 2 **cups water**
- 2 **teaspoons mixed Italian herbs, crumbled**
- 2 **teaspoons salt**
- ½ **teaspoon pepper**
  Hot cooked rice

1. Sauté peppers in oil until soft in a large skillet; remove to a large bowl.
2. Cook steak in oil remaining in skillet, turning once, 5 minutes on each side or until steak is as done as you like it. Slice steak into thin strips and add to peppers.
3. Stir water, Italian herbs, salt and pepper into skillet. Cook, stirring constantly, scraping to loosen cooked-on juices in skillet. Boil 3 minutes to reduce volume by one-third. Pour over sliced beef and peppers; cool.
4. Divide mixture among 12 freezing-cooking bags (10x8 inches). Close and label bags and freeze, following manufacturer's directions.
5. To serve: Place frozen bag into a large saucepan of boiling water. Allow water to return to a boil, then boil 20 minutes. Open bag and spoon over hot cooked rice in an individual casserole.

QUICK TIPS

FREEZE ▲

HOW TO MAKE YOUR FREEZER WORK FOR YOU

In these days of high utility bills, it is a benefit to your budget to follow these rules to successful home freezing:

• Never freeze more than one 4-serving casserole for each cubic foot of freezer space at one time.

• Cool hot foods to room temperature before placing in freezer to prevent the freezer from warming up.

• Package foods carefully for the freezer. Use plastic containers with tight-fitting lids and allow about ½-inch of headroom for food to expand. Use freezer-to-oven dishes with an over-

wrapping of aluminum foil, or better still, line the freezer-to-oven casserole with aluminum foil, allowing enough for an overlapping. When food is frozen, lift out frozen packet and have dish for other cooking. When ready to bake frozen casserole, remove foil and return food to same dish.

• Fast-freeze casseroles by placing them on the coldest part of the freezer.

• Stack packages of frozen foods after making a record of the food, servings and date for future menu planning.

• Plan to use home-frozen dishes within 2 to 3 months when held at 0°F.

• Keep frozen casseroles moving, store the newest to the back and push the older ones to the front.

• Never thaw a frozen casserole at room temperature. This is the perfect way to encourage the growth of those bacteria that cause food poisoning. Either place the frozen casserole in the oven and bake or thaw in refrigerator and then bake.

SWEDISH MEAT BALLS

This Swedish classic should be served with boiled potatoes and dill pickles.

Bake at 350° for 1 hour.
Makes three 4-serving casseroles.

- 3 **pounds ground beef**
- 2 **large potatoes, cooked, peeled and mashed**
- 4 **eggs**
- 1 **cup light cream or evaporated milk**
- 1 **large beet, cooked, peeled and chopped**
- ¼ **cup chopped dill pickle**
- 2 **tablespoons chopped onion**
- 3 **teaspoons salt**
- ½ **teaspoon freshly ground pepper**
- ½ **cup (1 stick) butter or margarine**
- ⅓ **cup all-purpose flour**
- 3 **cups water**

1. Mix ground beef, mashed potatoes, eggs, cream or milk, beet, dill pickle, onion, 2 teaspoons of the salt and pepper in a large bowl; shape into 72 balls.
2. Sauté the meat balls, part at a time, in butter or margarine in a large skillet.
3. Line three 6-cup shallow freezer-to-oven casseroles with heavy-duty aluminum foil, allowing enough overlap to cover food and make a tight seal. Divide cooked meat balls among dishes.
4. Blend flour and remaining 1 teaspoon salt into drippings in pan; cook, stirring constantly, until mixture bubbles; stir in water. Cook, stirring constantly, until gravy thickens and bubbles 3 minutes; divide among casseroles; cool; cover with overlap of foil; seal tightly. Label, date and freeze. When frozen solid, remove foil-wrapped food from casseroles; return to freezer.
5. To bake: Remove foil from frozen food and return to same casserole.
6. Bake in moderate oven (350°) 1 hour, or until bubbly-hot.

BUSY DAY STEW

Pop this frozen stew in the oven, heat and serve on those days when you are extra busy.

Bake at 350° for 1 hour, 30 minutes.
Makes two 6-serving casseroles.

- 3 **pounds ground round or chuck**
- 1 **clove garlic, minced**
- 2 **teaspoons salt**
- ½ **teaspoon pepper**
- ¼ **cup vegetable shortening**
- 2 **large onions, chopped (2 cups)**
- 1 **to 2 tablespoons chili powder**
- 1 **can (1 pound, 13 ounces) tomatoes**
- 2 **cans (1 pound each) cannellini beans (white kidney beans)**
- 2 **cans (1 pound each) red kidney beans**
- 1 **can (12 or 16 ounces) whole-kernel corn**
  Shredded Cheddar cheese
- 2 **tablespoons chopped parsley**

1. Combine ground beef, garlic, salt and pepper in a large bowl; mix lightly. Shape into 60 balls.
2. Brown, part at a time, in vegetable shortening in a kettle. Stir in onion and chili powder; sauté until onion is soft.
3. Stir in tomatoes, beans and corn and liquids. Line two 8-cup shallow freezer-to-oven casseroles with heavy-duty foil, allowing enough overlap to cover and make a tight seal.
4. Divide meat ball mixture between casseroles; cool; cover with overlap of foil; seal tightly. Label, date and freeze. When frozen solid, remove casseroles; return food to freezer.
5. To bake: Remove foil from the frozen food; return to same casserole; cover.
6. Bake in moderate oven (350°) 1 hour, 30 minutes, or until bubbly-hot. Top with cheese and parsley just before serving.

ANN GEFFROY'S CHICKEN CASSEROLE

Family Circle's own special cook shares this favorite of "her boys."

Bake at 250° for 3 hours.
Makes two 6-serving casseroles.

- 5 **cups diced cooked chicken or turkey**
- 5 **cups cooked rice (about 1¼ cups uncooked)**
- 2½ **cups frozen peas (from a 1½-pound bag), cooked and drained**
- 2 **cans cream of mushroom soup**
- 1 **cup light cream or milk**
- 3 **tablespoons bottled steak sauce**
- 2 **teaspoons curry powder**
- 2 **cups shredded Swiss or Fontina cheese (8 ounces)**
- ½ **cup grated Parmesan cheese**

1. Combine chicken or turkey, rice and peas in a very large bowl or kettle.
2. Combine cream of mushroom soup,

cream or milk, steak sauce and curry powder in a large saucepan; bring to boiling, stirring often; stir in shredded cheese until melted.

3. Pour sauce over chicken mixture and stir until well-blended.

4. Line two 8-cup shallow freezer-to-oven casseroles with heavy-duty aluminum foil, allowing enough overlap to cover food and make a tight seal.

5. Divide chicken mixture between casseroles; sprinkle with Parmesan cheese; cool; cover with overlap of foil; seal tightly. Label, date and freeze. When frozen solid, remove casseroles; return food to freezer.

6. To bake: Remove foil from frozen food; return to same casserole; cover.

7. Bake in very slow oven (250°) 3 hours, or until bubbly-hot.

COOK'S TIP: If you are in a hurry, bake in hot oven (400°) 1 hour, or until bubbly.

LAMB CURRY CASSEROLE

One of the best possible ways to use up lamb leftovers.

Bake at 350° for 1 hour, 30 minutes.
Makes two 4-serving casseroles.

- 1 **large onion, chopped (1 cup)**
- 1 **clove garlic, minced**
- 2 **tablespoons vegetable oil**
- 2 **to 4 teaspoons curry powder**
- 3 **cups cubed cooked lamb**
- 2 **jars (8 ounces each)**
  junior applesauce-and-apricots (baby-pack)
- 2 **envelopes instant chicken broth**
  OR: 2 chicken bouillon cubes
- 1 **teaspoon salt**
- 1 **teaspoon ground allspice**
- ½ **cup water**
- 1 **tablespoon lemon juice**
- 8 **cups cooked rice (2 cups uncooked)**

1. Sauté onion and garlic in vegetable oil in a kettle until soft; stir in curry powder; sauté for 2 minutes longer. Stir in cubed lamb, applesauce-and-apricots, instant chicken broth or bouillon cubes, salt, allspice, water and lemon juice.

2. Bring to boiling, crushing bouillon cubes, if used, with back of spoon. Lower heat; simmer 30 minutes.

3. Line two 8-cup shallow freezer-to-oven casseroles with heavy-duty aluminum foil, allowing enough overlap to cover food and make a tight seal.

4. Divide rice between casseroles; top with lamb curry; cool; cover with overlap of foil; seal tightly. Label, date and freeze. When frozen solid, remove casseroles; return to freezer.

5. To bake: Remove foil from frozen food; return to same casserole; cover.

6. Bake in a moderate oven (350°) 1 hour, 30 minutes, or until bubbly-hot. Serve with curry condiments such as tangy chutney, banana slices and chopped peanuts, if you wish.

DOUBLE-GOOD MACARONI AND CHEESE

It's made with two cheeses: cottage and Cheddar.

Bake at 350° for 1 hour, 15 minutes.
Makes four 6-serving casseroles.

- 1 **package (2 pounds) elbow macaroni**
- 1 **container (2 pounds) cream-style cottage cheese**
- 4 **cups shredded Cheddar cheese (1 pound)**
- 1 **container (16 ounces) dairy sour cream**
- 4 **eggs, slightly beaten**
- 1 **small onion, grated**
- 1 **tablespoon salt**
- ½ **teaspoon pepper**

1. Cook macaroni in a very large kettle of boiling salted water 8 minutes, or until firm-tender; drain and return to kettle.

2. Combine cottage and Cheddar cheese, sour cream, eggs, onion, salt and pepper in a large bowl; mix until blended; fold mixture into macaroni until well-blended.

3. Line four 8-cup freezer-to-oven casseroles with heavy-duty aluminum foil, allowing enough overlap to cover food and make a tight seal.

4. Divide macaroni mixture among casseroles; cool, cover with overlap of foil; seal tightly. Label, date and freeze. When frozen solid, remove casseroles; return food to freezer.

5. To bake: Remove foil from frozen food; return to same casserole; cover.

6. Bake in moderate oven (350°) 1 hour, 15 minutes, or until bubbly-hot.

COOK'S TIP: Casseroles can be uncovered after 1 hour of baking and topped with 1½ cups soft white bread crumbs (3 slices) tossed with 2 tablespoons melted butter or margarine. Bake until crumbs are golden.

WELSH CHICKEN AND LEEK PIE

Ideal to serve when the family is eating on shifts. For single and double servings, use your toaster-oven.

Bake at 400° for 40 minutes.
Makes 8 individual casseroles.

- 1 **broiler-fryer (about 3 pounds)**
- 2 **cups water**
- 1 **cup chopped celery with leaves**
- 1 **small onion, sliced**
- 3 **teaspoons salt**
- 1 **teaspoon leaf thyme, crumbled**
- ¼ **teaspoon pepper**
- ⅓ **cup butter or margarine**
- 1 **large leek, trimmed and sliced**
  OR: l large onion, chopped (1 cup)
- ⅓ **cup all-purpose flour**
- 1 **cup light cream**
  Sesame Seed Crust (recipe follows)

1. Combine chicken, water, celery, onion, 2 teaspoons of the salt, thyme and pepper in a kettle. Bring to boiling; lower heat; cover kettle. Simmer 45 minutes or until chicken is tender.

2. Remove chicken from broth; strain and reserve broth. (You should have 2 cups.) Slip skin from chicken; remove meat from bones; cut into tiny pieces.

3. Melt butter or margarine in a large saucepan. Sauté leek or onion until soft. Sprinkle flour over and cook, stirring constantly, 3 minutes. Stir reserved chicken broth into pan with cream and the remaining 1 teaspoon salt.

4. Cook, stirring constantly, until mixture thickens and bubbles 3 minutes. Add chicken and mix well.

5. Divide mixture among 8 individual freezer-to-oven casseroles or disposable aluminum pans. Top each pie with SESAME SEED CRUST.

6. Cover each dish with aluminum foil; label, date and freeze.

7. To bake: Remove chicken pies from freezer; unwrap; place on a cooky sheet.

8. Bake in hot oven (400°) 40 minutes, or until pastry is golden and mixture is bubbly-hot.

SESAME SEED CRUST—Combine 2 cups biscuit mix with 1 teaspoon sesame seeds in a medium-size bowl. Stir in ½ cup water until mixture forms a soft dough. Turn dough out onto a lightly floured pastry cloth or board; knead a few times. Roll out dough to a ¼-inch thickness; cut into 8 pieces slightly larger than the casseroles. Make several slits in pastry for steam to escape. Turn edges under; press pastry to rim casserole.

QUICK TIPS

● Have extra cheese on hand? Shred and spoon into a plastic container; seal and freeze. Measure out just as much as you need at cooking time.

● To remove foil or wax paper stuck to frozen foods, simply place the package in a 300° oven for 5 minutes.

● Kitchen clean-ups will be easier if you prevent grease from spattering while frying. The easiest way is to invert a colander over the skillet or flame-proof casserole. It will catch the grease, yet allow the steam to escape.

● Casseroles are international dishes. They are imported from all over the world and each country has its own system for measuring. Below is a chart to help you convert from one system to another.

Cups	= Pints	= Quarts	= Liters
1	½	¼	0.237
2	1*	½*	0.473
3	1½	¾	0.710
4	2*	1*	0.946
6	3	1½	1.419
8	4	2	1.892
10	5	2½	2.365
12	6	3	2.838
20	10	5	4.730

*In Canada 1 pint = 2½ cups
1 quart = 5 cups

BAKED BEANS ACAPULCO

Chips of pimiento and green pepper are simmered in this savory bean dish.

Bake at 350° for 1 hour, 30 minutes.
Makes two 4-serving casseroles.

- 1 **package (1 pound) dried pea beans**
- 6 **cups water**
- 1 **large onion, chopped (1 cup)**
- 1 **clove garlic, minced**
- ¼ **pound salt pork, diced**
- 2 **envelopes or teaspoons instant beef broth**
- 1 **bay leaf**
- 1 **small hot pepper**
- 1 **can (1 pound, 4 ounces) tomatoes, chopped**
- 2 **cans (4 ounces each) pimiento, cubed**
- 1 **large green pepper, halved, seeded and chopped**
- ¼ **cup firmly packed brown sugar**
- 2 **teaspoons hot mustard prepared**
- 1 **teaspoon salt**

1. Pick over beans and rinse; combine with water in a large kettle. Bring to boiling; boil for 2 minutes; remove from heat; cover; let stand 1 hour.
2. Add onion, garlic, salt pork, instant beef broth, bay leaf and hot pepper to kettle; return to boiling; simmer 2 hours; remove bay leaf.
3. Stir in tomatoes, pimiento, green pepper, brown sugar, prepared mustard and salt; remove from heat.
4. Line two 6-cup freezer-to-oven casseroles with heavy-duty aluminum foil, allowing enough overlap to cover food and make a tight seal.
5. Divide bean mixture between casseroles; cool; cover with overlap of foil; seal tightly. Label, date and freeze. When frozen solid, remove casseroles; return food to freezer.
6. To bake: Remove foil from the frozen food; return to same casseroles; cover.
7. Bake in moderate oven (350°) 1 hour. Uncover and stir well. Cover again and bake 30 minutes longer, or until beans are tender. Serve with a tray of crisp cucumber and green pepper slices.

CHICKEN AND HAM NEWBURG

Have party food for pennies.

Bake at 350° for 1 hour.
Makes two 4-serving casseroles.

- 3 **chicken breasts (about 12 ounces each)**
- 3 **cups water**
- 1½ **teaspoons seasoned salt**
- ¼ **cup (½ stick) butter or margarine**
- ⅓ **cup all-purpose flour**
- 1 **cup heavy cream**
- 2 **egg yolks**
- ⅓ **cup dry sherry**
- ¾ **pound cooked ham, cubed**
- ½ **cup quartered pitted ripe olives**

1. Combine chicken breasts, water and seasoned salt in a large saucepan. Bring to boiling, lower heat, simmer 20 minutes, or until chicken is tender. Lift out chicken; cool until easy to handle. Slip skin from chicken; remove from bones; cut meat into 1-inch cubes. Reduce broth by boiling rapidly, uncovered, over high heat, 10 to 15 minutes, to make 2 cups; strain.
2. Melt butter or margarine in same saucepan; stir in flour. Heat, stirring constantly, until bubbly. Gradually stir in broth and heavy cream; continue cooking and stirring until sauce thickens and bubbles 3 minutes.
3. Beat egg yolks slightly in a small bowl. Slowly stir in a generous cup of the hot sauce, then stir back into remaining sauce in pan; add sherry. Heat, stirring constantly, 1 minute. Fold in chicken, ham and olives. Heat gently 5 minutes.
4. Line two 4-cup freezer-to-oven casseroles with heavy-duty aluminum foil, allowing enough overlap to cover food and make a tight seal. Spoon in chicken mixture; cool; cover with overlap. Label, date and freeze. When frozen, remove dishes; return food to freezer.
5. To bake: Remove foil from frozen chicken mixture and place in same casserole; cover. Place in baking pan; pour 1 inch of hot water into baking pan.
6. Bake in moderate oven (350°) 1 hour, stirring once or twice, until casserole is bubbly-hot. Serve with refrigerated flaky biscuits, if you wish.

ROLLED STUFFED STEAKETTES

A trick for slicing raw meat is to freeze the piece about 45 minutes before cutting with a very sharp knife.

Bake at 400° for 1 hour.
Makes 12 individual casseroles.

- 1 **bottom round roast (about 3 pounds)**
- 1 **large onion, chopped (1 cup)**
- ½ **cup vegetable oil**
- 6 **cups soft white bread crumbs (12 slices)**
- 1 **cup grated Parmesan cheese**
- 1 **cup chopped parsley**
- 2 **teaspoons salt**
- ¼ **cup hot water**
- ½ **cup all-purpose flour**
- 4 **envelopes or teaspoons instant beef broth**
- 2 **teaspoons leaf thyme, crumbled**
- 5 **cups water**

1. Cut beef into 12 thin slices; pound slices with a wooden or metal meat mallet to a ¼-inch thickness.
2. Sauté onion in ¼ cup of the oil until soft in a large skillet. Add bread crumbs, Parmesan cheese, parsley, salt and hot water; toss lightly to mix.
3. Spread ¼ cup of the stuffing on each beef slice. Roll up, jelly-roll fashion; secure with wooden picks.

5. Stir flour, instant beef broth and thyme into drippings in skillet; cook, stirring constantly until bubbly; stir in water; continue to cook, stirring constantly, just until gravy thickens and bubbles 3 minutes.
6. Return beef rolls to skillet; cover. Simmer 1 hour, or until tender when pierced with a fork.
7. Place a beef roll in each of 12 individual freezer-to-oven casseroles or 1-cup disposable aluminum pans.
8. Divide sauce among casseroles ; cover each with heavy-duty aluminum foil; label, date and freeze.
9. To bake: Remove beef rolls from freezer; loosen foil around dishes.
10. Bake in hot oven (400°) 1 hour, or until bubbly-hot. Serve with French bread and a hearty red wine.

CHEESE AND VEGETABLE BAKE

Mixed vegetables and sliced frankfurters bubble in a rich cheese sauce for hearty supper eating.

Bake at 400° for 1 hour.
Makes three 6-serving casseroles.

- 2 **bags (1½ pounds each) frozen mixed vegetables**
- 2 **cups water**
- 2 **teaspoons salt**
- 2 **pounds frankfurters**
- 1 **can (4 ounces) pimiento, chopped**
- ½ **cup (1 stick) butter or margarine**
- ½ **cup all-purpose flour**
- 1 **teaspoon leaf basil, crumbled**
- 2 **tall cans evaporated milk**
- 2 **cups shredded sharp process American cheese (8 ounces)**
- 2 **tablespoons prepared mustard**

1. Cook mixed vegetables in water and salt in a large kettle 5 minutes; drain, reserving liquid. Return to kettle.
2. Cut frankfurters into ½-inch slices and add to kettle with chopped pimiento.
3. Melt butter or margarine in a large saucepan until bubbly; stir in flour and basil; cook, stirring constantly, just until bubbly; stir in reserved cooking liquid and evaporated milk. Cook, stirring constantly, until mixture thickens and bubbles 3 minutes; stir in cheese until melted; add mustard. Combine with frankfurters and vegetables.
4. Line three 6-cup shallow freezer-to-oven casseroles with heavy-duty aluminum foil, allowing enough overlap to cover food and make a tight seal.
5. Divide frankfurter mixture among prepared casseroles; cool; cover with overlap of foil; seal tightly. Label, date and freeze. When frozen solid, remove casseroles; return food to freezer.
6. To bake: Remove foil from frozen food and return to the same casserole; cover.
7. Bake in hot oven (400°) 45 minutes; remove cover. Bake 15 minutes longer, or until bubbly-hot.

MOUSSAKA ROMANO

Eggplant and lasagna noodles are layered with two sauces.

Bake at 350° for 1 hour.
Makes 10 servings.

    Béchamel Sauce (recipe, page 75)
1 container (15 ounces) ricotta cheese
    OR: 1 container (1 pound) cream-style cottage cheese
½ teaspoon ground cinnamon
3 eggs
1 medium-size eggplant, pared and sliced ¼-inch thick
3 tablespoons olive oil or vegetable oil
1 package (1 pound) lasagna noodles
    Tomato-Meat Sauce (recipe, page 75)
½ cup grated Parmesan cheese

1. Make BÉCHAMEL SAUCE: combine with ricotta or cottage cheese, cinnamon and eggs in a large bowl.
3. Fry eggplant lightly in oil in a large skillet; drain and reserve.
4. Cook lasagna noodles in boiling salted water (16 cups water plus 2 tablespoons salt) until not quite tender, about 12 minutes. Rinse with cold water; drain on paper towels.
5. Cover the bottom of a 15⅜x10⅜x2¼-inch lasagna pan or two 13x9x2-inch casseroles with part of the TOMATO-MEAT SAUCE, then eggplant, then ricotta cheese mixture and noodles. Repeat to make 3 layers, ending with meat mixture; sprinkle with Parmesan cheese; cover; refrigerate.
6. One hour before serving, place uncovered casserole in oven; set oven control to moderate (350°); bake 1 hour, or until bubbly-hot. Allow to set 10 minutes before cutting.

GOLDEN GATE EGGS

The individual casseroles can be popped into the oven as family members arrive.

Bake at 375° for 20 minutes.
Makes 4 servings.

3 cups hot cooked rice
¼ cup chopped parsley
1 can condensed cream of shrimp soup
⅓ cup milk
1 can (about 3½ ounces) tuna, drained and flaked
6 hard-cooked eggs, shelled
¼ cup finely diced celery
¼ cup mayonnaise or salad dressing
½ teaspoon salt

1. Combine rice and parsley; spoon into 4 individual glass-ceramic casseroles.
2. Heat soup and milk in a small saucepan for 2 minutes; add tuna; spoon half the sauce over rice.
3. Halve eggs crosswise. Remove yolks and mash in a small bowl; stir in celery,

---

8 FOR HURRIED DAYS

Everybody's in a hurry. That's why we've given a lot of thought to make-ahead casseroles—the kind you can prepare when you're not in a hurry, and cook when you are. Recipes for the make-aheads begin here, but you'll find others throughout this book.

mayonnaise or salad dressing and salt; pile back into whites; set three halves in each casserole; spoon remaining sauce over eggs; cover; refrigerate.
4. Half an hour before serving, place covered casserole in oven; set oven control to moderate (375°); bake 20 minutes, or until bubbly-hot. Serve with lemon wedges, if you wish.

BEEF A LA LINDSTROM

Everyday hamburger goes gourmet with slender green bean slivers and waffle-cut yellow squash.

Bake at 350° for 1 hour.
Makes 6 servings.

1½ pounds ground chuck
1 small onion, grated
2 eggs, beaten
1 cup soft white bread crumbs (2 slices)
1½ teaspoons salt
¼ teaspoon pepper
3 tablespoons butter or margarine
1 cup uncooked rice
2¼ cups water
2 envelopes or teaspoons instant chicken broth
2 large yellow squash
1 pound green beans
1 container (16 ounces) dairy sour cream
½ cup milk
2 tablespoons all-purpose flour
1 tablespoon chopped fresh dill
    OR: 1 teaspoon dillweed

1. Mix ground chuck, onion, eggs, bread crumbs, salt and pepper in a large bowl, just until blended; shape into 30 balls.
2. Brown, part at a time, in butter or

margarine, in a large skillet; remove.
3. Cook rice with water and instant chicken broth in a large saucepan, following label directions.
4. Tip yellow squash; cut with waffle-cutter into ½-inch diagonal slices; cut each slice into 3 sticks with waffle-cutter. (Or you can just use a paring knife, but they won't be as pretty.) Tip green beans and cut lengthwise.
5. Cook vegetables in separate medium-size saucepans in boiling salted water, just until crisply-tender; drain.
6. Spoon rice into the bottom of a 10-cup shallow casserole. Pile meat balls in center of rice; arrange piles of yellow squash and green beans around edge.
7. Combine sour cream, milk, flour and dill in a medium-size saucepan; heat slowly, stirring constantly, just until hot, but do not boil; pour over meat balls; cool; cover; refrigerate.
8. One hour before serving, place covered casserole in oven; set oven control to moderate (350°); bake 1 hour or until bubbly-hot. Serve with refrigerated crescent dinner rolls and a Boston lettuce and cherry tomato salad.

STEAK PIQUANT

Chunks of beef bake with noodles, limas and tomatoes. A touch of cardamom gives a Scandinavian flavor.

Bake at 350° for 45 minutes.
Makes 6 servings.

2 pounds boneless chuck, cubed
2 tablespoons vegetable oil
½ cup water
2 beef bouillon cubes
1½ teaspoons salt
½ teaspoon ground cardamom
¼ teaspoon pepper
1 tablespoon lemon juice
1 package (8 ounces) noodles
1 package (10 ounces) frozen baby lima beans
3 medium-size tomatoes, cut into wedges

1. Brown beef, a few pieces at a time, in oil in a large skillet. Stir in water, bouillon cubes, salt, cardamom, pepper and lemon juice; bring to boiling, crushing cubes with back of spoon. Cover; simmer 1 hour, or until meat is tender when pierced with a fork.
2. Cook noodles, following label directions; drain; place in a 12-cup casserole.
3. Cook lima beans, following label directions; drain; spoon over noodles to make a ring around edge of casserole.
4. Spoon meat in middle, then pour juices over all. Arrange tomato wedges, overlapping, on top of lima beans; season with salt and pepper, if desired. Cover; refrigerate.
5. Forty-five minutes before serving, place covered casserole in oven; set oven control to moderate (350°); bake 45 minutes, or until bubbly-hot. Sprinkle with chopped parsley, if you wish.

STEAK-AND-ONION SUISSE

Let your range do the work then you take the bows with this beef and beer dish.

Bake at 375° for 1 hour, 30 minutes.
Makes 6 servings.

- 2 pounds round steak, cut ¾-inch thick
- 1½ cups water
- 1 envelope (2 to a package) onion soup mix
- 1 can (12 ounces) beer
- 6 medium-size potatoes, pared and quartered
- 6 medium-size carrots, pared and quartered

1. Trim fat from steak; melt a few pieces of fat trimmings in a large kettle. Brown steak quickly in hot fat; remove.
2. Bring water to boiling in same kettle; blend in onion soup mix and beer; return browned steak. Cover; simmer 1½ hours, or just until meat is tender; place meat and juices in a 12-cup casserole; cool; cover and refrigerate.
3. One and a half hours before serving, place covered casserole in oven; set oven control to moderate (375°); bake 45 minutes. Lay potatoes and carrots on top of steak; bake, covered, 45 minutes longer, or until vegetables are tender when pierced with a fork.

FRENCH MARROW BEAN CASSEROLE

A hearty French provincial casserole that is even more delicious if baked one day and served the next.

Bake at 325° for 2½ hours,
then at 350° for 1 hour.
Makes 8 servings.

- 1 package (1 pound) dried marrow or Great Northern beans
- 8 cups water
- 2 large onions, chopped (2 cups)
- 1 pound boneless lamb shoulder, cubed
- 2 tablespoons vegetable oil
- 2 cloves garlic, minced
- 1 cup dry vermouth, dry white wine or water
- 2 envelopes or teaspoons instant beef broth
- 1 tablespoon salt
- 1 teaspoon leaf thyme, crumbled
- ½ teaspoon freshly ground pepper
- 1 bay leaf

1. Pick over beans and rinse under running water. Combine beans and water in a large kettle. Bring to boiling; cover kettle. Boil 2 minutes; remove from heat; let stand 1 hour. Return kettle to heat; bring to boiling; add onions and lower heat; simmer 2 hours, or until beans are firm-tender.
2. Brown lamb cubes in vegetable oil in a large skillet; push to one side; add garlic and sauté 3 minutes; stir in ver-

mouth or white wine or water, instant beef broth, salt, thyme, pepper and bay leaf; bring to boiling.
3. Drain beans, reserving liquid. Combine beans and lamb mixture in a 12-cup bean pot or casserole; add enough reserved liquid to just cover the beans; cover casserole.
4. Bake in slow oven (325°) 2½ hours, adding more reserved liquid, if needed, to prevent beans from drying; cover; cool; then refrigerate.
5. One hour before serving, place uncovered casserole in oven; set oven control to moderate (350°); bake 1 hour, or until beans are very tender.
COOK'S TIP: Beans can be frozen in serving-size portions in freezing-cooking bags. To serve, bring water to boiling in a large saucepan; add pouch of frozen beans. Return water to boiling; lower heat and simmer 20 minutes.

CHINESE PORK AND VEGETABLES

You can serve crisply cooked vegetables even though the casserole was prepared ahead when you follow this method.

Bake at 350° for 1 hour.
Makes 4 servings.

- 1 pound lean pork shoulder, cubed
- 3 tablespoons peanut oil or vegetable oil
- 1 small Bermuda onion, thinly sliced and separated into rings
- 2 tablespoons brown sugar
- 1 tablespoon cornstarch
- ¼ teaspoon ground ginger
- ½ cup water
- 3 tablespoons soy sauce
- 1 beef bouillon cube
- 4 cups finely shredded Chinese or green cabbage
- 1 small yellow squash, tipped and sliced
- 1 cup sliced celery
- 1 can (1 pound) bean sprouts, drained
  Hot cooked rice

1. Brown pork in oil in a large skillet; add onion rings; sauté lightly 3 minutes, or just until soft (do not let them brown); spoon meat and onions into a 12-cup casserole.
2. Stir brown sugar, cornstarch and ginger into same pan; add water, soy sauce and bouillon cube; cook, stirring constantly, until cube dissolves and sauce thickens and bubbles 1 minute; pour over meat in casserole.
3. Layer cabbage, squash, celery and drained bean sprouts over meat; cover; cool, then refrigerate.
4. One hour before serving time, place covered casserole in oven; set oven control to moderate (350°); bake 1 hour, or until vegetables are crisply cooked.
5. Stir vegetables into meat in casserole; serve over hot cooked rice; top with toasted shredded almonds and pass soy sauce, if you wish.

FETTUCINE CON ZUCCHINI

A Roman way to serve pasta and cheese. Belisimo!

Bake at 350° for 45 minutes.
Makes 6 servings.

- 1 package (1 pound) fettucine noodles
- 2 cups shredded Gruyère or Swiss cheese (8 ounces)
  Béchamel Sauce (recipe, page 75)
- 1 large onion, chopped (1 cup)
- ¼ cup (½ stick) butter or margarine
- 6 medium-size zucchini, trimmed and cut into ½-inch-thick slices
- 1 teaspoon salt
- 1 teaspoon mixed Italian herbs, crumbled
- ½ cup grated Parmesan cheese

1. Cook noodles in boiling salted water in a large saucepan, 5 minutes, or until firm-tender; drain; return to saucepan.
2. Stir cheese into BÉCHAMEL SAUCE until melted. Pour over noodles; toss to mix; spoon into an 8-cup shallow casserole.
3. Sauté onion in butter or margarine just until soft in a large skillet; stir in zucchini; sprinkle salt and Italian herbs over zucchini; toss, cover. Steam, stirring once or twice, 10 minutes.
4. Push noodles to edges of casserole to make a shallow well in middle; fill with zucchini. Sprinkle with grated Parmesan cheese; cool; cover; refrigerate.
5. Forty-five minutes before serving, place covered casserole in oven; set oven control to moderate (350°); bake 30 minutes; remove cover. Bake 15 minutes longer, or until noodles are golden.

MIDSUMMER CHICKEN

Summer favorites—chicken and corn—are baked in a creamy golden sauce.

Bake at 400° for 1 hour.
Makes 8 servings.

- 1 broiler-fryer (about 3 pounds)
- 1 cup water
  Handful celery leaves
- 1 small onion, sliced
- 1 teaspoon salt
- ¼ teaspoon pepper
- ¼ teaspoon ground ginger
- 1 package (8 ounces) elbow macaroni
- 1 large onion, chopped (1 cup)
- 1 clove garlic, minced
- ¼ cup vegetable oil or peanut oil
- 1 can (about 1 pound) cream-style corn
- 1 can (3 or 4 ounces) sliced mushrooms
- 1 can condensed cream of celery soup
- ¼ cup grated Parmesan cheese

1. Combine chicken in water with celery leaves, onion slices, salt, pepper and ginger in a large saucepan; bring to

boiling; lower heat; cover; simmer 45 minutes, or until tender; remove chicken and set aside until cool enough to handle.

2. Strain stock into a 2-cup measure; skim off fat; return stock to saucepan, adding water to make 8 cups; bring to boiling; stir in macaroni; cook 8 minutes or until firm-tender; drain.

3. While macaroni cooks, remove chicken meat from bones; cut into bite-size pieces (you should have about 3 cups).

4. Sauté onion and garlic until soft in oil in a large skillet; stir in corn, mushrooms and liquid, celery soup and chicken; layer with macaroni in a 12-cup casserole; cover; cool, then refrigerate.

5. One hour before serving, place covered casserole in oven; set oven control on hot (400°); bake 30 minutes; uncover and sprinkle with cheese; bake, uncovered, 30 minutes longer.

TARRAGON CHICKEN

Chicken becomes a special treat when sautéed in tarragon butter and sauced with a touch of wine.

Bake at 350° for 1 hour.
Makes 4 servings.

- 1 **broiler-fryer, cut up (about 2½ pounds)**
- 3 **tablespoons butter or margarine**
- 2 **tablespoons chopped fresh tarragon**
  OR: 2 teaspoons leaf tarragon, crumbled
- 1 **small onion, finely chopped (¼ cup)**
- ½ **cup dry white wine or chicken broth**
- 1½ **teaspoons salt**
- ¼ **teaspoon pepper**
- 3 **tablespoons all-purpose flour**
- 1 **cup milk**
- 1 **cup uncooked long-grain rice**
- ¼ **cup chopped parsley**

1. Brown chicken in butter or margarine with tarragon in a large skillet; remove and reserve.

2. Sauté onion in drippings until soft. Stir in wine or broth, salt and pepper.

3. Return chicken to skillet; baste with wine mixture. Cover skillet; lower heat; simmer 20 minutes, or until chicken is almost tender.

4. Combine flour and milk in a cup to make a smooth mixture. Increase heat under skillet until liquid bubbles. Add milk mixture, stirring constantly until sauce thickens and bubbles.

5. While chicken simmers, cook rice, following label directions; stir in parsley; spoon over the bottom of an 8-cup shallow casserole. Arrange chicken and pour sauce over; cool; cover; refrigerate.

6. One hour before serving, place covered casserole in oven; set oven control to moderate (350°); bake 30 minutes; uncover; bake 30 minutes longer, or until bubbly-hot.

MEDITERRANEAN CASSEROLE

Try this Southern European way of combining zucchini and sausage for a hearty main dish.

Bake at 400° for 1 hour.
Makes 6 servings.

- 6 **medium-size zucchini, trimmed and cut into 1-inch cubes**
- ¼ **cup olive oil or vegetable oil**
- 1 **pound small pork sausages**
- 1 **teaspoon curry powder**
- 1 **medium-size onion, chopped (½ cup)**
- 3 **tablespoons chopped parsley**
- 1 **teaspoon salt**
- 1 **teaspoon leaf oregano, crumbled**
- 2 **large tomatoes, peeled and cut into thick slices**

1. Sauté zucchini in oil in a large skillet until golden; remove and reserve.

2. Pan-fry sausages in same skillet, turning often, 10 minutes, or until lightly browned and fat has cooked out; drain sausages on paper towels; pour all but 1 tablespoon fat from pan.

3. Stir in curry powder and onion; cook until onion is soft; stir in parsley, salt and oregano; remove from heat.

4. Layer half the drained sausages in an 8-cup casserole; top with layers of half the zucchini, tomato slices and onion mixture; repeat layers of zucchini, tomato and onion mixture; arrange remaining sausages on top; cover; cool, then refrigerate.

5. One hour before serving, place covered casserole in oven; set oven control to hot (400°); bake 1 hour, or until bubbly-hot.

OLD-FASHIONED TURKEY CASSEROLE

Frozen turkey parts make it possible to serve turkey dishes often, and not just after roasting the whole bird.

Bake at 350° for 45 minutes.
Makes 6 servings.

- 1 **package (about 3 pounds) frozen turkey legs and thighs**
- 4 **cups water**
- 3½ **teaspoons salt**
- ¾ **teaspoon pepper**
- 1 **large onion, quartered**
- ¼ **cup (½ stick) butter or margarine**
- ¼ **cup all-purpose flour**
- ½ **teaspoon leaf thyme, crumbled**
- ½ **teaspoon leaf rosemary, crumbled**
- 1 **can (1 pound) onions, drained**
- 1 **can (1 pound) sliced carrots, drained**
- 1 **package (10 ounces) frozen lima beans, cooked**
- 1 **cup crumbled potato chips (from a 3½-ounce bag)**

1. Place turkey parts in a large heavy kettle or Dutch oven; add water, 2 teaspoons of the salt, ½ teaspoon of the

pepper and the quartered onion. Bring to boiling; lower heat; cover. Simmer about 1½ hours, or until tender. Remove turkey parts to a large bowl to cool.

2. Skim fat from broth; bring to boiling; boil until reduced to 2 cups; reserve.

3. When turkey is cool enough to handle, pull off skin and slip meat from bones; cut meat into bite-size pieces.

4. Melt butter or margarine in a medium-size saucepan; stir in flour, remaining 1½ teaspoons salt, remaining ¼ teaspoon pepper, the thyme and rosemary. Cook, stirring constantly, just until bubbly. Stir in turkey broth; continue cooking and stirring, until gravy thickens and bubbles 3 minutes.

5. Combine turkey, gravy, onions, carrots and lima beans in an 8-cup casserole; cool; cover; refrigerate.

6. Forty-five minutes before serving, uncover casserole and top with potato chips; place in oven; set oven control on moderate (350°); bake 45 minutes, or until hot and bubbly.

HARVEST PORK BAKE

Meat casseroles always taste more flavorful when you make them one day and bake the next.

Bake at 375° for 50 minutes.
Makes 6 servings.

- 2 **pounds boneless lean pork shoulder, cubed**
- 2 **tablespoons vegetable oil**
- 2 **large onions, chopped (2 cups)**
- 2 **tablespoons all-purpose flour**
- 1½ **teaspoons salt**
- 1 **teaspoon leaf basil, crumbled**
- 1 **teaspoon leaf rosemary, crumbled**
- ¼ **teaspoon pepper**
- 2 **envelopes or teaspoons instant chicken broth**
- 2 **cups water**
- 4 **medium-size sweet potatoes**
- 3 **medium-size apples, pared, quartered, cored and sliced**

1. Brown pork cubes, a few at a time, in oil in a large kettle; remove. Add onions and sauté just until soft, then return pork to pan.

2. Mix flour, salt, basil, rosemary, pepper and instant chicken broth in a cup; sprinkle over meat mixture; toss to coat evenly. Stir in water slowly.

3. Bring to boiling; lower heat; cover; simmer 2 hours, or until meat is tender.

4. While meat cooks, parboil sweet potatoes in boiling salted water in a medium-size saucepan 20 minutes. Drain; peel; cut in ¼-inch-thick slices.

5. Layer potato slices, pork mixture and apple slices in an 8-cup casserole; cover; cool; refrigerate.

6. Fifty minutes before serving, place covered casserole in oven; set oven control to moderate (375°); bake 50 minutes, or until bubbly-hot.

BEEF STEW CALCUTTA

Curried beef is even more popular in London than in India. This recipe will make it a favorite in your home, too.

Bake at 350° for 1 hour, 15 minutes.
Makes 6 servings.

  2 **pounds boneless beef chuck, cubed**
  3 **tablespoons vegetable oil**
  1 **large onion, chopped (1 cup)**
1½ **to 3 teaspoons curry powder**
  2 **teaspoons salt**
  ¼ **teaspoon pepper**
  1 **envelope instant beef broth OR: 1 beef bouillon cube**
  2 **cups water**
  3 **large carrots, pared and thinly sliced**
  1 **cup thinly sliced celery**
  1 **apple, pared, quartered, cored and sliced**

1. Brown meat cubes, a few pieces at a time, in oil in a large kettle or Dutch oven; remove and reserve.
2. Sauté onion in drippings until soft; stir in curry powder and cook 2 minutes. Return meat to pan, then stir in salt, pepper, instant beef broth or bouillon cube and water, crushing cube, if using.
3. Bring to boiling; lower heat; cover; simmer 1 hour, or until beef is almost tender. Spoon into an 8-cup casserole; cool; add carrots and celery; cover; refrigerate.
4. One hour and a quarter before serving, place covered casserole in oven; set oven control to moderate (350°); bake 1 hour; add apple. Bake 15 minutes longer, or until carrots are tender. Serve with OVEN BAKED RICE PILAF (recipe on page 84), if you wish.

PAPRIKASH CASSEROLE

The cooking of Vienna inspired this veal and noodle dish. You can substitute lean pork shoulder for the veal.

Bake at 350° for 1 hour.
Makes 6 servings.

  2 **pounds veal for stewing, cut into 1-inch cubes**
  ¼ **cup all-purpose flour**
  1 **tablespoon paprika**
1½ **teaspoons salt**
  2 **tablespoons vegetable shortening**
  2 **cans (1 pound each) tomatoes**
  1 **envelope (2 to a package) onion soup mix**
  ⅛ **teaspoon pepper**
  1 **package (8 ounces) medium-size noodles**
  1 **tablespoon butter or margarine**
  1 **container (8 ounces) dairy sour cream**
  1 **teaspoon all-purpose flour**
  1 **teaspoon caraway seeds**

1. Shake veal with the ¼ cup flour,

paprika and salt in a plastic bag to coat.
2. Brown, half the meat at a time, slowly in shortening in a large skillet; remove; return all meat to pan; stir in tomatoes, onion soup mix and pepper; cover tightly; simmer, stirring a few times, 30 to 45 minutes, or until meat is tender; pour into a 10-cup casserole.
3. While meat simmers, cook noodles in a large saucepan, 5 minutes, or until firm-tender; drain; return to saucepan; add butter or margarine; toss to coat well; spoon on top of meat in casserole but do not stir in (noodles keep their color best if not mixed with sauce); cover; cool, then refrigerate.
4. One hour before serving, place covered casserole in oven; set oven control at moderate (350°); bake 55 minutes, or until bubbly-hot.
5. Combine sour cream, 1 teaspoon flour and caraway seeds in a small bowl. (Let sour cream stand at room temperature, while casserole cooks.) Stir into bubbly-hot casserole; bake just 5 minutes longer to heat sour cream, sprinkle casserole with chopped parsley, just before serving, if you wish.

GLAZED PORK CHOPS

Treat the family to this fruit glazed pork recipe when there's a special on pork at the market.

Bake at 375° for 1 hour, 30 minutes.
Makes 6 servings.

  6 **rib or loin pork chops, cut ¾-inch thick**
  1 **large onion, chopped (1 cup)**
  2 **tablespoons all-purpose flour**
  2 **tablespoons brown sugar**
  1 **tablespoon curry powder**
  1 **teaspoon salt**
  1 **teaspoon ground cinnamon**
  1 **cup water**
  1 **envelope or teaspoon instant beef broth**
  2 **tablespoons catsup**
  1 **jar (about 4 ounces) baby strained apples-and-apricots**
  ¼ **cup flaked coconut**

1. Trim any excess fat from chops. Brown chops in remaining fat in a large skillet; place in a 13x9x2-inch casserole.
2. Sauté onion in pan drippings until soft. Blend in flour, brown sugar, curry powder, salt and cinnamon; cook, stirring constantly, until bubbly; stir in water, instant beef broth, catsup, strained fruit and coconut.
3. Bring to boiling, stirring constantly, then simmer uncovered, 5 minutes, or until thick. Spoon over chops; cool; cover; refrigerate.
4. One hour before serving, place covered casserole in oven; set oven control to moderate (375°); bake 45 minutes; uncover and baste with glaze; bake 45 minutes longer, or until chops are tender and richly glazed.

POLLO CON VEGETALI

Chicken baked with vegetables is a favorite of many cuisines. This is an Italian version.

Bake at 350° for 1 hour,
then at 375° for 45 minutes.
Makes 6 servings.

  2 **broiler-fryers, cut up (about 2½ pounds each)**
  ¼ **cup all-purpose flour**
  2 **teaspoons salt**
  ⅛ **teaspoon pepper**
  2 **tablespoons olive oil or vegetable oil**
  1 **large onion, chopped (1 cup)**
  1 **clove garlic, minced**
  1 **jar (14 ounces) spaghetti sauce**
  1 **cup dry white wine or chicken broth**
  ¼ **cup chopped parsley**
  6 **medium-size potatoes, pared and cut into 1-inch pieces**
  2 **large green peppers, halved, seeded and cut into strips**

1. Shake chicken pieces with flour, salt and pepper in plastic bag to coat well. Brown, a few pieces at a time, in oil in a large skillet; place in a 12-cup casserole.
2. Sauté onion and garlic until soft in same pan; stir in spaghetti sauce and wine or chicken broth; bring to boiling. Stir in parsley.
3. Pour over chicken in casserole; top with potato cubes and green pepper strips; cover casserole.
4. Bake in moderate oven (350°) 1 hour; cool; cover; refrigerate.
5. Forty-five minutes before serving, place covered casserole in oven; set oven control to moderate (375°); bake 45 minutes, or until bubbly-hot.

CHICKEN IMPERIAL

Chicken breasts and legs are stuffed with a ham and parsley mixture, then baked in an easy wine sauce.

Bake at 350° for 1 hour, 30 minutes.
Makes 8 servings.

  2 **cups soft white bread crumbs (4 slices)**
  ¾ **cup finely diced cooked ham**
  ½ **cup chopped parsley**
  ½ **cup (1 stick) butter or margarine**
  4 **chicken breasts (about 12 ounces each)**
  4 **chicken drumsticks with thighs**
  1 **cup milk**
  1 **cup fine dry bread crumbs**
  1 **envelope (2 to a package) cream of mushroom soup mix**
  1 **cup cold water**
  1 **cup dry white wine**
  ¼ **cup chili sauce**

1. Mix soft bread crumbs, ham and parsley in a large bowl; cut in butter or margarine quickly with a pastry blender; refrigerate stuffing.

2. Halve breasts, then cut out rib bones with scissors. Separate thighs and drumsticks at joints with a sharp knife. To make pockets for stuffing, pull each breast piece open on its thick side, and cut an opening along bone in each leg and thigh with a short, sharp-pointed knife.

3. Pack about ¼ cup chilled stuffing into each half breast and 2 tablespoons into each leg and thigh.

4. Place ½ cup of the milk in a pie plate and dry bread crumbs on a sheet of wax paper. Roll stuffed chicken in milk, then in bread crumbs to coat well; chill while making sauce.

5. Combine mushroom soup mix, water and wine in a small saucepan; cook, following label directions. Stir in remaining ½ cup milk and chili sauce; pour 1 cup into a 12-cup shallow casserole.

6. Place chicken pieces in casserole; drizzle remaining sauce between pieces. Cover; refrigerate.

7. One and a half hours before serving, place uncovered casserole in oven; set oven control to moderate (350°); bake 1 hour, 30 minutes, or until tender and richly golden. Garnish with parsley.

SICILIAN FISH AND SHELLS

The women of Sicily are surrounded by the sea. That's why they know how to make fish dishes to delight the family.

Bake at 375° for 50 minutes.
Makes 6 servings.

1 package (1 pound) macaroni shells or farfalle
1 medium-size onion, chopped (½ cup)
2 teaspoons basil
2 tablespoons olive oil or vegetable oil
1 envelope (1½ ounces) spaghetti sauce mix
1 can (1 pound, 13 ounces) Italian tomatoes
1 package (1 pound) frozen cod or pollock fillets, cut into cubes
⅓ cup grated Parmesan cheese
1 package (8 ounces) sliced mozzarella cheese

1. Cook pasta in boiling salted water in a large kettle, 8 minutes, or until firm-tender; drain.

2. Sauté onion with basil in oil in a large saucepan; stir in spaghetti sauce mix and tomatoes. Cover; simmer 10 minutes; add fish cubes and simmer 10 minutes longer; remove from heat.

3. Spoon half the macaroni shells into a 12-cup casserole; sprinkle with half the Parmesan cheese; top with half the fish-tomato sauce. Repeat layers; arrange mozzarella cheese slices on top; cover; refrigerate.

4. Fifty minutes before serving, place covered casserole in oven; set oven control to moderate (375°); bake 40 minutes; uncover; bake 10 minutes longer, or until bubbly-hot.

LAMB AND EGGPLANT PARMIGIANA

Our recipe calls for cooked lamb, but you can use cooked beef, chicken or veal as well. A great ending to Sunday dinner's roast.

Bake at 350° for 1 hour.
Makes 6 servings.

1 large eggplant, pared and cut into ½-inch-thick slices
¼ cup vegetable oil
1 large onion, chopped (1 cup)
1 can (1 pound, 13 ounces) Italian tomatoes
2 teaspoons salt
1 teaspoon mixed Italian herbs, crumbled
¼ teaspoon freshly ground pepper
4 tablespoons fine dry bread crumbs
3 cups cubed cooked lamb
1 package (8 ounces) sliced mozzarella cheese, cut into strips

1. Brown eggplant slices, part at a time, in oil in a large skillet; remove.

2. Sauté onion until soft in same pan; stir in tomatoes, salt, Italian herbs and pepper, then simmer 5 minutes.

3. Arrange half of the eggplant slices in a 10-cup casserole; sprinkle with 2 tablespoons bread crumbs. Top with half of the lamb and tomato sauce. Repeat with remaining eggplant, bread crumbs, meat and sauce; cover and refrigerate.

4. One hour before serving, place covered casserole in oven; set oven control to moderate (350°); bake 45 minutes, or until mixture starts to bubble in center; uncover; crisscross cheese strips on top. Bake 15 minutes longer, or until cheese melts and is golden.

BAVARIAN STEAK ROLL-UPS

Steak is wrapped around spicy sausages and simmered in tomato sauce. Serve with dark pumpernickel bread for an authentic German dinner.

Bake at 350° for 1 hour.
Makes 6 servings.

1 round steak, cut 1-inch thick (about 2 pounds)
6 sweet Italian sausages
OR: 6 smokie link sausages (from a 12-ounce package)
2 tablespoons vegetable oil
1 medium-size onion, chopped (½ cup)
1 can (1 pound, 4 ounces) tomatoes
1 tablespoon caraway seeds
1 tablespoon brown sugar
1 teaspoon salt
1 can (1 pound, 11 ounces) sauerkraut

1. Cut steak into 6 even-size pieces; pound very thin with a wooden mallet or rolling pin. Wrap each piece around a sausage, then fasten with one or two wooden picks.

2. Brown rolls slowly in oil in a large skillet; remove and reserve. Add onion and sauté just until soft.

3. Stir tomatoes, caraway seeds, brown sugar and salt into pan. Return meat and cover. Lower heat; simmer 1 hour, or until meat is tender.

4. Rinse sauerkraut well under cold running water; spread into a 10-cup shallow casserole; place beef rolls on top; spoon sauce over; cool; cover; refrigerate.

5. One hour before serving, place covered casserole in oven; set oven control on moderate (350°). Bake 1 hour, or until bubbly-hot.

SENEGALESE CHICKEN

Chicken is often a safe choice for the hostess—so many people like it. The cream-and-egg custard sauce makes this recipe special.

Bake at 325° for 1 hour, 15 minutes.
Makes 8 servings.

1 broiler-fryer (about 3 pounds)
1 small onion, sliced
Handful celery leaves
2 teaspoons salt
1½ teaspoons curry powder
¼ teaspoon white pepper
1½ cups water
Milk
1 package (8 ounces) fine noodles
1 package (10 ounces) frozen peas
4 eggs
1 cup heavy cream
Toasted slivered almonds
1 red apple, cored and diced
Flaked coconut

1. Combine chicken with onion, celery leaves, salt, curry powder, pepper and water in a large saucepan. Bring to boiling; lower heat; cover; simmer 45 minutes, or until tender.

2. Remove chicken from broth; cool until easy to handle. Strain broth into a 2-cup measure; skim off any fat, then add milk, if needed, to make 2 cups.

3. Pull skin from chicken and slip meat from bones. Cut meat into bite-size pieces; reserve.

4. While preparing chicken, cook noodles and peas in separate saucepans following label directions; drain. Combine with chicken in a buttered 10-cup casserole, mixing lightly.

5. Beat eggs slightly in a medium-size bowl; stir in the 2 cups chicken broth and cream. Pour over chicken mixture, then stir lightly so liquid seeps to bottom; cover; refrigerate.

6. One and a quarter hours before serving, place uncovered casserole in oven; set oven control to slow (325°); bake 1 hour, 15 minutes, or until custard sets. (Cover lightly with foil during last 15 minutes' baking if top becomes too dry.) Garnish with toasted almond, diced red apple and coconut. Serve with a hearts of lettuce salad topped with a creamy Green Goddess dressing.

make-ahead

109

BUYER'S GUIDE

Cover: "Evesham" oval casserole by Royal Worcester Porcelain Co., 11 E. 26th St., N.Y., N.Y. 10010.
Page 2: Pewter covered casserole by Wilton Brass Co., Columbia, Pa. 17512.
Pages 4-5: Large photo is "Potter's Wheel" 2½-quart casserole by Denby, Ltd., 4688 Paddock Rd., Cincinnati, Ohio 45229. Photo inserts from left to right: "Servalier" 20-oz. bowl by Tupperware Home Parties, Orlando, Fla. 32802; 6-pt. white Gourmet Porcelain casserole and "Pearsons" 6-pt. Dutch Pot by Milnor, Division of Denby, Ltd., 4688 Paddock Rd., Cincinnati, Ohio 45229; "Soup 'r Stew Pot" by Nordic Ware, Minneapolis, Minn. 55416.
Page 6: "Roan Mountain" casserole by Iron Mountain Stoneware, Laurel Bloomery, Tenn. 37680.
Page 9: "Pearsons" 3-pt. oval baker by Milnor, Division of Denby, Ltd., 4688 Paddock Rd., Cincinnati, Ohio 45229.
Page 12: Foreground: "Fall Bounty" Temperware 3-qt. casserole and roaster by Lenox, Inc., Pomona, N.J. 08240. Background: "Pearsons" storage crocks by Milnor, Division of Denby, Ltd., 4688 Paddock Rd., Cincinnati, Ohio 45229.
Pages 16-17: 7-pt. oval casserole of Cast Iron Cookware by Lauffer Co., Inc., Belmont Dr., Somerset, N.J. 08873.
Pages 24-25: "Potpourri" Blue 4-qt.

casserole by Milnor, Division of Denby, Ltd., 4688 Paddock Rd., Cincinnati, Ohio 45229.
Page 32: "Independence Ironstone" round casserole and meat platter by Franciscan, Interpace Corp., 2901 Los Feliz Blvd., Los Angeles, Calif. 90039.
Page 44: Large photo: "Beans & Stuff" 2-qt. Automatic Slo-Cooker by The Westbend Co., R.R. 6, West Bend, Wisc. 53095; small photo: "Superpot" #696 by Oster Corp., 5055 North Lydell Ave., Milwaukee, Wisc. 53217.
Page 45: Clockwise, beginning at top right: "Crock-Pot" electric slow cooker by Rival Mfg. Co., 36th and Bennington, Kansas City, Mo.; heat control is for Oster "Superpot" (pot shown on page 44); "Pot-Luck" Cooker by Nesco, Div. of the Hoover Co., North Canton, Ohio 44720; "Country Festival" 10″ covered skillet and table range by Corning Glasswares, Corning, N.Y. 14830; "Colonial Cooker" by The Westbend Co., R.R.6, West Bend, Wisc. 53095; 12″ square Automatic Skillet also by West Bend; "Crocker" Frypan #7-153 by Sunbeam Corp., 2001 So. York Rd., Oak Brook, Ill. 60521; Presto Slow Cooker #LC1 by National Presto Industries Inc., Eau Claire, Wisc. 54701; "Crock Watcher" #449 by Hamilton Beach, Inc., 100 Hope Ave., Byesville, Ohio 43703.

Page 65: "Evesham" oval casserole by Royal Worcester Porcelain Co., 11 E. 26th St., N.Y., N.Y. 10010.
Page 71: "Pearsons" 4-pt. oval casserole by Milnor, Division of Denby, Ltd., 4688 Paddock Rd., Cincinnati, Ohio 45229.
Pages 72-73: "Pond Mountain" casserole and pitcher by Iron Mountain Stoneware, Laurel Bloomery, Tenn. 37680.
Page 74: "Spal" pitcher by Milnor, Division of Denby, Ltd., 4688 Paddock Rd., Cincinnati, Ohio 45229.
Page 79: "American Colonial" Heirloom Stainless flatware by Oneida, Ltd., Oneida, N.Y. 13421.
Page 82: "Monterey" serving bowl by Lauffer Co., Inc., Belmont Dr., Somerset, N.J. 08873.
Page 87: "Martha's Flowers" casserole by Iron Mountain Stoneware, Laurel Bloomery, Tenn. 37680.
Page 90: Background: International Craftmetal Coffee Service and Tray by Internation Silver Co., 500 So. Broad St., Meriden, Conn. 06450. Foreground: "Woodspice" baker/server Temperware by Lenox, Inc., Pomona, N.J. 08240.
Page 96: "Palmyra" flame-proof porcelain soufflé dish by Royal Worcester Porcelain Co., 11 E. 26th St., N.Y., N.Y. 10010.

Editor's Note: All items not listed in the Buyer's Guide are part of a private collection and not for sale.

ACKNOWLEDGEMENTS

The editor gratefully acknowledges the help of: American Egg Board; American Lamb Council; California Raisin Advisory Board; Dole Pineapple; Frozen Potato Products Institute; Kretschmer Wheat Germ Products; Maryland Seafood Marketing Authority; National Fisheries Institute; Ore/Ida Foods, Inc.; The Quaker Oats Company; Spice Trade Association; Dixie Paper Products; Western Iceberg Lettuce, Inc; The Pacific Coast Canned Pear Service; Inc.; Farberware; and Alaskan King Crab Association.